More prais

Up U
Down Down

"Takes a firmly tongue-in-cheek approach to the existential crises of male maturity for the millennial generation . . . Knapp's philosophizing is kept lively by exuberant and sometimes acerbically funny descriptions. . . . This intelligent take on coming of age deserves to be widely read, if only for its effortless-seeming form and its expression of how style and content are irrevocably intertwined."
—*Publishers Weekly*

"A master of collage, both in subject and in tone . . . The essays are hyperarticulate, literary, and occasionally self-conscious, but Knapp uses these tendencies to masterful effect. . . . If you have a conclusion, Knapp will beat you to it, and if you have an expectation, Knapp will flip it; what you end with is pure delight."
—*Booklist*

"Knapp is a smart writer using the power of his pen to come to terms with no longer being a twenty-year-old."
—*Library Journal*, starred review

"Examining various subcultures—pro wrestlers, skateboarders, his college fraternity, his neighborhood—[Knapp] also turns his lens upon his own coming of age, in meticulously crafted prose that's alternately cerebral, coy, wry, and laugh-out-loud funny."
—Oregonlive.com

"With his debut collection, *Up Up, Down Down*, Cheston Knapp exhibits both a studied mastery of the form and a reverence for its artistry. In his capacious works, Knapp seamlessly weaves seemingly disparate topics. . . . He writes with great empathy for his subjects, an approach that eases the reader into sometimes uncomfortable territory."
—Bookforum.com

"Reading *Up Up, Down Down* feels like reminiscing with an old friend on a quiet night. It has jokes, philosophical digressions, and those sneaky moments of intimacy that dissolve into contemplative silence. Knapp's candor and vulnerability are inviting, and he humbly submits himself to his own rigorous interrogation."

—*Los Angeles Review of Books*

"These essays are rich. Persistent and entertaining in his interrogation, and often surprising in his insights, Knapp is an open, candid, and inviting writer, with a gift for striking and original descriptive language."

—One-Story.com

"Full of wit and disquiet . . . The path toward whatever we mean by 'maturity' is a flowering vine of fruitful discomfort in these pages, and so much grows from it: acute self-awareness, intricate curiosity, tender interrogations. This book made me laugh out loud in embarrassing places—a quiet Swedish train, a darkened redeye flight—and its insights will keep echoing in me for a long time."

—Leslie Jamison, author of *The Empathy Exams*

"*Up Up, Down Down* is an always smart, often hilarious, and ultimately transcendent essay collection."

—Anthony Doerr, author of *All the Light We Cannot See*

"Wow. Offering up a steady supply of perfectly chosen words in precision-guided sentences, Cheston Knapp will either break your heart or jolt your spine, and quite possibly bring some of us back to life. Congratulations, Young Man, on becoming the person you were meant to be, and thank you for sharing some of it with the rest of us."

—Joshua Ferris, author of *Then We Came to the End*

"Under Cheston Knapp's uncommonly tender scrutiny, no absurdity goes unnoticed."

—Sarah Manguso, author of *300 Arguments*

"Few writerly consciousnesses are as fun to inhabit as the limber brain of Cheston Knapp. With an ordnance of wit, acuity, and casual erudition, these essays explode the local and everyday into huge and moving human reaches. This is the sort of book you look up from to find the dull room around you newly charged with life's important particles."

—Wells Tower, author of
Everything Ravaged, Everything Burned

"Cheston Knapp's essays are exhilarating and funny and endlessly smart on dads, fraternities, southerners, drinking games, retribution, tennis, the anxiety of influence, guilt, authenticity, UFOs, aptronyms, revelation, uncertainty, nostalgia, diversity, identity, skateboarding, and community, and that's just to start. He reminds us we're all caught up in one another's stories, as he tracks one family's unraveling and another's genesis, and points our way from fussbudget to enthusiast, from detachment to compassion, and from regret to joy."

—Jim Shepard, author of
The Book of Aron

"Pierce the surface to get to the depths, then rise up from the depths to laugh on the surface—Knapp performs some amazing alchemy in *Up Up, Down Down* by letting the two planes coexist so beautifully. Here's a voice ever so light and generous and funny and yet the essays probe and get to real substance and resonance. It's like a great party conversation under sparkly lights with umbrella cocktails where you emerge with your mind a little better."

—Aimee Bender, author of
The Particular Sadness of Lemon Cake

Up Up,
Down Down

Essays

Cheston Knapp

SCRIBNER

New York   London   Toronto   Sydney   New Delhi

For A, E
I owe you.

Scribner
An Imprint of Simon & Schuster, Inc.
1230 Avenue of the Americas
New York, NY 10020

Certain names and characteristics have been changed.

First Scribner trade paperback edition February 2019

SCRIBNER and design are registered trademarks of
The Gale Group, Inc., used under license by Simon & Schuster, Inc.,
the publisher of this work.

For information about special discounts for bulk purchases,
please contact Simon & Schuster Special Sales at 1-866-506-1949
or business@simonandschuster.com.

The Simon & Schuster Speakers Bureau can bring authors to
your live event. For more information or to book an event,
contact the Simon & Schuster Speakers Bureau at 1-866-248-3049
or visit our website at www.simonspeakers.com.

Interior design by Kyle Kabel
Photographs in "Faces of Pain" copyright © Scott Binkley

Manufactured in the United States of America

1   3   5   7   9   10   8   6   4   2

Library of Congress Cataloging-in-Publication Data is available.

Many thanks to Harvard University Press for the permission to quote from
The Poems of Emily Dickinson: Variorum Edition, edited by Ralph W. Franklin,
Cambridge, Mass.: The Belknap Press of Harvard University Press, Copyright © 1998
by the President and Fellows of Harvard College. Copyright © 1951, 1955 by the
President and Fellows of Harvard College. Copyright © renewed 1979, 1983 by
the President and Fellows of Harvard College. Copyright © 1914, 1918, 1919, 1924,
1929, 1930, 1932, 1935, 1937, 1942 by Martha Dickinson Bianchi. Copyright © 1952,
1957, 1958, 1963, 1965 by Mary L. Hampson.

Earlier versions of "Faces of Pain," "Beirut," "Learning Curves" (nee "On The
Journal of Jules Renard"), and "Mysteries We Live With" (nee "True Enough")
appeared in *Tin House*. *Brick* ran an excerpt of "Far from Me." I'm grateful to the
editors of these magazines, whose taste is patently unassailable.

ISBN 978-1-5011-6102-5
ISBN 978-1-5011-6103-2 (pbk)
ISBN 978-1-5011-6104-9 (ebook)

O me! that being what I have been
I should be what I am.

—Samuel Taylor Coleridge

There was I: a stinking adult.

—John Ashbery

Contents

Faces of Pain

Bell time for the Keizer Klash was 7:30 p.m., sharp, and Scott and I had arrived early according to plan, after the hour drive south from Portland. It was October and already dark out and GPS directed us down the kind of driveway I thought only existed in horror movies—murdersome's the word. But there at the gravel's eerie end we found the Lions Club. A beat-up moving truck was parked next to the entrance, and by the halogenic glow of an exposed bulb we could see that its side was stenciled with DOA PRO WRESTLING. Turns out the acronym doesn't stand for "Dead on Arrival," as I first assumed, but "Don't Own Anyone," which, although it has a certain Wild West and existential laissez-faire, primarily refers to the promotion's business model, the fact that it doesn't put the talent under contract and so doesn't limit where they can wrestle. With at least three other professional wrestling organizations in Portland, not to mention those up in Seattle, the wrestlers hereabouts have options. But boasting is a big part of the business and when we spoke with them, the managers of DOA were

1

quick to assure us that theirs was the "premier" outfit in the Northwest. One went so far as to call their competition "just half a step better than backyard."

We made our way into a spacious wood-paneled hall that was haunted by the smells of America's past, an olio of boiled hot dogs and stale Hydrox and orange-flavored Tang. Scott affixed a flash to his camera and started to work the scene. He'd been talking about this for months, about how we should team up on a project, a combo of words and pictures à la the Agee-Evans opus *Let Us Now Praise Famous Men*. Thanks in large part to my reluctance—I'd settled into a prevailing MO of irresoluteness—this had all remained remote and abstract, idle chatter after tennis, that is until a few days before, when Scott put the screws to me and convinced me to attend the Klash.

"It'll be fun," he said. And after a lengthy silence, he added, "At very least it'll be an experience."

I stood off to the side and made some notes while Scott orbited the hall. He shot the swag table, the staff, the gathering crowd. He shot the ring, which sat under a ceiling low enough to preclude top-turnbuckle action, it seemed to me. Empty though it technically was, you couldn't help but feel it was full of promise, potential. It teased the imagination like a missed opportunity, like preingested drugs. The wrestlers themselves were out of sight, behind a makeshift screen of black fabric hung across an oversize portable clothes rack, on top of which were perched an assortment of party lights that looked like they'd been bought on clearance at Spencer Gifts. In 1999.

The card for the Klash looked promising. There was Draven Vargas, "the Plus-Sized Playboy," vs. CJ Edwards, "the Little Chocolate Drop." Rockin' Ricky Gibson was set to tussle with Eric Right. For the heavyweights, J_SIN Sullivan was tasked with wrangling Dr. Kliever, "the Lean Green Love Machine." And a tag team match would end it all: the Left Coast Casanovas vs. the Illuminati. It was struggle enough to keep one's imagination from overheating.

We were then met by a member of DOA brass. He referred to us as press and we soon found ourselves being escorted through the black fabric and into the Lions Club's kitchen, which is to say: backstage.

Not counting my elementary school plays, I'd never been backstage at anything before, and I immediately understood the thrill. The wrestlers were giddy, full of antic aggression. Every couple minutes one of them would peek through the screen to check on the crowd filling the hall and then he'd beat his chest or beat the chest of a compatriot or jump up and down or jump into another wrestler or pump his fist. One rapidly slapped his head with both hands like I've seen legit Greco-Roman wrestlers do, in high school and the Olympics. Watching them amp themselves up, I remembered I'd experienced something similar back when I played lacrosse, when my teammates and I would bang our helmets together and roar testosteronic roars while listening to backward-*R* Korn—in what feels like, and what I often wish were, another life.

Maybe it was because we were in a kitchen, but after the initial thrill wore off, I started to feel less like I was backstage and more like I was at a Halloween house party. Or in the Castro. Or at a Halloween house party in the Castro. J_SIN Sullivan's baggy pleather pants had flames down the sides and he was wearing a T-shirt that read GLADSTONE RUB-A-DUB, which I learned was an allusion to an old-school Northwest wrestler and not a business that specialized in car washes and hand jobs. Rockin' Ricky Gibson dressed like he was in a Twisted Sister cover band. They'd both bleached their hair the way skaters I hung out with in the nineties used to. "The Plus-Sized Playboy" Draven Vargas's face paint smacked of the Insane Clown Posse and he'd brushed his hair forward and styled it into a fine fin that rose from the front of his head. Bald but for a sad little island of hair at the top of his forehead, "Loverboy" Nate Andrews, the other half of the Left Coast Casanovas, had also styled what hair he had into a fin, which you could see only in the right light, at the right angle. Wearing a shiny pleather pin-striped blazer, a purple-sequined shirt and matching hat, and googly black sunglasses, Mister Ooh-La-La, their manager, looked like a cartoon villain. Dr. Kliever lists his weight as "242 lbs of surgical steel and sex appeal," and his signature moves include the Autopsy, the Wheelchair Bound, and the Morphine Drop. He had a Marvin the Martian Mohawk so thick and meticulously coiffured that I swear you could do trigonometry on it. It was dyed a shade of neon green I've only ever seen on psychedelic posters and maybe, for that matter, on certain psychedelics. Somehow even those who weren't seemed shirtless.

Scott focused on Dr. Kliever. When "the Lean Green Love

Machine" noticed the camera, his arms shot up reflexively, as though an electric charge had passed through him. He flexed his muscles in the classic strongman pose and smiled a smirky and startling and weirdly handsome smile. "The World's Sexiest Doctor" was missing prominent teeth.

"Don't get a picture with me and him together," J_SIN said, pointing at Dr. Kliever. "We're wrestling tonight."

Wouldn't want to spoil the notion that the show's all real, not staged and scripted. Not a "work," as they say. In the world of pro wrestling, sustaining this illusion of reality, this suspension of disbelief, is called "kayfabe." The word's etymology is uncertain but it's often said to be a corruption of the Pig Latin for "fake," and all the accounts I read traced it back to carny culture, in which professional wrestling has its historical roots. The opposite of a work is a "shoot," as in "straight shooter." The improvised moves and holds the wrestlers perform on one another in the ring, that is, the pain they inflict and endure—that's the shoot. The tension between this reality of the match, the shoot, and what the public knows or believes to be an angle, the work, is an integral part of the audience's fun. A fan who cannot or does not distinguish between the two is called a "mark." As in, "Guy there with the foam finger and nacho cheese goobers in his goatee, he'll believe anything. He's an easy mark."

I peeked through the screen myself and counted seventy-five people in the crowd, give or take. The adults who'd come alone outnumbered those with kids, I noted. And people were still arriving, finding their spots on the collapsible steel chairs set up around the ring—steel chairs that you could just tell everyone present wanted to see used later as weapons.

An "experience." I wasn't entirely sure what that meant anymore. What'd always been an obvious idea had become a kind of phenomenological conundrum for me. A very simple part of the problem was wrapped up in the fact that, in English, we have a single word for two ideas. On the one hand, we register the sensational intensities of the world around us, and this is accomplished through perception of a prereflective sort. What senses we have build us a world. Immediately, automatically. And on the other, we gain experience over time. It's an aggregate of everything we've gone through, which, with reason and memory's help, implies a learning process, the development of wisdom, at least of a sort. The Germans, unsurprisingly, distinguish between these ideas.

They call the first one *Erlebnis*, which contains their root for "life," *Leben*, and the second *Erfahrung*, which includes their word for journey, *Fahrt*, as in Ralph Waldo Emerson's famous dictum "Life is a *Fahrt*, not a destination."

My misgivings started with a vague intuition that my *Erlebnis* machine had malfunctioned. I wasn't experiencing the immediate world as I once had. I was a newlywed and had recently bought a house and been transferred at work and my puppy had grown into a dog and the grass I'd planted had come in thin and patchy and I was startled to discover I actually cared about that and I was about to turn thirty and had all those clichéd and ramifying little anxieties that attend turning that age and my face was looking increasingly like my father's face and my parents had shocked the family by separating after more than three decades of marriage. All the things of promise in my life had become some version of what they'd promised to become, and something about the way these possibilities had resolved into reality had turned my days palpably strange. New and foreign names populated my inbox. Furniture that my wife, Alexis—Alexis: my wife?!—and I had brought to the relationship didn't fit in our new house. I wasn't a hundred percent on what all my light switches controlled. It unnerved me. Felt like I was living my life in translation. And having lost a handle in this basic way, I found myself having doubts of the *Erfahrung* variety, getting caught in eddying and abyssal questions I thought I'd put behind me. Real ponderous things like "How did I get here?" and "What's it all mean?" Because outside the obvious temporal continuity, I didn't sense there was any narrative coherence to my life. Events from my past were punctuated by a question mark, an interrobang. Were any the result of my having made a concerted effort to "become someone"? To "make something" of myself? Or had these things just like, you know, happened? In other words, there seemed to be unproblematic and "authentic" experience out there in the world to be had, of both the *Erlebnis* and *Erfahrung* sort, only not by me.

During the worst of this, I went to a barbecue at my buddy Kyle's house. Kyle casts an unmistakable aura. When you're around him, you begin to feel that life has a certain texture or grain or weave that otherwise—for me, at least—doesn't exist. He always seems so full of fucking life. It's intoxicating. So many people come to his BBQs that his backyard starts to look like the thoroughfare of a shantytown. That night, I wandered around talking to Kyle's friends, people who play in bands and make art and casually know all about good music and movies and books, people who ride their bikes everywhere they go, even if that means they show up a little sweaty, people who are apparently so at home with themselves that they're unbothered by the fact that they show up places a little sweaty. My mind felt buffered, as if it were in a padded cell, and I was hounded by a passage from *The Ambassadors*, in which Lambert Strether says, "Live all you can; it's a mistake not to. It doesn't so much matter what you do in particular, so long as you had your life. If you haven't had that, what HAVE you had?" By which I really mean to say I was hounded by that part in *Dazed and Confused* when Matthew McConaughey says, "You just gotta keep livin', man.

L-I-V-I-N." I ended up in a corner of the backyard, by the chicken coop, wondering what instinct tells a baby chicken to peck free of its shell, while Kyle moved from group to group and high-fived all the handsome guys and hugged all the pretty girls and told jokes and laughed and talked plans for his bike crew and his many bands. Everyone looked like they were having the time of their lives.

Kyle and I ended up at a twenty-four-hour Mexican restaurant not far from our houses. It was two in the morning. We got our food and sat at a booth in the big front window and we could've been in a Hopper painting, except we were in Portland, at a Mexican joint, so Hopper would've had to paint us on velvet. Kyle was about to start a new job working for a high-end bicycle company, what he called the "Rolls-Royce of bikes," doing a mix of advertising and publicity. For as long as I'd known Kyle, he'd managed a bike shop, and for exactly that long he'd talked about doing something else—whatever they're doing, twenty- and thirtysomethings in Portland are always talking about doing something else. Kyle's dream job was to work in a room with a whiteboard, beanbag chairs, and maybe a beer fridge or kegerator. Ping-Pong or foosball or arcade games or all of the above. An ideas room. And for five years he'd worked toward making this happen. He talked about the choices he'd made and would make, changes out on the horizon he'd set a course for—what an enviable sequence of cause and effect his life seemed.

"So what about you?" he asked when he was done. "What are your plans for the future?"

For as long as I'd known Kyle, I'd worked as the majordomo

of a summer camp for writers and as a magazine editor, and for exactly that long I'd talked about writing myself. So I said I'd probably continue to look for ways to prioritize that. But really I wanted to say that the future, like everything else in my life, wasn't quite what it used to be.

Listening to Kyle talk, I knew, at least intellectually, that I too had a history. A history of decisions, decisions that lacked the fundamental sense of choice but were decisions nonetheless, that ended with me moving to Portland, many thousands of miles from my home in Richmond, Virginia. A history in libraries and with books that had landed me a job at a literary magazine. A history of love affairs that'd ended in a marriage. An accordion-like history that would continue to open out and to end in this moment and this one and this. Only this history, this quasi-chaotic chain of events that stretched behind me through time, didn't feel like mine.

In addition to advertising "Live Pro Wrestling," the flyers for the Keizer Klash indicated that the event was a benefit for a kid named Hunter. Hunter's dad is the manager of a local Jiffy Lube, where "Loverboy" Nate Andrews works when he's not wrestling professionally. Backstage, Nate said that everyone at work, their hearts really went out to his boss and his family. They felt his pain. And he wanted to do what he could to help them.

Hunter has a rare condition called paroxysmal skew deviation, a term all the wrestlers said with studied nonchalance, though none of them could tell me what it meant. What they knew was they were there for him, "the sick kid," and that the night's proceeds, including their pay, would go toward sending him to the Mayo Clinic.

Before the show, Scarlett, the DOA ring girl, whose breasts and bottom looked as though they'd been inflated and who seemed almost criminally sweet and caring in her role as Team Mom, invited the family into the ring.

She handed the mike to Hunter's mother, who explained that something was wrong with her son's brain. His brain stem. Doctors didn't know much about his condition, including the cause, but it affected Hunter's eyes, his vision and ability to focus. One eye would sometimes move spontaneously upward, against Hunter's will, and roll away from the other in what essentially sounds like a lazy eye from hell. Worse still, sometimes it'd happen to both eyes at once. Hunter, who was maybe ten and stood between his mom and dad with his hands buried deep in his pockets, frequently suffered headaches of such terrifying acuteness that they reduced him to tears. He experienced blurred vision and general fatigue. Seizure activity hung about him as a when-not-if. And he rarely slept through the night because of all the pain, which had also forced him to be homeschooled.

"That's the story," she concluded. "The *short* story," she added, giving a sense of her exhaustion, her own pain.

I've lived pretty much my whole life with a tacit yet strict understanding of pain: at all costs it is to be avoided. Fuck pain, really. Fuck physical and emotional pain. Fuck spiritual pain. Pain *hurts*, after all. The assumption here was that the opposite of pain is pleasure or joy, and that if I minimized the former, I would, ipso facto, maximize the latter. But while pleasure may be pain's antonym, it's not its lived opposite. That'd be something more like nonfeeling, a value-neutral blankness. And by so vigilantly avoiding pain, I wasn't being prudent, as I thought, but timid, maybe even cowardly.

Which brings me to this: When I was around Hunter's age, I overheard an argument my folks were having. They fought infrequently enough then for their fights to be memorable mostly by virtue of their strangeness. An electric and dangerous mood would settle on the house and my brothers and I would sit where we'd been caught when it all started and we would listen. This one, I was in my room, and I put my ear to the door I'd closed when I knew things were going to get worse before they got better. One of my brothers or I must've lately been fussing, because Dad said we were getting to be too sensitive. That Mom was ruining us with her coddling. He accused her of turning us into mama's boys. Dad grew up on Long Island and, despite the fact that he'd been in Virginia longer than New York, continued to valorize northerners for what he held to be their chief characteristic: they were hard, "tough as nails." A characteristic sorely lacking from southerners, who were, by his estimation, duplicitous and weak. The syllogism he must've feared isn't hard to complete: southerners are weak, my sons are southerners, ergo my sons are weak. As a way of combating this, he didn't brook any complaining or crying when it came to frustration and pain. We were to have a "stiff upper lip," to "act like a man." "Yes, sir," we were to say. "No, sir." His philosophy seemed to be that pain was no more than a problem of perspective, its severity (or very existence) hanging on how (or whether) you chose to acknowledge it. And as I backed away from the door that afternoon, I tried to act accordingly, tried to forget what I'd heard, to go on acting like I'd never heard anything at all.

But God, that phrase. Mama's boy. For years it'd return to me with a sharpness unblunted by time. An example: it's fifteen-ish years later and I've been in Portland about a year. For several weeks I've been experiencing mysterious and unsettling episodes. Mood swings sing through me. Anger and anxiety and loneliness and fear and a deep unutterable sadness. There's somatic stuff, too. A sudden and inexplicable paresthesia in my arms and palpitations in my chest that make me worry, like "Perfect. A stroke *and* a heart attack." I pace and stomp about and I smoke. I take long walks in an effort to calm my underskin. I weep at TV commercials, at nothing at all. I feel like I'm going crazy. Like I'm turning into somebody else. So disturbing are these episodes that I have trouble believing the doctor when she tells me they're called panic attacks—whatever was happening to me definitely deserved a less prosaic name. Weeks later, after more of these neural shock waves, these full-body flails, I finally cave and commit myself to a daily regimen of meds that promise to stabilize my moods and reduce both the likelihood and intensity of my episodes. But before they begin their work, they turn my mind into an empty castle, and it's in those stilled and foreign corridors of thoughtlessness that I hear it softly taunting me, a thin persistent whisper: mama's boy, mama's boy, mama's boy.

Before their Three Year Anniversary show, the DOA wrestlers held a meet and greet at Pattie's Home Plate Cafe in St. Johns, one of the northernmost neighborhoods in Portland. Primarily a fifties diner–cum–soda fountain, Pattie's is also a music venue, sock-hop dance hall, gift shop, clothing store, video store, costume-rental shop, meeting place, and, I'm pretty sure, more. St. Johns has always seemed to me to be a living reminder of what this town must have been like before it became so hip and cool to live here. There's none of the yuppie influence that pullulates in the Pearl District or the hipster-doofus aesthetic that teems elsewhere. There's no upmarket flannel or fashion-statement glasses or knowing facial hair. Although it may be read onto the place, irony has not yet invaded and colonized St. Johns as it has much of the rest of this city. When you're there, you feel it's safe to take the place at its word. Work boots are worn to work and big-framed vintage glasses are just the glasses people have had for thirty years and mustaches are grown to make a face look *better*. Pattie's hosts a regular Bigfoot believers meeting.

It was a Saturday afternoon and sunny and the wrestlers had set up a card table with two gold-plated black leather belts, T-shirts, DVDs, and flyers for the Three Year Anniversary show the next day. J_SIN Sullivan sat in a chair built for a much smaller man. To call him simply "big" would be a silly understatement. In the ring, yes, he looks big. But when you're next to him, he's beyond big. Upright, he's a hair shy of six and a half feet tall and weighs 380 lbs. You'd shudder and avert your eyes and pray little please-God-not-next-to-me prayers if he boarded your plane. All-you-can-eat buffets must factor people his size into their P&Ls. He's gigantic.

A fan—the only one who stopped by in the two hours I was there—approached for a photo. J_SIN slung the Tag Team Champions belt he and Big Ugly hold over his shoulder. Together, they are "Ugly as Sin" and weigh 650 lbs. In the ring, they are like two parts of one person, and are unstoppable. J_SIN posed his menacing pose and pictures were taken and the fan thanked him and walked off.

Now, there's J_SIN and there's Jason and the difference between the two is at once subtle and pronounced. After the fan moved on, J_SIN relaxed back into Jason, the man who by day works at a printing plant and who's a founder and star of an independent wrestling promotion. Jason's bigness isn't really intimidating. Rather, he suggests a soul-comforting equipoise, more Buddha than the bad guy he plays. I sort of wanted him to give me a hug and tell me not to worry, that everything was going to be all right. I imagined being hugged by a MINI Cooper. But Jason's bigness was still intimidating enough for me not to suggest we try it out.

"Some people just have it," he said. The "it" he was referring to is the it factor, those characteristics an entertainer or person possesses that make him compelling, magnetic. For some wrestlers, it's a physical talent, the way they carry themselves, a move they do in the ring. For others, it's mike skills, their swagger and charm, the way they talk. Either way, it's how a wrestler manages and engages the crowd—it's the crowd, after all, with its response or lack thereof, that decides how long a match goes and whether a character makes it. "If they're not feeling it," Jason said, "we cut it short. No one's bigger than the show." As a "heel," a bad guy, in DOA, Jason's job as J_SIN is to inspire the fans' derision and hate, to rile them up and get them rooting for the "faces," the good guys.

"I've got this thing I do with my eyes," he continued. He cocked his head to the side and made movements with his brow and then said, "I can't really do it out here. The sun, it's too bright. But you get the idea."

A group of kids BMXed lazily by and shouted something I didn't catch.

"Nothing fake about this," Jason called back as J_SIN, patting the belt he still had over his shoulder. "Come over and I'll show you. Or are you too scared?"

The kids moseyed on.

"People are always like, 'Well, it doesn't matter, it's all fake anyway.' But is this fake?" He held up his forearm and pointed to a four-inch pink scar that looked like a gummy worm. "That's from barbwire."

In his essay on professional wrestling, Roland Barthes writes, "The public is completely uninterested in knowing whether the contest is rigged or not, and rightly so; it abandons itself to the primary virtue of the spectacle." The gist of the essay is that professional wrestling is a "spectacle of excess" and a species of morality play, and though highly athletic, it is decidedly not a sport. Unlike the crowd at a boxing or mixed martial arts match, the one at a professional wrestling production wants an image of passion, not passion itself. What is enacted and played out in the ring is "the great spectacle of Suffering, Defeat, and Justice . . . Everyone must not only see that the man suffers, but also and above all understand why he suffers." The shows may be scripted, but they're not choreographed, and while some of the suffering and pain are amplified for effect, "sold," that hardly makes it all fake.

Jason said he's bled in the ring twelve or thirteen times. At an event where the fans bring weapons for the wrestlers to use on one another—mostly pizza cutters and tenderizers and other kitchen utensils, but some real creatively sadistic shit, too, like an old keyboard with thumbtacks glued to the buttons like a miniature bed of nails—he got a cut on his back deep enough to demand medical attention, but he didn't go to the doctor. "I just EZ-stitched it," he said, meaning—I had him clarify—that he'd superglued the wound shut. Two years ago, he partially tore his MCL and he still hasn't had the surgery he knows he needs, but continues to wrestle regardless. He said Home Boy Quiz (HBQ) recently underwent a fearsome procedure known as back fusion surgery. Two rods and six pins now stabilize his spine and he's set for a comeback in a matter of months. I saw a picture of Wade "By God" Hess from the Taipei Death Match a few years ago. He and Thunder had dipped their taped-up hands in glue and rolled them in broken fluorescent tube lights, then punched and chopped each other until that grew stale, at which point they started smashing the fluorescent tubes over their heads and across their backs. In the picture, Hess is on his knees and his back looks like a river delta of pulpy skin and blood. Everyone has a bad back or bad knees or a bum shoulder or a crooked nose or broken ribs that didn't heal right. Dr. Kliever said he has to do yoga every morning to make it through the day. For a time he also had burns all over his back from a show where he was slammed onto a table that had been lit on fire and, consequently, caught fire himself. Plus and all there's the situation with his teeth.

"Concussions are so common that they're, that we, wait. Hold on. Where was I going with that? Anyway, every time you're slammed to the ring, it's like you're putting yourself through a fifteen- or twenty-mile-per-hour car crash," Jason said. "In order to deal with it you need a lot of mental toughness. That's more important than physical toughness, really. You have to condition yourself to deal with it."

One of the managers came out of Pattie's to tell Jason there was a girl inside who wanted an autograph, but she was too shy or scared or awestruck to ask for it herself. Jason signed a picture of the DOA logo, smiling a smile more private than public.

When I asked why he puts himself through all the pain,

what he gets out of wrestling, Jason said, "There's that, the fans, of course. And I just love the sense of community I get from wrestling. I met my girlfriend through wrestling. I've met my friends through wrestling. It's also just fun as hell."

Another of the managers—they came in such a number that I got the sense that "manager" also meant "friend who wishes not to wrestle"—said they should probably wrap up. They had to head to the airport to pick up "Maniac" Matt Borne (of Doink the Clown fame) and Raven, who were coming in especially for the Three Year Anniversary show. Before we disbanded, I asked Jason whether he thought DOA could ever support him and the other wrestlers full-time.

"It's a dream, of course. Because, I'll be brutally honest," he said, as though he could be honest any other way. "It's really humbling, going from being the boss to being the grunt. Monday morning back to work. It's hard. That's the reality of it."

After five-plus years, when the acuteness of my initial episodes had long since faded, I began to fear that the meds had
leveled me into a listless, anhedonic, das Manian existence.
So in an effort to purify my experience and gain access to
what I imagined were deeper realms of myself, realms more
vivifying and significant and "authentic" than any I'd recently
inhabited, I decided to go off them. Because I didn't know
any better, I tried quitting cold turkey. By day three I was
having vertiginous fits so bad I had to lie down for a half
hour or longer. The dizziness was of a deeper, more severe
sort than any I'd ever experienced, qualitatively different
from what happens when you childishly spin around a lot of
times. There were shocks and jolts that ran up and down my
spine, to and from the base of my brain. They're called "brain
zaps" or "cranial zings," which makes them sound a lot more
whimsical and fun, like some cartoon bubble out of Adam
West–era *Batman*, than they really are, in reality. My head
ached. My mind went as mushy as a cake half cooked. Some
kind of akathisia alighted and I felt as though I'd had too
much coffee when I hadn't even had any. I couldn't keep still.
I allowed myself to visit a handful of medical websites—after
a spate of hypochondriacal false alarms I'd been advised to
give them a wide berth—and read that the white-knuckling
I was engaged in is ill-advised. Doctors instead recommend
a process of gradual reduction called a taper. So again I took
up the regimen and decided to think long and hard before
I gave quitting another shot.

After the Keizer Klash match with J_SIN, a victorious Dr. Kliever stood sweaty and breathless by the ring. He leaned against one of the ring's posts, signing autographs and posing for pictures with kids from the audience, most of whom came up to about his waist. There was a thrilling and transgressive cultural exception about all this. Parents letting—no, rather encouraging their kids to get close to this man wearing nothing but little leather undies, who's missing prominent chompers and who has a large crustacean tattooed on his chest, which was red and welted from J_SIN's chops, and who was breathing suggestively and had sweat so much that he glistened and whose verdigris Mohawk had lost its initial pluck and verve and was now flopped over and matted and sad in a way that's probably best signified by the sudden diminuendo of a slide whistle. The atmosphere was charged.

In line with the kids to have his picture taken was an

older fan. Disheveled in his loose jeans and Hawaiian shirt and unbuttoned flannel jacket, he walked with a cane and looked like he could've seen action in Vietnam. When it was his turn, he congratulated Dr. Kliever and said J_SIN was a whale and a jerk and it took balls to get in the ring with him. He asked Dr. Kliever how he felt, after a win like that.

"You never get used to it," Dr. Kliever said. "You never get used to the pain."

I lied to my dad, said I was getting in on Friday, when really I had arrived in Charlottesville the day before. I was in town briefly and wasn't sure I wanted to see him, what with all the anger and disappointment, the annoyance and confusion— the rawness of all the shit I preferred not to reckon with. But I felt bad, guilty, and from a friend's back porch I told him I was calling from the train, couldn't talk long. Could we meet for coffee later that afternoon? After he'd moved out of my mom's place but before he'd subleased a cheap room in a house with UVA graduate students younger than his three sons, he'd asked this friend if he could live with him and his wife. He doesn't know I know this and even if he did I'm not sure he'd see the problem. On the phone he said Mom had Airbnb guests coming that night and he had to drive out to the house to cut the grass. So we made plans to meet for half an hour the next morning, at seven, before he headed to College Park, Maryland, to watch a UVA lacrosse game. Later that day I learned that Mom had already cut the grass, that he, too, had lied. And then, feeling bad and guilty himself, I guess, he went to pick me up from the train station, thus catching me in my own lie. I didn't answer his phone calls and the voice mail he left only made me squirm: "Where are you, bud? Which train were you on? I'm standing by the entrance, the exit. . ." I just texted back that I'd see him in the morning.

We met at Spudnuts, a fifties diner famous in Charlottesville for its dense potato-flour donuts and thin coffee. I was a little hungover—for a while there I'd been drinking in order to bring on a mild, manageable hangover. The symptoms of a mild hangover were the physical analog, the literal embodiment of the itchy-edged ache and estrangement of my normal mental state; and they were strangely soothing, in that they quieted the dissonance I typically felt while walking around. The wrongness felt right, evened me out. Dad was wearing an old T-shirt and, like me, was carrying a little extra weight and, who knows, maybe he was a little hungover, too. We got good donuts and bad coffee and talked.

It can often seem like the world or someone in it has either executed an injustice against Dad or fallen well short of his expectations. No bone seems to go unpicked, no ax unground. This time, he wanted to discuss how my brother had shown up late for a lacrosse game someone had given him tickets to. Good seats. Box seats. He'd missed the first quarter and a few minutes of the second. What did I make of that? Wasn't it messed up? Rude? (Was this really what we were talking about?)

When he got around to asking about the train station, I came clean. I hadn't been sure I wanted to see him, didn't know what to make of what was going on—the separation but also everything that'd led up to it. I put some questions to him, was direct. Confusion bloomed on his face, for ours is a relationship that thrives nearest the surface. Behind the door I'd nudged open lay a mess of knottily complicated emotions. And for a second I was ten again, waiting in terror for his reaction to something I'd said or done. But I was also almost thirty, by any metric a man now myself, and wanted an explanation, an accounting of some sort. A story. How had Dad come to be a man with a marriage on the ropes? Broke with no reliable job? Was it really possible for life events of this magnitude to just like, you know, happen? But I also knew that nothing he could point to—depression, booze, laziness, pride, hebetude, booze—would undo or absolve the pain of the last few years. At bottom it wasn't really about undoing or absolving the pain anyway, but honoring it as real, acknowledging that the rest of us hadn't simply imagined it.

We sat for a spell in silence. Donut particulate dusted

Dad's ratty tee. I don't know why or exactly how I expected things to be different now, but I did and so his deflection bummed me out. He said Mom needed to get help. "I'm getting help. All kinds of help." He said that word, "help," like he resented even it. And before I knew it our half hour was up, as though this had been some sort of prison visit. We hugged outside and he said, "Pray for your mother, bud," and I said I would, even though I hadn't prayed in years and probably wouldn't start again anytime soon. And then I turned away, not wanting to see him get into his dinky little truck and blow into the pneumatic doohickey I'd heard he had to blow into in order for it to start. I didn't want that experience. Walking back to my friend's house, a heavy, donut-sick feeling in my stomach, the sun working its way through the morning haze, I wondered what alchemical substance is added to time that makes it possible for us to forgive.

I spent my time at the first few wrestling events looking for socially or sexually or politically charged shit I could write about. And it's everywhere to be found. Take, for instance, the wrestlers' obsession with the microphone. In the face of working-class anonymity, of a system that renders them all but powerless, "voiceless," controlling the mike could be read as their way of asserting control over their situation, their lives. When they got their hands on it, nearly all of the wrestlers first said something like "Shut up! I have something to say!" This all seemed symbolically complicated by the fact that the cordless mikes often cut out abruptly, mid-insult, and that even when they did work they amplified and distorted in equal measure, muffling the wrestlers' voices into the nonsense, muted-trumpet language adults speak in Charlie Brown cartoons. Everyone would've been totally lost were it not for the fact that we were all sitting close enough to the ring to hear through the distortion. I thought of the improvisational nature of professional wrestling as a field of play and an embrace of pain that Nietzsche would have associated with his übermensch, and probably would have admired. Then I thought professional wrestling could be seen as a metaphor for our own normal and mediated lives, some of it real, sure, but a lot of it scripted, posed, fashioned for other people to observe and assess, to "like." And that maybe folks get so up in arms about pro wrestling being "fake" because they're acutely sensitive to and insecure about all the ways their own lives are a work.

After my third event, though, I began to sense that looking for these signs and "readings" was, at bottom, dishonest. I could continue to shyster together language that masqueraded as insightful, but in the end I knew that that language would only amount to a form of avoidance, of hiding, namely from my own pain. But, further still, I'd also started to tire of the idea that all experience aspired to significance, to meaning of one sort or another. The idea that an experience was somehow only completed by insight. Because I'd had enough of insight—what had once promised an endless unfolding symphony of self-knowledge had lately taken on the tinny jangle of Muzak. Insights had come to be as easy to have as they were hard to live by. Know thyself? I'd been knowing on myself for years and yet here I was, almost thirty and still waking up feeling like I was in a stranger's bed, a stranger's life. Wasn't reasoning like this just another form of storytelling and so, by definition, a work? Didn't it betray the very nature of the experience? Barthes was very much on my mind here, particularly when he writes, "What matters is not what [the crowd] thinks but what it sees." And as part of the crowd at the many events I attended, sometimes alone, I saw a lot.

I saw "Loverboy" Nate Andrews introduce himself by stuttering the first syllable of his name with an overactive tongue—"Luh-luh-luh-luh-luh-luh-LOVERBOY. . ."—in a way clearly meant to signify cunnilingus. I noticed then that he'd shaved most of his stomach and chest, leaving one long center strip of hair from his neck to under his belly button. When it was his turn with the mike, Thunder called it an "unhappy trail" and we all erupted.

I saw C. W. Bergstrom, who's fifty-four years old and whose prime dates back to the days when Rowdy Roddy Piper wrestled here, come out and say to another tag team, "I hope

you packed a lunch, because we're taking you to school."
To which his opponent from the Honor Society responded,
"My partner and I are the true masters of the double team.
Just ask this girl," and he pointed to a woman in the front
row, which drew cheap heat, halfhearted jeers and boos, but
didn't seem to register any actual offense.

I saw Mister Ooh-La-La on a YouTubed episode of
Springer and learned that when he was eighteen, he'd changed
his legal name to Mister Ooh-La-La.

I saw Dr. Kliever throw J_SIN into the ropes and then
clothesline him when he bounced back into the ring, and I
saw all 380 lbs of J_SIN go horizontal in the air and fall to
the mat with the sound of a cannon, after which Dr. Kliever
walked around the ring pointing to his chest with his thumbs
like I'm the Man.

I saw a number of head butts to the groins of spread-eagled
men that looked like deranged and hellish fellatio.

I saw crowd members with what must have been seventy-
inch waists hold up homemade signs that said FOOD STAMP
TRAMP when the Left Coast Casanovas came out with their
escort, Mary Jane Payne. As they entered the ring, I saw the
Casanovas hold down the middle rope for Mary Jane, who
paused for an awkward and long few seconds when her head
came close to Draven Vargas's crotch and her bottom came
close to "Loverboy" Nate Andrews's crotch, at which point
the two wrestlers posed a high five to complete the pantomime
of a sexual maneuver known as the Eiffel Tower, at which
the audience collectively groaned.

I saw J_SIN point to a much smaller opponent and say,

"I've had bowel movements bigger than him," and really almost believed that.

When I arrived early at an event, I saw wrestlers warming up and going over their moves. They were wearing T-shirts that hung over their little spandex undies in a way that made me think they might not actually be wearing little spandex undies at all, that they might be Porky Piggin' it.

I couldn't help but see that some of the wrestlers' little spandex undies looked more full than other wrestlers' little spandex undies and wondered why the less endowed wrestlers didn't opt for shorts.

My heart went out to one wrestler, gone generally flabby and a little gynecomastic, when a twelve-year-old girl in front of me started to chant, "Get a sports bra!"

I saw Big Ugly stand in the ring wearing a plastic neck brace and tell a story about having been in a bad car accident with a semi. He'd had to spend time in the hospital, where some of the other wrestlers had visited him. Though he was in a lot of pain, he guaranteed that he'd be back in the ring as soon as he could. He made a point of saying that a lot of guys in the business, they spend their lives on painkillers to numb themselves. He didn't want that life. J_SIN said he would wrestle their tag-team match against the Left Coast Casanovas alone, in honor of Big Ugly's pain. And I felt a great wave of tension and then shock and then confusion wash over me when, during the match, Big Ugly rushed out from backstage, doffed his neck brace, picked up a collapsible steel chair on his way into the ring, and used it to smack J_SIN across the head. This betrayal, this twist in the angle, stupefied the crowd. J_SIN lay stunned on the mat and Big Ugly hit him another time. Then Big Ugly got another collapsible steel chair and put it on top of J_SIN's head and hit that chair with the first one. "I can't believe they let this happen," said someone behind me. "Nothing fake about that," said another. And I completely marked out, bought it. I was genuinely confused. Was J_SIN okay? Had Big Ugly been faking his injury all along? What just happened? After the managers got Big Ugly out of the ring, three wrestlers came to help J_SIN backstage. Scott got a picture of the four of them walking away from the ring, and when we looked at it later, we saw that Dr. Kliever is smiling at the camera, and his smile is different from the one I'd seen on him before. It is full of gleaming and perfectly white teeth and he looks movie-star handsome and I didn't know what to think.

I saw so many incredible things I almost couldn't believe my eyes.

Six months after the Keizer Klash, I found pictures online that a local journalist had taken that night. Sure enough, I spotted myself in one of them, standing in the back of the Lions Club, leaning against the wood paneling, an out-of-focus ghost taking notes as grown men pantomimed a primal struggle. This picture convicted me. In the months intervening I'd been dutiful about my reporting, attending events and interviewing the wrestlers, but had only recently begun to understand how much of myself this project was demanding I give. All along I'd been fighting the personal turn, afraid that naming or narrating certain hurts would both cheat and cheapen them. Amount to no more than complaining. But watching alone would no longer do, of that much I was sure. A line of Hölderlin's kept coming to mind: "But where danger is, grows the saving power also." And a little etymological sleuthing turned up that danger and risk are literally embedded in the word "experience"—I knew I was going to have to put myself in harm's way, that is, in *peril*.

The DOA training facility is in Troutdale, Oregon, about a half hour east of my house in Portland. It also serves as a school where Dr. Kliever teaches new wrestlers the ropes, as it were. I drove out I-84, the Columbia River on my left, and I was thinking about time and experience. I mean, I was thinking about Dad. How much of our relationship is a work? How much a shoot? And would its being a work make it any less real? Any less painful?

Mount Hood rose outside my windshield. Clouds crossed it. It looked like something Ansel Adams might photograph. In the nearly seven years I've lived here, Hood has never looked real to me. Against the sky, it looks flat and matted, too much like what it is, and this subtle irreality has always led me to think of it as a symbol. How large and how small. Grandeur. Awe. Ineffability. Far-reaching singleness. Timeless time and eternal return.

Behold! A mountain.

There was an accident on the highway and three lanes became one and traffic slowed to a creeping pace as everyone passing tried to assess the damage, counted their stars. I grabbed my phone and checked my Instagram account to see whether any of my seventeen friends had liked the photo I'd posted earlier. Kyle was one of three who had, and he'd uploaded a new photo for his many hundreds of followers. I thought of posting a shot of the accident. There were fire trucks, police cars, and ambulances, a dizzying display of spiraling light. Surely there was a good filter for that. The rescue workers had lobotomized one of the cars that had come to a crumpled rest on the right shoulder. Its roof was peeled back like the lid of an anchovy tin. On the embankment, an abrasion of fresh red paint stretched behind it. I would put a knowing caption on my photo, an allusion, play to the Pacific Northwest crowd with "Randle Patrick McMurphy" and get tons of likes, or tens of likes at least. I slowed, assessed, and only after I had taken a picture that came out blurry and smeared-looking did I consider that it was probably in bad taste anyway, the situation too, well, real. As I drove on, I thought about how, at an earlier time in my life, like Dad, I would have prayed for the safety of the people involved.

I got off the highway and drove past the semitruck

dealership and then the Troutdale airport, where two small helicopters were either taking off or landing, just indecisively hovering there. I passed a sprawling and enervated office complex no different from one I remembered at that moment I used to work in. And then development abruptly ended and I was in the middle of nowhere and I almost missed the turn. I searched in vain for address numbers on a street that had large garages on the left and semitruck trailers behind chain fences on the right and knew I had arrived when I saw an SUV with a DOA sticker across its entire back windshield. I parked behind it. When I got out, I saw hanging from its rearview mirror what looked to be shrunken heads. The training facility's windows and door were cheaply mirrored and I stood a moment in the thoroughfare between the two strips of garages. My face was imperfectly and fuzzily reflected in the DOA insignia on the door. I walked up and my reflection grew larger. At the door, though, gripping the handle, I hesitated, imagining the world of hurt that would be revealed to me in the ring. But I pulled it open because I had decided that, more than anything, I wanted a piece of the action.

Beirut

Every Thursday night was Games Night. That is, every Thursday night was Games Night so long as we weren't on probation for our last Games Night. And a certain mood enveloped the fraternity those afternoons. Call it a tincture of excitement and aggression.

The brothers would band together to ensure there were enough Solo cups and beer, to get the music set up and to check whether anyone had remembered to invite some girls this time. A pledge would layer printer paper over the windows on both of the doors to the basement—the sides facing out were Sharpied with BROTHERS ONLY. The intention here was equal parts secrecy and exclusivity: we wanted to protect our paddled asses from Campus Security and to invite everyone else to kiss them. Our informal slogan? "Whether you like us or don't like us, learn to love us, because we're the best thing going today."

Arrive after eight on such a Thursday in the early aughts and you would've heard the muted hubbub as you entered the house, which was a three-story dorm "unit" owned by the school. You would've descended the rubber-nosed stairs, rapped on the door with the proper cadence, and a pledge would've admitted you into the basement. You'd've made your way past the bathrooms and through a doorless portal on your left and into the claustrophobic charter room, where under a low ceiling there sat a pool table, but not quite enough space around it to really play. Against the far wall was the huge-screen TV funded by alumni donations, which would've been playing *Stop Making Sense* or *The Last Waltz*, possibly (oddly) on mute. Brothers and their guests would've been arrayed on the leather sectional couch, cards and empties strewn across the coffee table before them. This was surely some version of Kings or Asshole. The faces of brothers past looked nostalgically on from the composite pictures that hung on the walls. Then a pledge behind the chest-high bar would've proffered you a beer from one of two thirty-gallon garbage cans, which held ice and water and the many cases of Beast or Natty Light that one of the brothers would've bought earlier with membership dues that some of us paid at the beginning of the semester and others of us never. Back out on the basement's open floor, lit with a fluorescence that made even the best complexion look a little *Children of the Corn*-ish, you would've surveilled the action.

By the far door would've been a homemade table, warped and wobbly due to poor or hasty craftsmanship. Four or five washed-out-looking young folk would've been lined up on either side, chanting some variation of "Go, go, go," as another person on their side endeavored to flip an empty Solo cup from the table's edge and get it to land upside down, after which the next person in line would chug his or her drink and attempt the same. On an adjacent table, two people would've been struggling to bounce a quarter up into a single centered Solo cup—succeed and your opponent had to drink the contents, typically beer but sometimes rotgut liquor poured from a plastic handle, not to mention whatever microbial ickiness had been on that quarter.

But all this action was merely incidental, a footnote to the main event. Because to speak of Games Night is to speak almost exclusively about one game, conducted in the center of the basement on two specially designed tables, both emblazoned with our Greek letters. We called this game Beirut.

Because he feels very far away from me now, I often have to remind myself that I'm the same person who pledged this fraternity, who puked and pissed into a communal garbage can with twelve other shaggy-headed young men, who learned trivia about older brothers' hometowns (e.g., the lighthouse in Sea Girt, New Jersey, is forty-four feet tall) and memorized "family trees" detailing how all the brothers were "related," who went on four-in-the-morning sandwich-and-condom runs for older brothers, am the same numbass who sat upon a block of ice while drinking liter after liter of a chunky concoction the primary ingredients of which were warm beer, cocktail onions, cayenne, and bananas. With time it's getting harder to believe these are among the things wrapped up nice and tight in my hobo sack of experience. Why did I allow preppy manboys to spank me with a shoddy paddle

I'd fashioned myself? Why, in front of a crowd of shrieking sorority girls, did I strut gamely upon a table, removing my clothing, article by article, to the tune of Ricky Skaggs's "Country Boy"? Why did I swallow so many live goldfish? Why did I submit myself to the quaffing of nuked vodka? To humiliating vitriol? To running twenty-two miles one evening while holding on to a pole just long enough for all twelve of my fellow pledges to hold on to as well?

Cue the harp music, watch the wavy lines play across your mind. I remember it all like it was yesterday. . . Though it pains me to admit this, I too was once a preppy manboy. I too once believed, and deeply, in the idea of fraternity, in a community of young men assembled, according to the preamble we all knew by heart, "for the establishment of friendship on a firmer and more lasting basis; for the promotion of brotherly love and kind feeling; for the mutual benefit and advancement of the interest of those with whom we sympathize and deem worthy of our regard." All our literature was written in this semiarchaic language, which for me lent it the weight of longevity, of history. It was so earnest, full of sepia-toned notions of capital-V Values, capital-C Character. Its unapologetic bid for significance seduced me. As did all the secrecy, the elaborate handshakes and the candlelit rituals. But I was an easy mark, already a true believer.

In high school I'd been on the margin of a number of friend groups, but hadn't been an integral member of any one. Having been excluded from these core relationships, I was invited to imagine them as penetralia of a sort, intimate places where inside jokes flourished, where a cup of ambrosial acceptance was passed around, and where, possibly, people were getting laid. As evidence of this exclusion I submit a thing that would sometimes happen at parties: if they started to get too big or loud or unwieldy, if there was any threat of the cops being called, the host would walk around his or her house thinning the crowd. So while I'd go to these parties, I'd be nervous pretty much the whole time that I'd again be classed among the broke dicks asked to split early. It's nothing special, of course, this not feeling special. But because it'd been denied me, I was possessed of the notion that my insecurity and anxiety and self-doubt, the Gordian knot of my identity, might be allayed or undone by being open-armed into a community. I wanted to be deemed worthy of regard, to be absolutely positive I'd make the party's cut. There's all that and, of course, there was a girl.

I met Cara during rush, which was when you were supposed to go around meeting the brothers of all the different houses. They'd ply you with booze and drugs and show off the caliber of tail that hung around and you'd then decide whether they were the sorts of guys for whom you might freely befoul yourself. She was sitting in Luxton's room with a couple of friends while Luxton was on his computer, his back to us. She was sporting a pink polo shirt with the collar popped up and athletic shorts that inched up her sunbrowned legs, revealing a penumbral tan line. Her long, dirty-blond hair was parted on the side in the manner of all the southern girls who haunted my dreams then, who through my tortured adolescence had been responsible for so many mucked-up sheets. She'd grown up in one of the richest little pockets of minimansions in Richmond, and had attended the "old-money" private all-girls school not far from my house. Every so often throughout middle and on into high school, my public school would catch fire with rumors about these girls. Everyone knew they were the hottest—they seemed, to a girl, to possess the heart-hurting beauty that I came to associate with casual wealth; their hair and skin, their clothes and postures, the only word was "rich"—but these apocryphal stories also suggested that they actually put out.

Around the house Luxton went by Lucky. He was a blond lifeguard type, a triathlete. Catalog handsome with a jaw you could've used as a protractor. Like a number of the other brothers, Lucky exhibited a host of Stoic Southern Guy personality traits I wished I had. He greeted people with an upward nod of his head that I found appealingly Tourretic. His wardrobe consisted of Wallabees and roughed-up khakis, well-worn T-shirts and Lacoste polos. He always looked so at home with himself, so imperturbable—he'd drink and drink without ever appearing to get all that drunk. And he dated Cara. It was hard not to be intoxicated by the idea of being part of a group of such good-looking people. To maybe even be mistaken for good-looking myself.

Beirut \bā-ˈrüt\ *n* : *A drinking game common to college campuses the nation over.* Four people play at a time, in teams of two. There are twelve cups on either end of the table, divided into two tight pyramids of six, which go 3-2-1 from the back edge of the table. Each team gets two beers and pours them evenly among the twelve cups. Before the game begins, the two Ping-Pong balls bob in separate cups of water at either end, used periodically (uselessly?) as a rinse. The point is this: you want to land your Ping-Pong ball in one of the dozen cups at the other end of the table. You may toss or bounce the ball, but if you choose to bounce, a member of the other team may swat the ball away. (House wisdom also held that only bitches bounce.) When a ball is made, a member of the other team must drink the beer in the cup and remove it from the pyramid, leaving an empty space where the cup used to be. When six cups have been made, the remaining six are "reracked" into the 3-2-1 pyramid shape and shot at until all the cups are gone. Each team member gets to shoot on a turn, and if both shots are made, they get the balls back. When the last cup is made, the losing team must then chug however many cups are left on the winning team's end. Winners stay on the table.

And there end most definitions of the game, which sometimes goes by beer pong and has evolved from the Norman Rockwelly days when you'd play on an actual Ping-Pong table and use paddles to hit the balls into the cups. But we played a mutant form of this game, one that was surely dreamed up in the crunked crucible of a state university somewhere. We played "full-contact" Beirut. Gone is the Ivy League decorum, the letter-jacket probity. Welcome instead an element of danger, a danger that allowed the game to achieve an exalted form of frattiness.

Say you shoot your ball and it plunks off a cup's rim and

goes plink-plinking across the floor. That ball is live. Until one team possesses it, it's a free-for-all. You may use any means you see fit to retrieve the truant ball—slides, dives, swim moves, tackles—but once someone has it in hand it's game on and you have to return to your side of the table.

The linoleum floors of our basement unit would soon grow slick with water and beer and dirt and other fluids, which combined to form an amoebic mess we called, flatly, "frat-sludge." So slick would the floor grow that some brothers liked to run a couple feet and drop to their stomachs and haunches and glissade across it—our own meningitic slip-and-slide. And with two games going at once, the result was a manufactured mayhem that most of us couldn't get enough of.

A brief digression: your more evolved drinking games will typically demand some specially developed skill, something more than drinking alone, and they will, more often than not, entail making *someone else* drink. We're not talking the Neanderthal-like Edward Fortyhands or Roxanne here. Try lobbing a Ping-Pong ball seven feet into a Solo cup. It's not easy. And then try doing so under threat of physical harm—harder still. So you could say the final point of full-contact Beirut is to inflict drunkenness upon the other team by sinking your shots. While you're at it, though, you're also trying to put a literal hurt on them, which also happened. Often.

Whitaker chipped his two front teeth and for more than a week, before he could fix them, they presented an interesting parallelogram of empty space. After a second concussion, Hicks had to wear an old motorcycle helmet when he played. Doctor's orders. L'il Dave was six-six and 250 lbs and known house-wide to be the descendant of African royalty—he left cartoonish indentations in the metal door one night when he dove for a ball, but got up and just stared confusedly at the door, not a scratch on him. At another Games Night, Whitaker slammed the back of his head into the table during a scrum for the ball, and so added blood to the ingredients of that night's frat-sludge, blood so thinned by booze that the doctors couldn't give him painkillers when they stitched him up. There were countless bent-back or broken fingers. Elbows to stomachs and nuts. Knocked heads and knees. Bruised coccyges. The Zookeeper fly-tackled Squeak, sending him hospital-bound with a punctured lung. Gerritz busted Ashley's big-ass nose with a strategically thrown shoulder. And Pig Nuts up and punched Pruitt in the face, which yielded approximately nothing by way of kind feeling.

Incidents like this typically went down late-night, after all the booze had transmogrified the brothers into Hyde-like ag-bros. By that time I would've long since stepped away from the table, having sheepishly retired to the relative safety of our slip-and-slide or excused myself to the charter room, where mellower herbal delights could sometimes be found on offer. In fact, that I never broke a bone or left blood on the floor now seems an odd portent, a telling piece of evidence that I'd never really fit in.

First semester junior year I spent so much time around Lucky and Cara I could've been charged with loitering. By then I'd started running with the same crew as Lucky. The fraternity was split, roughly, into two factions, divided by what side of the Mason-Dixon line you called home. We were the Southern Assholes. We wore our beat-up khakis and sweat-stained white baseball hats and ate blue crab by the bushel and were vaguely proud of our "history," a history none of us really wanted to get too specific about. It wasn't about the history itself anyway, not really, but an attitude it allowed us to project, the tight-lipped sanctimoniousness of those who have brooked a whupping. The Northern Assholes, those fucking carpetbaggers, wore their hair short and sometimes "styled" it with gel, which was among the most egregious no-nos we could imagine. We held an annual Civil War–themed party to honor and stoke this intrafraternity rivalry. We'd break off to separate sides of a backyard and call regional-centric insults across an imaginary dividing line while attempting to discover which faction could more swiftly empty a keg. By the end of the night the war would end and we'd reenact our own version of Appomattox, gathering together in corners of the backyard to throw up.

For a short time, I'm ashamed to say, I dated Cara's close friend and housemate, Addy, just to be closer to her. I took Addy to formals, bought Addy drinks, said nice things to Addy, even made out with Addy a little, my mind mostly on the time I got to spend around Cara. Lucky and I grew closer, too, and the four of us ended up going on a few dates together. At that semester's Civil War party he held my legs aloft for a keg stand like he was signaling a field goal good. I did likewise. He gave me an old pair of his Wallabees. I used to go to parties at Cara's house and play civilized, noncontact Beirut with him and some other brothers, looking forward to when the cameras were brought out, because it was then that Cara would drape herself on me as part of some inscrutable pose. I read sub rosa intimacy in the tiniest of gestures—the faintly flirtatious touch of a hand, a chesty hug hello or good-bye, the throaty way she'd sometimes say my name. And with them I'd entertain elaborate fantasies about her, many of which ended in the spontaneous combustion of her clothing. A combustion that didn't terrify her and left her lustrous hair unsinged and her buttery skin free of abrasions and burns—whatever, I wasn't majoring in physics.

The next semester Lucky studied abroad in Australia. Not long after the semester's start, I went to a party and found Cara slung about the waist of a soccer player, a guy as handsome and seemingly self-assured as Lucky. What could she possibly see in him? The guy was practically nothing more than a flawless jawline, a six-pack, and surfer hair. I mean, for fuck's sake, did he even have pores?! After I'd made sure she'd seen me, I left. I told myself I was disgusted with her willingness to betray Lucky, but really it was that she hadn't chosen to do so with me.

She and I shared an English class that semester, though, and I ended up helping her write a couple of essays. I assured her I was but a humble midwife for her good ideas, that once she got started there was no stopping her, and so on. Sometimes during these sessions she got to talking about Lucky and from her stories I started to see that all the coolness and effortless self-assuredness that I wanted, that defined how he and the others in the fraternity interacted, actually put

45

up a wall. He was distant, cold. Could be a dick. And soon I was advising her to break it off, saying she deserved better, someone who'd appreciate her. Jesus, was I really ever such a milquetoast?

My already ambivalent feelings about the fraternity—deep down I probably always knew that it couldn't provide me with the freedom from self-doubt I was looking for—were further adulterated by my desire to see Cara naked. Because I still agreed, at least in principle, with one of the fraternity's basic tenets: you don't fuck with another brother's girl. No matter what.

Then one night after discussing the finer points of *Our Mutual Friend*, we decided to watch a movie. We both lay on the couch. I kicked off Lucky's Wallabees and they thudded Tell-Tale-Heartishly on the floor. We'd never been horizontal together before and I got nervous. I decided to fall off the couch.

I'd grown up in the church, as the saying goes, and was, at twenty-one, still unlearning the most draconian and shame-baiting lessons about *le sex* that'd been urged on me as an adolescent, namely that it was something that I, a boy, did to (not with) a girl. (I suspect the girls were operating with even more disturbing wisdom: that it was something they let happen to them. And God literally forbid you *choose* to identify as anything other than straight. . .) As an exemplar we were presented with a parishioner couple who'd shared their first kiss at the altar. Not that I had that many opportunities, but thanks to these rules and to the eternal consequences associated with violating them, I'd once been a champion self-sabotager, master of the auto-cockblock. My pièce de résistance came when I faked untimely gooage, choosing the thrum of blue balls over the hellish shame I knew would've dogged me had the young woman and I, you know, 👉👌. And while much reformed, every so often during a hook-up I'd fall prey to a proleptic fit of guilt and hit abort. Odd habits die hard.

"What are you doing?" Cara asked.

"I fell off the couch," I said, looking up at her.

"Come here," she said, and leaned down over the cushions. She took my face in her hands, and when she kissed me with lips I'd inflated in my mind to the size of those made with candy wax, when after a few minutes she suggested we go upstairs, when once there she unveiled her gravity-defying whathaveyous and her famous sculpted backside, barely bound by the pasta-thin ribbons of her miraculous underwear, when desire then subsumed me like drunkenness, I wondered how it was that anything in this world ever managed to go wrong.

Fraternity life isn't all paddling asses and elephant walks. It's not all ritual coitus with billy goats and baking-soda-and-vinegar volcanoes exploded on your johnson. No. There's bad stuff, too. You gather fifty or more bro types together and not everyone is going to get along, no matter how much brotherly love and kind feeling the fraternity intends to promulgate. Grudges are cultivated, often over the pettiest of shit. There is deceit and anger and chest pounding and no shortage of derision and insensitivity. And these grudges, this anger and aggression, fueled the most intense showdowns at the Beirut table. Because, see, according to the implicit system of ethics that governed the house, forgiveness was not something one could simply give verbally. It couldn't come at the expense of all the cool self-assuredness. It had to be worked out, had to be earned. And the logo-emblazoned tables in the basement provided the space where the ever-present tension in the house was allowed to flourish and erupt and, finally, be dispelled.

I was sorely disappointed when that first night with Cara didn't usher in some new order, full of as much such-and-such as I could imagine. How close I came to avenging all those sheets! Instead, for a time after, she was inexplicably distant. She ignored my many calls and e-mails. I suspected she and Soccer Guy were off somewhere washing each other's hair or whatever and grew paranoid, borderline obsessive. Then, out of the blue, she called me up and acted as though nothing had happened. And with that a pattern was established. After a thawing period she'd be caring and touchy again and my heart would race with my mind in expectation, but you could almost hear the squelch of brakes after each flurry of limbs. Crime and punishment, in this, were one. And then, at the end of the term, Lucky resurfaced from Down Under.

It wasn't until late second semester junior year, after figuring we must've learned our lesson for the Games Night that sent one brother to the hospital and another to jail, that the college lifted its iron curtain of probation.

We were free! It was time to celebrate! Time for Games Night!

By then I'd more or less fully distanced myself from the fraternity. I'd started hanging out with some arty kids from my cultural studies classes. They didn't judge me for being in a fraternity and I didn't judge them for more than tolerating our school's sketch comedy troupe. But while I was pulling away, I saw that something was developing between many of the guys in the house. A sense of togetherness. Community. They were proud to watch Lembo's short film and to give him notes before he sent it off to festivals. They rallied around Rags when his dad got sick. And when Hunter's brother was in a bad car accident, some of the guys sat up all night listening to him tell stories from his childhood. They were *there* for one another. I heard not a pinch of irony in their voices when they said "brother." And when I came by the house for that Games Night, the coolness from the brothers no longer felt like part of our code, but genuinely cold. I got some "hey"s and some "where you been?"s, some pointed "what's up, stranger?"s. I wasn't sure the brothers liked me much anymore. Maybe they never had. Though I was deep in arrears, for example, no one mentioned my dues—maybe they didn't even want my money anymore. But I showed up early that Thursday, because, well, I mean, it *was* Games Night after all. The chiasmus practically completes itself: you can take the boy out of the frat, but not the PARTYBEERTITSPARTYPARTYPARTY!!!!!!!!

I started off the night by playing a number of games of Kings in the charter room. The center of the TV screen now presented a large *Videodrome*-ish hole—I was told that Holtz had thrown a D battery through it, thus turning it into an alumni-funded art installation. More people arrived. Word had spread in that way word would mysteriously spread before Facebook and Twitter, before texting became de rigueur, by a kind of drunken osmosis, on the ether. I went back out on the floor and tried my hand at Quarters. "I signed us up for Beirut," Overdorff said, gripping my shoulder after a few rounds. "Old times' sake." When we took the table, I didn't recognize the shaggy-headed pledge in roughed-up khakis who scurried off to get us beers. Our first game got under way and I found that even though I hadn't played in a while my shot was on. It was a curious piece of house wisdom that you sometimes got better at Beirut the more you drank. The booze and adrenaline would combine and complement each other and deliver you into a rarefied zone of attention, coordination, and aggression. And it was in such a zone that I found myself that night. I sank cup after cup and was ready to fend off any charges with quick grabs and a wiliness I'd cultivated as the fraidy-cat small kid on the lacrosse team. I, for once and finally, allowed myself to dissolve into the game's logical chaos. And it was just as thrilling as it had always looked from the sidelines.

Overdorff and I dominated for six or seven games. After a win, I made like I was dusting rubbish off my shoulders and chest and walked over to where the list was posted.

"Next victim?" I said, running a finger cinematically

down the list of crossed-off names. I couldn't bring myself to call out the next team: "Ring/Lucky."

There were so many people and so much noise that I hadn't seen Lucky come into the basement. When he stepped up to the table, everyone made a big to-do about welcoming him back. He and Ring were still the reigning champs, after all—there was a house-wide tournament and they'd held the title three consecutive semesters. They took little comedic bows and waved Princess Di waves around the floor. The brothers clapped and woo-hooed and laughed and those closest high-fived him.

We met halfway down the side of the table and, in accordance with the code of the Southern Asshole, we clasped hands and brought each other close with a one-armed hug and patted each other's back like nothing had changed. I was wearing his shoes. He was deeply tanned, his hair more sun-bleached than normal. My mind had played a sick trick on me: in my memory he'd grown small, atrophied.

"Welcome home, brother," I said. "Can't wait to hear about your trip."

"Thanks, man," he said, smiling. "Heard I missed a lot, being gone."

He turned about-face and went to his end of the table. Ring held out a beer for him to fill his pyramid. Lucky took it and tipped his head in my direction and Ring shook his slowly.

I knew Lucky knew. I hadn't gone to great lengths while he was away to hide what I'd been up to.

As we got going I felt I'd played maybe one or three too

many games. I'd been eighty-sixed from the zone. The cups started to blur and I had to concentrate very hard to keep them from looking like one big buckety cup. And the hand that only moments ago had delivered dialed-in parabolas? It felt heavy and foreign and my first shot landed at least six inches in front of the cups. Lucky nabbed it with a swift magician's pass of his hand and asked, "So what? you bouncing now, too?"

Ring and Lucky started the game by doubling up, so they got the balls back. They performed their special high five/handshake before taking their next shots. The mark of a good team, like that of a family, is that it takes them no time at all to pick up where they left off. By the time we reracked, they had only one cup gone from their pyramids, a shot Overdorff made.

Brothers I'd met maybe once were on the table next to ours. I didn't remember their names, if I'd ever known them in the first place. Their polo shirts were wet-spotted and torn. One of them spoke with a southern accent but had gel in his hair and I thought like what the fuck is that about? From across the basement I heard "*Go, go, go.*" Coeds lifted red Solo cups to their washed-out-looking faces as though smelling roses. In order to be heard over the music and the chanting and cheering, people were using outside voices and the basement became a symphony of small talk. Through it all and as though from somewhere far off I heard the distinct plunk of a rimmed shot. The hollow plink-plink of a ball skittering across linoleum. I couldn't tell, had it come from our game or the other one? I glanced around, scanned the floor. And then my legs were ripped clear from under me and there was the weight of a body across my chest and I was far more horizontal than vertical and I saw the ceiling lights rise in front of me, lambent with their hideous fluorescence, and as gravity seized me and I thudded to the ground and all the breath left my lungs and the frat-sludge soaked through my shirt, I knew that I was, at least for the moment, right where I belonged.

Learning Curves

The task of the writer is to learn how to write.

—Jules Renard

I didn't know I would ever want to be a writer when, at seventeen, I started to keep a journal. And if those early entries reveal anything, it is the near crystalline insanity of that dream. They take as their subjects things like how much I'd partied at Beach Week and how certain friends (that they were not really my friends deserves mention—I recall setting out to convince my future self that they, who numbered among the popular kids, had been my friends, such was the level of self-deception I was operating on) had cried as they headed off to college. In one entry I announce that I'm a cynic and a misanthrope and then, mere entries later, I declare, without a hint of irony or self-awareness, that I'm a born people person. Then there are the girls, my nauseating desire for, my persistent lack of success with, their names light as sundresses: Allison, Katie, Lindsey, Ginny, Kristine, Katie, Katie. "Girls are so dumb!" I lament. "I just want someone to hold hands with," I emote. But sometime during my freshman year of college, the record shows, I started to transcribe poems and quotes from whatever I was reading. (I was reading!) There's some Dickinson and Eliot and Frost. Vonnegut and Kafka. I practiced what only by the loosest of definitions qualifies as explication. Observe my inchoate insight: "I finished Kafka's 'The Metamorphosis.' It was an interesting short story that I thought contained many underlying meanings and themes." It wasn't long before I was writing descriptions, full of dashes, of my solitary walks through snowy Virginia woods, peppered with phrases in Latin, a language I'd never studied. I composed metered lines about stars and the moon that used the word "sublunary" as though I'd bought it at cost. Reading back through these entries now gives me a sensation something like when you put your hand up against another person's and massage the twinned middle fingers, a charge of the familiar and the utterly mysterious. This is and cannot be me.

These notes are my daily prayer.

—Jules Renard

Jules Renard, a French novelist, poet, and playwright, started keeping a journal in 1887, when he was twenty-three. This was roughly two years after Victor Hugo died. Literary historians tend to cite Hugo's death as the end of an era, at least for the French, and what followed was a renaissance that combined, say, the economic boom of our jazz age and the experimental creativity of the sixties. The French call it *la belle époque*. It's when Alfred Jarry was waddling the streets of Paris as his creation, Ubu Roi, a pair of six-shooters slung from his hips. When Henri Rousseau was painting his primitive paintings and Picasso was turning perspective on its head. But despite all the flutter and buzz of artistic revolution, Renard remained unfazed. He never hitched himself to any clique or wave or ism. On this point his journal shows him getting a little chippy and defensive: "You can be a poet and still wear your hair short. You can be a poet and pay your rent. Even though you are a poet, you can sleep with your wife." Point is, Renard set his sights on himself, on exploring and rendering the weave of his experience. It makes sense that in his lifetime he was best known for an autobiographical novel about his troubled childhood, *Poil de carotte*. And he might have first intended his journal to act as a shadow to his art, a companion to his novels and plays—the success of which won him admittance into the prestigious Académie Goncourt—but through a Peter Pan–like thaumaturgy, the shadow broke off and became the work of art itself.

> *I spread out my memory like a map and strive to see again what I have seen: and am continually astonished.*
>
> —Jules Renard

I discovered *The Journal* at about the same age Renard began keeping it. I was twenty-two and had just graduated college.

That summer I stayed on in Williamsburg and worked at a seafood restaurant, where I served buttery-ass clam chowder to tourists getting their anachrono-historical highs off all the Coloniality. I was also falling in love with an old friend, Grace. We'd met the summer after my sophomore year as part of an experiment in Christian community—we and nine other young adults had lived in a large Victorian house on Martha's Vineyard. I'd started to think that maybe she was the woman for whose protection (and the protection of whose "virtue") I'd been taught to pray for growing up—my future wife. In addition to thinking about her, I spent my free time obsessively reading and writing. I'd started to write fiction my senior year and was encouraged when my college awarded me a couple of prizes for my first stories, which were rip-offs of the contemporary writers I was reading at the time. That they were rip-offs meant that for some time to come there hung about me the noxious feeling of fraudulence. I'd built according to others' designs and imitating their work in this way had given me the first inkling of how much effort would be demanded of me to do my own. And so I became consumed with work. When I wasn't working, I was alternately anxious and depressed. Was I working hard enough? Did thinking about work count as work? Was I losing my hair? Renard returns to feelings like this throughout *The Journal*: "Work is treasure; I know it by counter-proof." During bouts of procrastination, I listened to a radio show that had as its guests the very writers I was ripping off. I listened for murmurs of profundity, shit I could steal. And in one interview the host said Donald Barthelme had at one point carried *The Journal* everywhere he went. Hooked as I was on Barthelme's stories then, I went off looking for secrets. See, I believed then that one could catch genius, as though it were an exotic virus.

My style, full of tours de force that no one notices.

—Jules Renard

Early on in his life, Renard writes, "I am convinced it is through observation that poetry must renew itself." And later: "Truth is not always art; art is not always truth; but truth and art have points of contact, which I am seeking." He is everywhere concerned with Truth in a way that feels charming and nostalgic now. But we still talk about small-*t* truth, how an image or a thought can ring true. And *The Journal* brims with brilliant descriptions and aphorisms that do just that. "Happy people have no right to be optimists: it is an insult to sorrow." "Spiders draw plans of capital cities." "I am never bored anywhere: being bored is an insult to oneself." He manages to restore a flavor of mystery to things or feelings that, for many of us, time and familiarity have dulled and muted. He has this to say about his style: "I always stop on the brink of what will not be true." And at their best and most economical, Renard's sentences give the illusion they've stood for all time, as though it was his phrasing that was used to forge whatever he's describing. I like to imagine him, after writing one, reaching for a cigarette.

Any good writer will achieve moments of small-*t* truth like Renard does in *The Journal*—it's for such moments of recognition, the uncanny feeling that it is the writer who has read us, that most of us read in the first place. But there was an aura of inevitability to his details, one that demonstrated to me the powerful alchemy writers fiddle with. Coming to understand this power language wields was for me a lot like falling in love with an old friend. A foundational shift in perception occurs. And this shift was scales-from-the-eyes revelatory for a person who at the time was writing shit like "Then my shirt is off and her pants are off and my pants are off and I'm feeling good."

Suppose I were called upon to possess all the women I am in love with!

—Jules Renard

The summer I discovered *The Journal*, one of the girls from the Martha's Vineyard house got married in DC. Besides the couple who'd been our leaders, Grace and I were the only people from the house to attend. We'd spent the two years since that summer keeping up through letters. Real letters. Hers would arrive in handmade envelopes, intricate collages of images she'd cut out of magazines—glorious vistas abutted the airbrushed features of Abercrombie models. And while there was an intimacy to them, there'd never been any over-tures of attraction, not a lick of tension, sexual or otherwise.

"8/2/04: We spent the day before the wedding doing all the touristy things she wanted to do. The Vietnam Memorial. The Smithsonian. We flirted in that second-grade way, making fun of each other. She really is beautiful, and, remarkably, maybe totally oblivious of this. We shared a bottle of wine in the hotel room, whose lone bed had a thick red comforter and stuck out from the wall like a tongue. In bed, we talked for a while about our summer on the Vineyard, certain nights and discussions we wished we could relive, and then about her Fulbright—she leaves for Germany in a couple months. Then she said something so deeply penetrating about me that only she could have said it, something that had the weight of our history behind it, which I of course can't remember now, and my head a little light from the wine, I leaned over to her side of the bed and kissed her. She kissed me back. Our knees touched under the sheets like a rock and flint. And then, well, et cetera. Say what they will about creams or lotions, incense or whips, there's no aphrodisiac like nostalgia."

Death appears to me as a wide lake that I am approaching and of which I am beginning to see the outlines.

—Jules Renard

The Journal "develops" in two ways. The first is obvious: chronologically. We can talk about Renard's early years, about the year his son was born or his father died, the years his plays were produced, or the years when he was most social. Our inner art-dork, star-fucker mentality is coddled during these social years. Like some fantastic cocktail party, we're always surprised who pops up: the Edmonds, Rostand and de Goncourt, Toulouse-Lautrec, Oscar Wilde ("He has the oddity of being an Englishman. He gives you a cigarette, but he selects it himself. He does not walk around a table, he moves a table out of the way."), Mallarmé, Valéry, and Rodin. And then, of course, there's the magnificent Sarah Bernhardt: "Near a monumental fireplace, she reclines on the pelt of a polar bear. Because in her house you do not sit, you recline." Some of the pleasure in following this chronology has to do with the curiosity and charm of encountering a living history, as though *The Journal* were a necromantic terrarium. The fascination here, for me, may also have to do with an embarrassing, solipsistic tic I have: I am still dumbly baffled by the fact that people, hundreds upon hundreds of people, have lived their lives before me, lives more or less like the life I'm living *right now*. Renard had a wife and kid; I have a wife, have friends with kids. He started a literary magazine; I work for one. He cared about plays; I care about plays and movies. He wrote sentences, was frustrated whenever he couldn't or didn't; me too! He died; _____.

The second, subtler development is much harder to talk about, at least in any satisfying way—articulation being the curse of our deepest intuitions. ("Disgust with the literary métier, with life bent to fit the written rule, with truth amended for the reader.") This has to do with the way Renard grows, as a writer and a person. But "grow" is perhaps too simpy and superannuated a word for what I'm trying to get at. Ditto "deepen." I mean to say something as broad and boring-seeming as that time gets into him, that experiences make and remake him. Life happens, both to and through him. And maybe this is the principal pleasure of reading a writer's journal—watching how he or she contends with the relentlessness of those two human fundamentals, time and experience. How a perspective emerges in a manner not unlike sedimentary rocks, slowly and certainly, bound by an inscrutable glue. Renard's insights and descriptions themselves come to convey this acquisition of time and experience. Time, for example: "Several times during our lives we have our seasons, but their course is not well known." And experience: "The death of my father makes me feel as though I had written a beautiful book."

At bottom, though, this has to do with the limit of time and experience, i.e., with death, with Renard's lifelong internalization of the imminence of his own. Here are two paragraphs from 1906, one of his blooming seasons:

If I were to begin life again, I should want it as it was. I would only open my eyes a little more. I did not see properly, and I did not see everything in that little universe in which I was feeling my way.

But if I were to try to work again regularly, every day, like a student of rhetoric who wants to be the first in class;

not in order to make money, not to be famous, but in order to leave something, a little book, a page, a few sentences? Because I am not at peace.

These occur right after one another, presumably written in the same sitting. The self-assured acceptance he begins with becomes, very quickly, something more like resignation, acceptance with a caveat. Enter anxiety. What will he leave? And could he ever be satisfied with what he's done? Not plagued by what he has not? Moments like this present some of the most "truthful" writing in *The Journal*, because they seem to embody our own state of being-toward-death, to borrow a phrase. He says, "What most surprises me is this heart which keeps on beating." It's as though the simplest, most basic aspect of his life is a haunting reminder of what he's approaching. But this seriousness is always undercut by Renard's wit, his ability to sculpt a perfect aphorism. "Imagine life without death. Every day, you would try to kill yourself out of despair."

At a sign of Sarah Bernhardt I would follow her to the ends of the earth, with my wife.

—Jules Renard

I spent the flight to see Grace in Germany exhausting my imagination with the permutations our bodies would combine to form. That I didn't feel guilty about our relationship's physical turn seemed a promising augur, to suggest that maybe we had approval from on high. We made dinner that night—during prep, she taught me a neat new way of mincing garlic. After we'd eaten and cleaned up and were hanging out on the couch in her apartment's small living room, I kissed her. She stopped me. Said she wasn't sure she was attracted to me like that anymore. What had happened? Was it the garlic? I nearly threw up my spaghetti.

"12/2/04: We're in Heidelberg. Spent the early afternoon walking around the city. Then hiked up to Heidelberg Castle, which overshadows the city like a family legacy. It was struck by lightning and sustained numerous cannon assaults during I don't know how many dead wars. Wings and turrets are in shambles, broken and crumbled like a dry, half-eaten wedding cake. We looked out over the city.

"'Are you upset? I don't want you to be mad at me. About last night and all.' She hugged me just long enough to arouse and murder my hope.

"I quoted Jules to her: 'I have built such beautiful castles that I would be satisfied with their ruins.'

"'What?'

"I felt her looking at my profile. I kept looking out over the city and the Neckar River, which has a system of locks that reminded me of bracelets. Heidelberg lies between two steep, green mountains that cascade down toward the river. In the cradle between these mountains, the city seems to have sprouted up like prodigious, orange-capped fungi. I knew Grace wanted a real response.

"'Doesn't the city remind you of a brain from up here?'"

This evening, memories are using my brain as a tambourine.

—Jules Renard

It's now been more than a decade since I went to Germany. The trip and Grace have been relegated to a deeper, less accessible level of memory. Last time we corresponded— our mail now came prefaced by an *e*—I learned that she'd moved to Seattle, gotten married, and was pregnant. Given all the ways that time and experience have gerrymandered our lives in the meantime, it's somewhat astonishing to recall that Germany is still somewhere between Paris and Asia. And for a heartbreak that was once so painful and real, I'm surprised it takes reading through my journal entries to summon any emotion in me. Again, the me there is and is not me. To my delight and relief, though, this same heart keeps beating behind my ribs.

Looking back on his journal, Renard says, "What surprises me is that I did not give more details. Today my eye would have taken in everything. My apparatus is better. But you become aware that you have, after all, lived, and that it is natural for life to pass and, even, for it to end." It's hard to imagine what more details he could have given, but what he acknowledges here is how deeply intertwined, inextricable even, are his life and work, like some double helix of his being. "You can recover from the writing malady only by falling mortally ill and dying." And the sharper his perception, the closer he comes to experiencing his Truth. "The moments during which, like a fish in the water, I move with ease within the infinite."

Like Renard, I think I continue to keep my journal because I'd like to learn how to be at home in the infinite ocean, to accept the fact that I can be just this one fish, even if it's not a gigantic whale shark or a manta ray or a humpback anglerfish with its big teeth and bioluminescence. Even if it's just a plain old tuna. I'd like evidence of a sort that time has gotten into me, proof that experience has made and remade me. Because before my own reckoning, at some point in the hopefully distant future, I'd like to be able to look back on all my anguish and joy and sorrow and pain, everything about my infinitely small tuna existence, and be grateful for it.

Far from Me

Born Originals, how comes it to pass that we die Copies?

—Edward Young

I.

You know us by sight, have seen us out on the courts of your neighborhood park or local high school, and, perhaps, been baffled. You who've had to wait on benches or behind windscreens for us to tire and finish, we've taxed your patience, I know—I apologize. We are the tennis players who do not properly play, who send the ball back and forth over the net without serving, without keeping score. If asked, we'd say we're working on our strokes. Just some good old proprioceptive fine-tuning, endless preparation for a match that will never be played. This isn't to say that competition between us doesn't exist, though, only that it isn't measured by something so brutely positivistic as a score. By the subtler metric of body language and mood, then, shifts in the ether. As a result of these shifts, tensions will sometimes rise unaccountably and every now and again we'll howl out in frustration. We'll curse our rackets or air our grievances with the wind. Decry a passing siren or bitch about the glare coming off a car's hood. But for all that, we don't refer to each other as opponents. Never would. We are "hitting partners," twinned in an elaborate rumba of angle, pace, and spin. And the point of it all? What can the endgame be when, properly speaking, there is no game? Though we are legion, I speak only for myself when I say that as much as is humanly possible, I want my groundstrokes to resemble those of Roger Federer.

II.

For this ridiculous ambition my hitting partner, Scott, can be held largely responsible. We first met on the courts of Irving Park here in Portland, when he invited me over to be the fourth in an amicable set of doubles, one of the few we've ever played. He was part of a crew that regularly gathered there—almost every day of the week they'd turn at least one, though often more, of the four public courts into a private club of sorts. A members-only type deal. And I was excited to get the call, had seen them all before and wanted in. I'd discreetly admired Scott's strokes, in particular, from the safe distance of a few courts over. Watching his long one-handed backhand could prompt a driblet of envy-drool to trickle down my chin.

And the state of my game? It'd been nearly a decade since I'd played with anything like regularity, but I'd been seized by an urge as mysterious as it was sudden to get back into it. From the neighborhood pro-shop I picked up a racket on the cheap, a seasons-old midplus model from Prince. And a trip to the local Nike outlet yielded a baroque pair of purple sneakers and a matching headband that I thought quite smart—quite smart, that is, until I saw a picture of myself wearing it. I used to cart a grocery bag of balls to the park and serve to ghosts until my shoulder went sore, and then I'd rally with myself against the backboard, trying all the while not to think of myself as kin to that most forlorn of souls, the lone rider of a tandem bicycle. I'd played enough growing up to have a meager aquifer of muscle memory to tap but hadn't progressed much past the war of attrition stage of youth tennis, when kids can mostly be found hitting great parabolic moonballs and waiting for their opponent to miss. My game, in other words, was mine only according to the laws of grammar. And though I'd continued to watch tennis, I'd never considered modeling my strokes after those of a pro.

Enter Scott, who's about ten years older than me, though he'd say about eight. He grew up in Northern California, where he surfed and skateboarded, played music and tennis, activities he's kept up into adulthood. He's an accomplished photographer and has a master's degree in English and used to write poetry and, time to time, still does. He's been collecting midcentury modern furniture since well before it was trendy and will surely continue to after it's not. He's one of Those People. You know, annoyingly above average at everything he does. And whatever that happens to be, he always looks good doing it, is always accoutered with the finest gear. His several surfboards are practical works of art. He had Leica custom build him a camera. He commissioned a guitar to be made of wood reclaimed from a New York apartment once inhabited by Jim Jarmusch. And his tennis racket? His tennis shoes? They're the models used and endorsed by Roger Federer. Even his string job is the same as Roger's, down to the leather power pads and little plastic string savers, features whose utility is, at best, questionable.

After one of our earliest hitting sessions, Scott took me aside and informed me that I'd accidentally bought shoes endorsed by Rafael Nadal, the southpaw Spaniard whose buggy whip forehand makes him rather resemble a male stripper twirling undies above his head. His voice betrayed embarrassment on my behalf. He didn't want to have to mention the ankle socks I'd been wearing in the hopes of avoiding weird leg tans—a fashion choice, I was told, espoused only by lesser players like Mardy Fish. And what of the Adidas crew neck I'd got on clearance? It was the get-up of the ATP's resident Eeyore, Andy Murray. About my poor racket, the less said, the better. Scott likes to refer to this as the time in my life when I was confused.

Now, after a Ship of Theseus–like transformation, I, too, wear only Roger's shoes, I, too, use his racket. I guess I now have to specify his *old* racket, the Wilson Pro Staff 90, a version of which he used to win each of his record seventeen major championships. That Roger no longer uses this racket, having lost a step to age and switched to a considerably larger frame, means that Roger isn't quite Roger anymore. Or so Scott's argument—and probably mine, too—would follow. And I've come to understand the weird tan lines my legs now bear in summer as something like a monk's tonsure:

in striving for tennis purity, one may be called to sacrifice a calf or two.

That I'm so impressionable, so easily influenced, has over the years been the source of much irritation and hand-wringing, and to dwell on it for any length of time is sure to bring on a mean case of the collywobbles.

III.

Outfitting myself like Roger is but a small part of the deeper ongoing project, a project that's practically metaphysical in its ambition: to get my body to move like his, so much so that an unsuspecting passerby might mistake me for the Maestro. Absurd, I know. But only *logically*, according to *reason*. How does this work? you might be wondering. When I'm on the court? It's not that I imagine I *am* Roger, as when growing up, playing basketball, I'd imagine I *was* Michael Jordan. I do not picture myself at Wimbledon, for example, up a break in the fifth and serving, 19–18, for the championship, my player box filled with stalwarts: my wife, my coach (the affable ghost of Arthur Ashe, a fellow Richmonder), and a clutch of my closest friends, Michelle Obama and Randy Newman and Joey from *Full House*. No—such fancy is rightly left to those with undescended testes. Rather, it's more like there's a hologram of Roger projected on the court, superimposed on my body. While Scott and I are hitting, I am aware of the degree to which my body's movements conform to those of hologram-Roger. Have I properly timed my split-step? Has my forehand's backswing described a capital *C*? Has my head stayed still through contact? Readying for a backhand, did I correctly measure my steps and transfer my weight from right heel to toe? And after releasing the racket for the swing did I keep my left arm down and by my side for balance? A session is good or bad depending on how much in the positive I can answer a whole battery of questions like these.

It was no minor feat, either, acquiring hologram-Roger. To get him into my head, to have a clear enough understanding of what my physical aspirations should be, took hours and hours of observation, study, and practice. Through various European streaming sites, I watched every match of his I could, and not just at the four majors, but at the smaller tournaments, too, including ones played on surfaces like carpet. When there were no matches to be watched, I'd get on YouTube and binge on highlights, supercut after supercut, a practice that'd lull me into dumb wonder. I'd then visit a tennis-teaching website that had videos of Roger warming up on the outer courts at Indian Wells, tuning his serve, his backhand, and his greatest weapon, his forehand, that liquid whip. These videos were in high-def and had sections in ohhh-nooo slo-mo that allowed one to observe and process his body's every movement. The mechanics of how this happened are unclear to me, but over time I found myself to be in possession of a strange form of bodily knowledge. Almost literally possessed by it, actually. When hitting, I no longer simply knew that I'd made a mistake, but knew its cause, knew precisely how my body had failed to live up to my expectations for it. And with this knowledge in place, I began the long work of refining my movements and shrinking bit by bit the distance that lay between hologram-Roger and me.

IV.

Preposterous as this desire may sound, set down like this, a quick survey of the players at your neighborhood park or local high school or club would show that I'm not alone in it. Not by a long shot. You can't huck a rock where the sport's played without dinging a Fedhead. We even have a representative on the pro tour in Grigor Dimitrov, the Bulgarian phenom whose strokes so closely resemble Roger's that the press often refers to him, sportively, as "Baby Fed."

So what is it about Roger that casts such a spell? To what can we attribute his tremendous influence?

I don't think this can be reduced to something as simple as his success, to the fact that he's won more majors and spent more time at the top of the rankings than any other player in history. Go back a tennis generation and you find folks admiring Sampras for not much other than his domination. Unfair as it may have been, I recall there being quite a bit of fuss and bother then about how boring he was to watch.

Much to-do, on the other hand, has been made about Roger's game. And maybe more written. Not a season goes by, it seems, without some new appraisal of his greatness, without some writer rehashing what sets him apart from the rest of the field. The dominance, the stats—welcome icing. And while we're never fully satisfied with the explanations given, while we always find them wanting in some way, tiresome and full of clichés, Scott and I can't help ourselves. With unspoken relish, a relish that masquerades as disdain, we read them. And of a session we, too, indulge. We moon over his footwork, over the apparent effortlessness of his movement—he so rarely looks rushed or out of place. We go gaga for his forehand, how he manages to create angles with it that one would have thought impossible given his position on the court. We wax dreamily about his serve, about how well he can put it out wide to either court or play it mean and deadly up the T. His feathery slice and occasional tweener thrill us. And his drop shots? His touch around the net? Only a neonate's tuchus rivals the softness of his hands.

What all this talk amounts to, in the end, is the unshakable belief that Roger plays tennis the way it's meant to be played. We know it in our bones, such that acknowledging it feels foregone, almost redundant. In this it's maybe closer to Platonic anamnesis than anything else, a form of deep remembering. A fleet of nerds coxswained by Mark Zuckerberg himself couldn't program a more complete tennis player. And so it shouldn't be surprising that there's a multitude of us out there trying to emulate him. To aspire to play better tennis is, *eo ipso*, to aspire to play more like Roger. For a handy analog we might look to yoga. Yoga's promise is that by disciplining one's body to hold different poses, what amount to bodily archetypes, one may achieve a certain measure of mental quietude or spiritual lightness. Likewise, so long as I'm not playing matches and therefore not afraid to fail, not tempted to resort to a safer and more limited form of the game, I am able to nourish the illusion that progress is being made, that I'm on the road to the sort of total attunement and deep self-forgetting that one used to be able to call, without an ironic sneer, transcendence.

V.

"Liquid whip"—much as I wish it were, the description isn't mine. It's Wallace's, from his now canonical essay "Federer as Religious Experience," collected posthumously as the more gnomic and koan-like "Federer Both Flesh and Not." The tween girl inside me has never been able to shake a giddy fascination with the fact that, for half an hour or so in a nondescript ATP office at the All England Club, Roger and Wallace met. I'm not a hundred percent sure what, if anything, it means, but where I naturally and casually call Federer Roger, sometimes even Rodge in fits of pique or passion during a match, I don't refer to Wallace as anything but Wallace. Not by the publishing world's freight train, "David Foster Wallace," and not by the hipster-dipshit acronym "DFW." And certainly not "David," or, worse, "Dave"—having known and loved only the work, I cannot bring myself to affect such familiarity with the man. But of course the question's begged: how did their introduction go? The scene's been an endless source of homosocial woolgathering for me. Did a tournament official present them to each other with a semiformal exchange of surnames? "Mr. Federer, meet Mr. Wallace. Mr. Wallace, Mr. Federer." Or was the vibe more relaxed and chill than that? Was Wallace nervous? Presuming he was nervous, how did those nerves manifest? Did he fidget? Shuffle his notes? Was he literally sweating it? And if so, did Roger do anything special to put him at ease? A joke? A gesture? Maybe a way of crossing his legs or relaxing into his chair? And the questions keep coming: Was Wallace just another journalist to Roger? Or did Roger have a sense of his accomplishments? From the questions Wallace asked, we know he was trying to figure out whether Roger was aware of his own greatness, and, if so, how, but did Roger perceive the possible reflexivity of those questions? Did he know that he was more or less sitting across from the belletristic equivalent of himself? There's no caboose to this train of questions, it keeps on chugging along.

We do have an inkling of what Roger made of the meeting. When after Wallace's suicide he was asked about the interview, Roger said, "One of the strangest I've ever done. As I was leaving I was still wondering what we had talked about." And when later prompted by another reporter, he added, "I wasn't sure what was going to come out of it because I didn't know exactly what direction he was going to go. The piece was obviously fantastic. You know, yeah, it's completely different to what I've read in the past about me anyway."

And the piece is fantastic, obviously. If you're wondering how or why, feel free to hop online and read it. And if you're still curious after you finish, you can plug any variation of "Wallace Federer" into your search engine of choice and scroll through page after page of appreciations and thoughtful exegeses. Let your tolerance for conspiracy theories and your stomach for mind-boggling insensitivity determine whether you read the articles that aver a correlation between Federer's "decline" and Wallace's suicide. There's all this and more about Wallace out there now, including a movie starring the guy you may remember from such films as *The Muppets* and *Sex Tape*. So swiftly plaguelike has writing about him spread in the wake of his death, in fact, that it's hard not to imagine it all as an electronic rat king. And as aware as I am of this ever-growing corpus, as hesitant as I am to join my hairless tail to the many hairless tails Twizzlered together in cyberspace, I'm also equally aware that it's become all but impossible to write anything essayistic or ruminative about Roger without first acknowledging a debt to Wallace. It's not only his writing about Roger, either, but tennis more generally, too. To write about the sport at all is pretty much to write oneself squarely into the long, dark shadow of his influence and, therefore, to court the easy dismissal that familiarity encourages, almost demands. We seem fixed in our belief that the worst sin an artist can commit is that of being unoriginal and, ergo, inauthentic. How else are we to explain the work of someone like Richard Prince, who's made a career out of needling this very idea? And yet with that said, every year, come late June, some magazine with a budget sends a writer to London to cover Wimbledon, the fortnight, surely hoping that one of them might return with something like Wallace's magic. And many of them do. They come back with *something like* Wallace's magic. Indeed, there are passable mimics out there, accomplished ventriloquists. (You likely encountered them in the now-defunct "pages" of Grantland, the sports and culture website conspicuously designed to accommodate footnotes, Wallace's stylistic calling card.) But the spiritual equivalent of reading essays like these is listening to a cover band or someone really fucking nail a song at karaoke. It's not that they're not admirable or that writing them doesn't take a measure of talent and hard work—they are! they do!—only that there's a ceiling to how much one can appreciate such performances, a ceiling so low you can't really stand up all the way. The pre-Romantic poet and critic Edward Young, whose work influenced Coleridge, and later Emerson, is great on this. "Suppose an *Imitator* to be most excellent (and such there are), yet still he but nobly builds on another's foundation; his debt is, at least, equal to his glory; which therefore, on the balance, cannot be very great." This is all to say that what interests me here isn't Wallace's work, at least not quite, and it's not his life—with time the considerable allure both once had for me has diminished. Considerably. ("We cloy of the honey of each peculiar greatness," Emerson wrote. "Every hero becomes a bore at last.") What interests me, recovering *Imitator* that I am, is his influence and its residue. And furthermore, that notion's very pith: that you can, in the career of your life and one way or another, fall under the sway of another person.

VI.

Junior year of college James lived in the crappy little carpeted apartment next to mine, in a complex that went by the manifoldly deceptive name of Governor's Square. This was Williamsburg, Virginia, so Governor's Square was just off Ironbound Road, right behind the Bucktrout Funeral Home.

Given how much space James takes up in my memory of that time, it's surprising that I can't remember any particulars about meeting him—it's almost like he was already there. And in a way he was, in the form of cultural archetypes I'd long since internalized and was still incredibly in thrall to: James was part Cool Older Brother and part Reclusive Genius. I first learned of his existence from my roommate. Had I met the guy next door who was taking time off school to write? Who sold his plasma to help make rent? Whose Russian girlfriend with an achingly exotic accent would drop by every so often to smoke pot and erotify and listen to records? I had not, but I'd glimpsed him, had seen him down in the parking lot getting in and out of his black early-nineties Isuzu Rodeo. It ranks among the failures of our latently homophobic culture that we're discouraged from honoring the flint-spark of attraction that ignites even the most platonic relationships, but fuck it, James was beautiful. He was tall and rocker-lean and his chestnut hair hung in waves and practical goddamn ringlets down past his shoulders. He wore dandyish monk-strap boots that clip-clopped on the concrete steps as he came and went, taking them, both up and down from the sound of it, two at a time. I knew that he was older than me, but didn't know by how much, and still don't—that James can be cagey about the strangest shit was one of the many things about our friendship I had to learn to live with. He was cloaked in dusky obscurity, seemed always to have a smoke going. And by the time we finally met, sometime later that fall, he'd attained in my mind the mythic status of Writer.

Now, there is a form of envy that afflicts a certain kind of young person, the kind of young person studying Literature in college, whose writerly aspirations are amorphous, wispy intuitions that haunt the mind, who sorta thinks, I don't know, that maybe one day, after I've studied enough, read enough, maybe then I'd like to write something myself. For such a young person, Literature is always capital *L*. It is a giant temple inside of which sit a whole bunch of smaller temples, and by the entrance to each, a great marble bust looms: Tolstoy, Woolf, Dostoyevsky, Austen, Faulkner, the Eliots, etc. One is led through these temples by docents, by professors, professors who may on occasion be heard to proudly declare, "I don't read living authors." The dream of writing for such a young person culminates in an imagined quid pro quo, in having one's name burnished on a syllabus, to finally and at long last be studied oneself. And the envy this young person can fall prey to is that of another writer's calling, of the relative certainty with which that person inhabits his or her artistic identity. How unproblematic is that person's relationship to their promise and ambition! And how uncertain my own!

The fall I met James I was still at least partially bent on achieving yet higher levels of bro: I was still semiactive in my fraternity, still playing lacrosse, still wearing plaid on plaid and saddle shoes and pants embroidered with sundry fauna. But I'd also fallen hard for the poetry of T. S. Eliot and had buckled down sophomore year and decided to count schooling among the priorities of my time at school. The first of many Grand Academic Endeavors I'd embark on, all of which time would swiftly abort, was a thesis exploring the philosopher F. H. Bradley's influence on Eliot—the latter wrote a dissertation on the former while at Harvard, before WWI broke out and prevented him from defending it. (And how very proud I was to have grasped that grammatical construction. Former, latter; latter, former: no longer would I wander blindly the path of misidentified antecedents!) Plan was I'd then use my credentials to score a position on the English faculty of a hoity-toity boarding school in the Northeast, where I'd stroll the manicured grounds contemplating the Verities, writing poems, nay, writing *verse* in the rusticozy lodgings the institution provided me, all the while inspiring a generation of wealthy children who would remember me throughout their lives, perhaps most fondly whenever they confused Emerson and Thoreau at art auctions or on their yachts. In the privacy of my Governor's Square apartment, which had come furnished, I wore a crimson old-man cardigan and sheepskin slippers while attempting to memorize long passages from *The Four Quartets*—a practice I thought might help me understand them. Also sometimes, sincerely, I smoked a pipe.

My apartment had the anodyne vibe of a low-rent beach house. I wasn't home very often then but even when I was it still seemed empty, maybe more so with me in it. But James's? His place was for me the prototypical locus of writerly divination. State of his floor, it was like someone had busted a piñata packed with holey jeans and threadbare T-shirts. Dirty plates and empty cereal bowls were always Jengaed in his kitchen sink. And in his living room you were likely to find a number of his floral-patterned antique china cups, in which soggy cigarette butts floated, extinguished in the cold remains of the milky tea he favored then. On his walls, though, actual art: a painting of a man sitting in a chair wearing only a flocculent beard, his not inconsiderable dong somehow more intimidating for being limp, hung next to another of an erect naked woman whose feral black pubic thatch stirred in one equal parts desire and fear. In addition to a simple tribal mask on the wall near the front door, James owned a five-foot bamboo blowgun. I gathered that he'd picked them up while in South America, but because he never told me why he'd been there or how he'd acquired them, my imagination was allowed (encouraged?) to run wild. I pictured him in a remote Amazonian village, participating in an obscure initiation rite, one that entailed visionary drugs administered via the tip of a blow dart achooed into his ass, followed by some inconspicuous bit of body modification. Most important, though, were the books. They were always strewn about in a way that suggested they'd been seized in a moment of inspiration and then summarily discarded. Pick one up and open to a random page and you might find a cater-pillar of cigarette ash gathered in the spine, a physical trace of the ghostly and immaterial act of reading, evidence he'd been there. The names on the spines were foreign to me then and, by virtue of the transitive property, were an extension of James's mystery and further evidence of his considerable power over me. I arranged them all alphabetically in my mind, where they sat in a row like the world's most intimi-dating admissions board: Acker, Auster, Baldwin, Barthelme,

Carver, DeLillo, Didion, down on through Gaddis, Munro, Murdoch, O'Connor, and Pynchon. And of course, finally, there was Wallace.

VII.

It's a phrase that zaps the mind, like biting into tinfoil—"the anxiety of influence." Like other Big Ideas that devolve into idioms (Relativity, String Theory, Communism, etc.), it gets mentioned more often than it gets discussed. Do we skip over it so quickly because we've all accepted it as fact? Or do we quietly distrust or resent it? In a way it's easy to dismiss or ignore. It's almost willfully oblivious of writers who aren't white or male, for example—a big-time no-no nowadays. But there's also the simple fact that Harold Bloom's theory comes to us via Harold Bloom's prose, which smells of oniony-ripe academic BO. His syntax gets so gnarled in places and he repurposes so many words from Latin and Greek that at times *The Anxiety of Influence* reads like a parody of bad scholarly writing. What it's like? It's like watching Barysh-nikov dance in combat boots. Because the core idea is striking, elegant even: young poets ("ephebes" (of course)) begin their artistic journeys nervy and afraid that the achievements of previous poets will always overshadow their own. In order to protect and nurture their gifts, their originality, to ensure they aren't swallowed up and subsumed by the splendor of their "Great Originals," they must creatively "misread" them. And their work, their poems—this is key—they *are* those misreadings. They're artifacts and instances of living anxiety, not proof that that anxiety has been overcome. And so literary history, at least from Shakespeare to the present, isn't simply a Connect the Dots of anchoritic geniuses but a complex and tessellated game of Telephone. The bulk of Bloom's little book is taken up with outlining six "revisionary ratios," i.e., the ways a poet misreads his Great Original, and exploring the psychological ramifications of each. But the phrase itself, "the anxiety of influence," has since outpaced all these particulars. It now lives a life abroad in the culture, a much diminished and maybe even bankrupt life, one in which it means something like: a fruitful creative life is begun only after an ephebe kills his artistic father.

You don't hear the question of influence put directly all that often—we seem to skirt it, almost as if it were a taboo. But every now and again an interviewer will trot it out like a Trojan horse. Much of the time it's harmless, driven by innocent curiosity, but still there are instances in which you hear it loud and clear, the accusation in the question. "Is there not the shibboleth bequeathed to us by Eliot," Bloom puts it, "that the good poet steals, while the poor poet betrays an influence, borrows a voice?" If the writer doesn't simply slough the question off, he (because in my experience it's largely pygmy-weinered, mommy-issued men we're talking here) will likely qualify and evade. Act cagey. He might offer some bit of braggadocio, a helping of humbug or humble-brag on the order of "I thought about Nabokov a lot in my latish teens." Or he might reach for the heavens and claim an influence so grand as to border on the delusional, like when I heard a novelist, unfamous for his experiments with genre, assert, "Proust? I count him among my influences." These answers are never satisfying, most likely because they amount to little more than the writer's bid for influential power of his own.

But the question's always confused me. Because when we ask a writer about his or her influences, what are we really angling after? What would a good answer look like?

Do we want to hear about their initial thrill of discovery? About how the Ephebe, at the riperound age of a score, borrowed a hip and smart friend's copy of, say, *Girl with Curious Hair*, prepared to like what he found there because it came stamped with that friend's seal of approval, and spent a weekend feverishly reading and rereading it? Do we want to know that he may have experienced a mild form of the vaunted Stendhal syndrome? That he literally swooned, the words blurring and pulling apart on the page in a way that forced him to put the book down? Do we really want to hear that he'd been unaware that language could feel as alive, as playful and inventive and fresh and funny, as welcoming of all modes of contemporary experience, as what he encountered in those pages?

Not really, I don't think. It's the same first lesson every writer must learn, one way or another: literature is alive, ongoing. Language, like history, is always making room. Always ending in this moment and this one and this.

But if it's not this itty-bitty epiphany we're hankering for, then what? Maybe we're hungry for what the Ephebe did after that experience. The obsessive bits, then, the embarrassing shit. How he wrote down every word he didn't know on a note card and kept the growing stack in a case on his desk, a case he came to think of as a treasure chest. How before writing essays for his classes he'd choose half a dozen of these cards at random and force himself to use them, often to preposterous and cringe-worthy ends. How he happened upon Wallace's writing process, one that involved doing five drafts of whatever he was working on, and forthwith began doing that, believing it would solve the Rubik's Cube of genius inside him. Maybe we want to hear how wildly stilted his fiction was then, how it was so full of footnotes that the text proper was practically on stilts. Or how on a cross-country trip with the hip and smart friend he found a copy of Wallace's then hard-to-find first novel, *The Broom of the System*, in a Haight-Ashbury bookstore and felt a soaring sense of power over the friend, who'd never read it. Or about how the Ephebe audited a Wittgenstein seminar and a Calculus class because he thought one needed more than a passing familiarity with Analytic Philosophy and capital-*M* Mathematics in order to produce Serious Writing. And so on (and on and on. . .).

There's something delightfully deranged about behavior like this and such details come close to what we're after, I think, when we ask about "influence." We like to hear that the writer—tickler of our risibilities, puppeteer of our heartstrings—wasn't always in full possession of his or her powers. Which is to say that we like to hear that there was a time when he or she wasn't quite fully him- or herself. To ask about "influence," then, is to ask for an explanation, an origin story. For as much as we talk about genius, for as thoroughly as we've invested our artists with qualities once culturally reserved for prophets and hierophants, we still seem to favor the view that great art is the result, at bottom, of hard work. Questions of talent and spiritual awareness and vision (in the deepest sense of that word) make us squirrelly, so we place our faith in the process, in the discipline that self-knowledge and -transformation demand—and in, finally, the very idea of selfhood and its expression. There's even a whole genre devoted to the development of an artist: the Künstlerroman. And in her fantastic one, *The Song of the Lark*, Willa Cather sums this idea up nicely: "Every artist makes himself born. It is very much harder than the other time, and longer."

We're happy to treat our athletes, on the other hand, as outliers, as physical mutants or avatars. The freakishly graceful ways they move, in real time, right before our eyes, necessarily blind us to the tremendous amount of work they've invested into moving that way. And so we chalk their achievements up to something that lives in the genes, that's gifted to them more than earned. This would help explain the hiccup of dissonance we experience when we hear elite athletes talk about how hard they work at their "craft."

And while of course hard work and natural aptitude are integral to both, the difference in how we emphasize them fascinates me. By stressing that great art is the result of hard work, we shore up the notion that it's attainable. We've come to put such a high premium on individuality and self-expression, and have brought those into an asymptotic relationship with art, that we have to ensure art remains democratic, accessible—hence the popularity of books that claim to explain "creativity," that promise mastery to those willing to put in ten thousand hours of practice. Hence MFAs. Said differently: more people believe they have a great book in them than believe they could win, say, Wimbledon. No amount of later-in-life work could prepare Joe Sixpack or Plain Jane for the latter, but the former? If they had enough free time, on the weekends maybe, if they didn't have to make money, if they weren't burdened by the kids, if they could read everything they needed to read to prepare themselves, then they could articulate what makes them special, authentic. Then, at long last, they could tell their story.

This is a long way of saying that, early on, I thought a writer's influences were a blueprint of sorts, a record of the work they did to become themselves and therefore a road map of the work I'd need to do to become myself. So after I got through all Wallace's books and all the uncollected work I could run down online in the dread latter days of Web 1.0, including short stories he'd published in his college's literary magazine, humor articles he'd written for its paper, I went off in search of something like a developmental record. I was looking for anything that bore a trace of where Wallace had come from. I scoured interviews for mentions of other writers he admired, folks he may have read as closely as I was reading him. All at once I became a truffle pig, snuffling for sources, clues. And I was thrilled when I thought I stumbled upon them, when I caught stylistic or spiritual echoes in work that he'd either mentioned or that I was sure he'd read. There's a scene in Walker Percy's *The Moviegoer*, for example, where Binx returns to a theater to look for a seat he'd long ago carved his initials into, and there's an almost identical scene in *The Broom of the System*, only if I remember right it's a bathroom stall. Vonnegut's story "The Euphio Question" features a radio signal that produces in those who hear it a euphoria so intense it stupefies them, leaves them as but blissed-out husks of their former selves, which is precisely the conceit of the eponymous movie at the heart of *Infinite Jest*. And Madame Psychosis's suicide attempt in that book might as well have been written on onionskin laid atop an indelible party scene in Gaddis's *The Recognitions*. Don DeLillo's work makes many cameos, especially nuggets from his lesser-known novels like *End Zone* and *Ratner's Star*. Nicholson Baker's use of footnotes in *The Mezzanine* set bells off, as did Lee K. Abbott's knowing way of spelling out "quote unquote" in dialogue. I could go on and on. Point is I found what I'd been looking for, which is to say, I found other writers, a whole lot of them. "For a time, our teachers serve us personally, as meters or milestones of progress," Emerson wrote. "Once they were angels of knowledge, and their figures touched the sky. Then we drew near, saw their means, culture, and limits; and they yielded their place to other geniuses." But what I thought would empower disturbed me in the end. I wallowed for a while. By this point I'd dropped out of the frat and grown my hair long and cultivated what I could of a beard and bought a corduroy bomber jacket that seemed like something James might wear, or at least approve of in his tight-lipped way, and I'd swapped my pipe for cigs and my contact lenses for big, doofy glasses, and I'd sometimes sit around my bland apartment ruefully excogitating: all this evidence, did it mean that Wallace was unoriginal and, therefore, inauthentic? And if so, I fretted, what hope could there ever be for me?

VIII.

Authenticity. It's the Big Word around which so many of our anxieties orbit, the standard against which we're asked to judge our experiences of people, places, food, and art, which is to say experience itself. You hear it so often nowadays that you could turn it into a drinking game: after every mention, take a shot of small-batch artisanal bourbon, chase it with a quaff of craft beer. Authenticity is at the top of a class that includes other buzzwords like empathy, community, human, and organic. Concerns about these things intensify, of course, when the conditions of existence conspire to make them difficult or impossible to achieve. So the more mediated our lives become, the more we'll stress the value of the organic. The more automated we ourselves become, the more we'll worry over what's human. The more dislocated and uprooted we feel, the more we'll talk about community. And given how neutered and disembodied, how literally superficial people are online, lost as they get in the endless clown hanky of a social media feed, it's no wonder that we've got folks out there rah-rahing empathy. But the ubiquity of these words shouldn't be mistaken for a mark of comprehension. Situation's quite the opposite, it seems to me: the more they're used, the less they're understood. It's more than that, though. The more they're used, the less they need to be understood at all.

Asked to define authenticity, for example, most of us would probably start small. Something is authentic when it is, in fact, what it professes to be. This is what we mean about eighty or ninety percent of the time and it doesn't really trip us up. We roll right on by Mexican and Ethiopian food that claims to be authentic because we know that it means genuine, the real deal. At a restaurant that boasts authentic Sicilian pizza, we can expect to find za on the order of what we'd get in Sicily. And so on. Same holds for garments claiming to be made of one hundred percent authentic cashmere or Mulberry silk or Japanese denim. Concerns about this type of authenticity grow out of our awareness of and sensitivity to phonies and fakes. We like hearing food is authentic because we've eaten tacos whose shells are waffles, burritos swaddled by quesadillas, pizza whose crust is gravid with cheese. Knockoff clothes have burned us, so much so, apparently, that eBay has felt compelled to offer tutorials on how to identify, say, a bogus Lacoste polo shirt. (For what it's worth, on an authentic one, the alligator logo is dark green and sits between the bottom stitch of the collar and the bottom button. . .) This simple meaning of the word comes to us from the art and auction world, the museum, where experts are trusted to certify a piece's origin and originator. Think of *Antiques Roadshow*, which shouldn't be anywhere close to as compelling to watch as it is. It generates its surprising tension by stoking our desire to know whether, e.g., a chair that's been in the family four generations is an authentic Chippendale, whether the vase purchased for the plant it held is an authentic Lalique. Replicas, counterfeits, impostors, facsimiles—they impart upon authentic shit its aura and appeal (and, therefore, its value).

It's when authenticity comes to be applied to people that things get dicey. Pressed for a definition of it in this sense, we'd likely have to MacGyver one. With Scotch tape and spit we'd affix a dim notion of truth to a considerably dimmer one of selfhood, that blessingcurse modernity bequeathed us. It means being true to yourself, we'd say, not caring what other people think of you, not needing their approval. You do you or whatever. We might go on to claim that some things about us are really us, while others are only incidentally us, and that to live authentically is to live in such a way that the real things are tended to and nourished more than the incidental ones. Only then can we declare, proudly, that we're self-fulfilled or self-actualized or self-realized. We don't really learn this ideal of authenticity so much as we absorb it, don't choose so much as inherit it. And once internalized, it recedes to the background, where it serves as the screen upon which we project our wildest hopes and dreams for ourselves. It's burrowed so deeply into our understanding of how we should aspire to live that it's easy to overlook the fact that it has a history, both a personal and philosophical one.

Everyone has a fund of experience with this—it's the sort of thing that you find everywhere once you start looking for it. Here's but one example from mine: for my fifth-grade banquet, a get-down thrown for graduating elementary school, the youth pastor from my church was called in to deliver the keynote. While my cohort and I ate our single-serving ice cream tubs with wooden infinity spoons, he held forth about the difference between thermostats and thermometers. A thermostat controls the temperature, while a thermometer only reflects it. Thermostats influence the environment around them; thermometers are influenced by the environment. "Which one are you going to be?" he concluded, and the question hung so heavily in the cafeteria that even the festive helium balloons seemed to bum out a little, to droop upon invisible shoulders. His tone and manner conveyed the message more effectively than words alone ever could: to become a thermometer was to fail in a very special way. We knew deep in our bones that this failure was far worse than showing up to a test unprepared. It was failure in the form of betrayal, a betrayal of our potential and, therefore, our greatest gift, our selves. Between influencing and being influenced lay an unbridgeable chasm, one you didn't want to find yourself marooned on the wrong side of. The deeper implication was also clear, given that we were listening to a recruiting agent for the Presbyterian church: on one side lay heaven, on the other, hell.

This talk was a mental splinter for me—it slid right into my cerebral cortex, where it sits to this day, embedded alongside the innumerable other times I was urged to be myself, to let my little light shine, to dance my own dance, etc. And together they coalesce to form a mother lode of shame, a massive vein of self-abasement I tap whenever I find myself caring what other people think of me. Whenever I try to manipulate someone's impression of me during a routine tête-à-tête or parrot an opinion I filched rather than formed myself or deploy a mannerism that doesn't fit my manner or when I succumb to an ad campaign or feel the nauseating tug of brand loyalty. Whenever, in other words, I let the "out there" infiltrate, and so corrupt, the "in here." It is in these moments that I feel farthest from myself and most like a fraud. That I doubt, down in my guts, the very credibility of my existence. Lo! I am become Thermometer. My mercury rises and falls with the environment or according to the sick climatological whims of a powerful and self-possessed Thermostat. And so, alas, I'm bumped out back to the sad bunkhouse of inauthenticity, where the furniture is made of particleboard and pleather, where of a Friday evening my sad sack amigos and I are forced to share nacho pizza and drink Sam's Cola while watching late-career Spielberg flicks, and where, because the place is kept colder than we'd like, we must don sweaters of ersatz angora. On they swarm, the collywobbles. . .

I know it might seem like I'm getting a little loosey-goosey here, carelessly conflating authenticity and influence, but it's impossible to talk about one without the other, and that's borne out by a quick glance at the history of the idea, or at least a couple branches of its family tree. Authenticity got its teeth into Being as part of a massive cultural shift that took place during the mid-to-late eighteenth century. Ta-da! Romanticism. The Phil 101 story here would go something like: as our faith in traditional avenues of significance and meaning (e.g., the Good and God) eroded, we were cast back upon ourselves. We turned inward, acquired a sense of inner depths, became "individuals"—and this was a real brain buster for me, learning that there was a time when we didn't consider ourselves thus. Under this new way of thinking, moral salvation was no longer achieved through religious or philosophical institutions but through intimate contact with yourself, through the passionate embrace and experience of your own existence. Rousseau was the first person to popularize this idea. He called it "the sentiment of existence." Other folks chimed in, too, and it's from a man named Herder, ironically, that we get the idea that each of us has an original way of being human. This frees us to discover and articulate and live according to whatever it is that makes us unique. But freedom of this magnitude, as the saying goes, isn't free. Because now the discovery and articulation of what makes you you is also a duty. Fail to do so and you effectively miss out on the point of your life.

No story would be complete without a compelling antagonist, of course, and this awareness of ourselves as individuals grew alongside our awareness of other individuals, alongside the emergence of that faceless mass, the public. And so our endeavor is hopelessly complicated, because the more we're exposed to the thoughts and feelings of others, the harder it is to suss out those thoughts and feelings that are only our own, and so the more we'll worry about being sullied, tarnished, *influenced*. "The anxiety of influence," Bloom writes, "is strongest where poetry is most lyrical, most subjective, and stemming directly from the personality." Imitating another person, plagiarizing someone else's way of being, caving to some societal pressure, conforming—these are new cardinal sins, the penance for which is a zombified existence, a form of living death. It is in this spirit that we understand Wallace

Stevens when he says, "I am not conscious of being influenced by anybody and have purposely held off from reading highly mannered people like Eliot and Pound so that I should not absorb anything, even unconsciously."

Another wrinkle here is that our inwardly generated authentic identities depend on being recognized. And in order to be recognized, we must submit ourselves to the assessment of other people, to the public. Here's an illustrative snippet from *The Simpsons*:

> HOMER: Maybe if you're truly cool, you don't need to be told you're cool.
> BART: Well, sure you do.
> LISA: How else would you know?

Exactly. How else would you know? One needs to be affirmed in one's authenticity. Authentic selfhood is worked out and achieved *in relation to* other people. This is the constant tension under which we must now negotiate our identities, because not being recognized as authentic is another form of failure. This is the paradox at the heart of the ideal of authenticity: "Other men are lenses through which we read our own minds," Emerson wrote. And of Bloom's theory: "The poet is condemned to learn his profoundest yearnings through an awareness of *other selves*." Wherever a person broods over the number of likes a selfie got, there lies the paradoxical ideal of authenticity. It lies wherever an indie band derides another indie band for its newfound popularity. Wherever an experimental writer champions his obscurity in one breath and bitches about how no one understands him in another, there it skulks, heavy-footed and husky-breathed.

Navigating all this can be treacherous business. Here's an e.g.: I once wrote a short story that took place at a famous tennis match. When I showed it to James, he had a few faint words of praise, but went on to say that the story reminded him too much of Wallace's work and therefore he couldn't properly respect it as art. Be yourself, he advised, find your own voice. I'd unknowingly invited the easy dismissal that familiarity encourages, even demands, and so was crushed. This alone was enough to keep me from showing my writing to anyone for years. The risk of losing, of failing, was too much for me to handle, so I preferred not to play the game at all.

IX.

There are only a handful of decent public courts around Portland, ones whose surfaces aren't webbed with cracks and whose nets don't sag like ruined elastic waistbands, and your more serious players have searched them out. The result is that Scott and I end up seeing a lot of the same faces about town. And every so often, after a session, a member of the group taking our place will compliment us on our strokes. It's another subtle form the competition between us can take: I'm sure Scott believes they mostly mean his strokes, while I believe they mostly mean mine. Either way we're grateful for the attention—it affirms us in the absurdity of our ambition. The interactions will typically end there, but every so often someone will ask for our phone numbers, try to set up a session. My phone's full of contacts filed under the last name Tennis. Ross Tennis. Ry Tennis. Chris Crazy Hair Tennis. Farhad Tennis. Vinny Tennis. And then there's Tennis Father.

Tennis Father is a lithe and wiry Serbian who can always be found on the court with his two daughters, who I'd guesstimate are nine and fourteen. His MO is he'll hit with the younger one while the older plays sets against boys and girls from the area high schools and colleges, as well as select men and women from the Community of Decent Courts. But then he'll let the younger girl go off and do her own thing and he'll cross his arms over his racket like he's embracing it and he'll watch the older daughter play. He cuts an undeniably martial figure, standing there, one that makes you think he probably goes around the house correcting everyone's posture. Often after a long rally or an unforced error, he'll call out unsolicited instruction or admonishment, and always in a brusque and barbed Serbian. She'll bark back, too, also in Serbian, throwing her arms up or swatting her racket at the air between them, and for a while they'll go at each other with the verve of an Eastern Bloc Itchy and Scratchy. It's worth noting that while they bicker, her opponent has to stand there just dumbly waiting, bouncing the ball or peppering it against the fence or whatever, until they've exhausted themselves and she's ready to play again. She doesn't seem as embarrassed by this as you'd maybe expect and what irks me is that she never raises a hand in apology, never acknowledges what a bleb on the ass the hiatus must be for her opponent.

One afternoon Tennis Father stopped Scott and me after a session. He wanted to talk about how they were no longer allowed at the local youth academies. The coaches and the rich parents don't want his daughter embarrassing their kids. Not to mention that they were all liars and cheaters and worse. Could we believe that, in order to beat her, the coaches had encouraged their kids to cheat? We tsk-tsked with feigned sympathy, sure there was another side to this story. But what this amounts to practically is that he has to rustle up hitting partners, anyone he can find to challenge her. He nodded toward the court and asked whether either of us would be up for a match. Scott begged off, but I surprised myself by saying sure, why not, and gave him my number. "I call, I call," he said, in lieu of giving me his. Days later, when my phone buzzed "Unknown" and the voice on the other end sounded like a KGB interrogator, I almost hung up. It was next to impossible to understand what he was saying.

"I don't understand what you're saying," I said, the phone some nine inches from my ear. "Who is this? I'm hanging up."

"Tennis Father," he said. "Tennis Father!"

We settled on a date for the following Sunday and at once the jitters alighted. I hadn't played competitively in ages and now wondered how my strokes would hold up under pressure. How well would I execute? What should my game plan be? Would I be tempted to resort to a lesser form of the game, to become a gutless pusher, a chickenshit moonballer, and in so doing invite shame upon not only myself but the sport of tennis, too? I tried to calm myself by asking, over and over, WWRD? (What would Roger do?)

But that mantra proved a fruitless remedy and my nerves only redoubled. Why had I agreed to play in the first place? Part of me thought that maybe I was doing it for the story. Tennis lore is full of yarns about how, as kids, Andre Agassi and Serena Williams and other greats had opened industrial jars of whoop-ass on the players at their local clubs. Was this my chance to play someone bound for the tour? For greatness? But maybe something else was percolating, something that had to do with submitting myself to the game's rigid schema of win vs. lose. Maybe all along I'd been cutting my nose to spite my face. No matter how good my strokes got, no matter how much they might resemble Roger's, wasn't I dooming myself to a lesser form of the sport by not competing? Wasn't I, in this way, an inauthentic tennis player?

On the Friday before the match, I met two former students for happy hour, guys who had, after graduation, interned at the little magazine I work for. They were readying themselves for their great reverse migration back east, home, where they planned to enroll themselves in the workforce and begin their own careers in writing and editing and publishing. They're among my all-time favorite students, mostly because they led me to believe I had something, however meager, to offer them, which is to say that they allowed me to feel like I'd influenced them. And I can hardly own up to the cliché without squirming, but they reminded me a little of myself, eightish years back.

We gathered our discount cocktails and took up around a picnic table on the back patio. The fellas weren't interested in talking about anything but Wallace. Back in class I'd had them read "Federer as Religious Experience," the original version, and now they were chasing the dragon, deep in the brambles of the Project. They were bent on reading everything he'd written, most of which was now available between covers or, if not, readily accessible on a host of websites and blogs. One had recently finished *Infinite Jest*—and oh, how relieved I was that he didn't refer to it as *IJ*—and the other said he was two-thirds of the way through. They wanted to know had I read it? Wanted to know what were my favorite parts? Wanted to know had I come across the guy online who re-creates its most famous scenes using Legos? Wanted to know what was my favorite Wallace book? Was I one of *those* people, you know, who claimed only to be able to stomach the nonfiction? And what did I make of the book about infinity? They'd heard there were mistakes, ones that undercut his putative standing as a math wunderkind. Would I see the movie that they'd read about?

Though the sensation's grown less keen with age, less pointed and gaggy, I still feel I slip into an electrical storm of paranoia whenever someone asks me about Wallace. It's as though I stood accused of some unspecified crime (Indebtedness? Inauthenticity? Influence?), the punishment for which is a manner of spiritual nullity or irrelevance, some obviation of being. And listening to them moon over his work set off the old alarms. "Danger. Danger." Small comfort though it admittedly is, it pleased me to discover in my research that strife and tension are the very soil out of which that word authentic shoulders forth. One of its Greek roots is *authenteo*, which means to have full power over—though also, interestingly, to murder. And the other's *authentes*, which denotes not only a master and a doer, but also a perpetrator, a murderer, even a self-murderer. To have full power over is the limit case of influence. And suicide's an interesting, if extreme, metaphor for the deferral of self that happens when you find yourself under the thumb of another person.

"Tread lightly and beware the rip," I advised. "You might could find yourself swift and sudden out to sea."

"Sounds like you speak from experience," one said.

"Something like that," I said. "Yeah."

It was true. I'd been lately regretting how deep down the rabbit hole I'd let myself fall when I was their age and beyond, how hard I'd made it for myself to surface again, and I encouraged them to temper their reading of Wallace with other folks. I directed them toward the Edward Young and Emerson essays I'd been grooving on. And though I didn't, it would've been a nerdy baller move if I'd then quoted them some Young: "Illustrious examples *engross*, *prejudice*, and *intimidate*. They *engross* our attention, and so prevent a due inspection of ourselves; they *prejudice* our judgment in favour of their abilities, and so lessen the sense of our own; and they *initimidate* us with the splendor of their renown, and thus under diffidence bury our strength." Or this choice canapé from Emerson: "We have never come at the true and best benefit of any genius, so long as we believe him an original force."

And I know this might sound a little woo-woo, but bear with me: for a moment there with the fellas it was like I was allowed to grasp or glimpse the diaphanous filament of Being that threads us all together. I'm not sure how to describe it, really, but as an instantaneous montage, a mash-up of scenes and images charged with deep sentiment, all laid upon one another as though time had abruptly accordioned together, like Borges's aleph or the peak of a shroom trip or something. There I was at twenty-one, sitting with a cup of milky tea in James's apartment, listening intently as he read to me from "The Depressed Person," but at the same time I was nine-teen and waking in the loft bed in my dorm before the sun to read "Little Gidding" by penlight so as not to disturb my roommate, and twenty-four, on a road trip, with a busted copy of Barthelme's *Forty Stories* in the backseat of a car being driven by my uncle, navigated by his friend, rolling through Big Sky country, and twenty-two, sitting in the booth of a parking lot I monitored in Charlottesville, Virginia, getting busy with the compelling commonplaces of Lydia Davis. But I was also thirteen and cutting the acres of grass at my grandmother's house in the exurbs of Richmond, my ass swampy and numb on the tractor's seat, and experiencing then a new thing: there rose in me unbidden a series of words, words that tried to assert the wet-tangy smell of the grass and the sun incubating my neck and the flutter and sting of cricket-missiles pinging my calves and the electric singe of the seat's hot vinyl on my hammies, that is to say, a poem, an attempt, no matter how bad and gropey, to capture the grass-cutting experience in language. This great sprawling kinship map of everything I'd read and everything I'd written opened before me. But the intuition or vision or whatever it was concerned more than matters just fussily literary. It was all the ways other people have influenced and continue to live on in me. Pinch any opinion, tug any mannerism, pull at any insight and you'll find someone else. You'll find James in the way I sometimes say "adios" or stomp my feet amusedly when someone disagrees with me. You'll find Garth whenever I consider someone's point by looking skyward and Christian whenever I'm iconoclastic, whenever I doubt the hype. I could go on and on. And to be filled with anxiety about this suddenly struck me as childish and immature. Our culture's prevailing notion of individuality itself seemed childish and immature. "We are tendencies, or rather, symptoms, and none of us complete," Emerson wrote. "We touch and go, and sip the foam of many lives." What makes us individuals, in this way, is the people we've been treated to know and what I felt then was gratitude, a cockles-level appreciation of every book, movie, piece of art or music that'd ever moved me and every person I'd ever meaningfully interacted with. Everything, that is, that makes me me.

The fellas and I wrapped up. I told them to keep in touch, to know that if I was good for anything, it was a glowing rec-ommendation. They'd been my students, my interns, and now, soon, they'd be my peers. I left them with a misremembered quote from Jean Rhys, which correctly goes: "All writing is a huge lake. There are great rivers that feed the lake, like Tolstoy or Dostoyevsky. And then there are mere trickles, like Jean Rhys. All that matters is feeding the lake. I don't matter. The lake matters. You must keep feeding the lake."

"The lake matters," I repeated, really more for my benefit than theirs. "Adios."

Two days later I met Tennis Father and his daughters at a complex in Vancouver, Washington, about fifteen minutes from my house. Inside were six courts, three on either side of a waiting area whose many windows lent it an aquarium-like, *Jaws 3* vibe. You could head upstairs, too, though, to a balcony that afforded one an overhead view of all the action.

Tennis Father met me at the check-in counter. He didn't shake my hand but put his arm around my shoulder and steered me to the window, where he nodded toward his daughter, who was on the court closest to us, warming up with an Asian man.

"A show court," he said, and smiled conspiratorially. His younger daughter was at a table with a coloring book, a rainbow of crayons fanned out in front of her.

"I guess we'll see," I said, and made my way out.

Taking the field in baseball has been well documented, well praised, but decidedly less has been made about debouching through the synthetic folds of an indoor tennis court's backdrop. The way the thwack-pops sharpen and clarify over the electric hum of the industrial lights overhead. How your vision recalibrates to allow for the open space, to account for the presence of so many white lines. The pissy sibilance of popping a new can of balls and their Band-Aid-ish smell. There should at least be a subgenre of light verse devoted to cataloging such phenomenological delights.

The Asian guy left the court unceremoniously and the daughter met me at the benches courtside. Taller than I expected, and thinner, she had on a skirt over warm-up pants, which was oddly intimidating. I'd worn my favorite tennis shirt, a white polo with pin-tuck pleats that made it look like a tuxedo shirt or guayabera. I'd hoped it would convey elegance and seriousness of intent—it was the shirt Federer had worn during a poor showing at the 2010 Wimbledon—but next to her I looked overdressed, which suggested I'd been thinking about the match in a way she had not. While I composed myself, put on a wrist- and headband and opened a can of balls, she put herself through a prematch routine, running backward around the court and doing various calisthenics and stretching. My lack of such a routine suggested another deficiency, was another piece of evidence that I might be in over my head.

We got under way. Warmed up with a few minutes of dinky minitennis from the service line before moving back to the baseline, where we drilled. Forehand to forehand. Backhand to backhand. Forehand to backhand and vice versa. I was tentative, rolling balls in with generous topspin, not going for too much. Tennis Father had moved from behind the lobby's windows to the balcony up top. He didn't lean against the railing but stood straight-backed and stiff, and he seemed a little naked without a racket to embrace. The tableau could've been lifted right off the cutting-room floor of *Infinite Jest*. And can I take a moment here to confess a dream I once nurtured? Pause to say that I once entertained fantasies about playing tennis with Wallace? I'd grown close with the novelist Curtis White, a friend and colleague of his from the Illinois State days. They'd played together on the regular and this fact, early on, was reason enough for me to court Curt's friendship. I'd pussyfooted for a while, talked around the elephant, but after the last time we hit, I put the question to him straight. How would I have fared? What would the match-up have been like? And sick vindication though I know it to be, a pathetic piece of cheap machismo, I was overjoyed when he said that there was little doubt in his mind that I would've taken him.

"He didn't have the firepower to deal with a player like you," he said. "But he was also in terrible physical shape when we were playing."

During our drills, both the daughter and I made mistakes. We hit balls well wide or long or into the net and so broke the soporific rhythm of our exchange. After one, Tennis Father called out something that sounded like a waterbed set a-sloshing.

"In English, please," I said. This came out a lot harsher than I'd intended it to, and practically without passing through my brain. I recognized at once the thorny bile of competitiveness, the selfsame thorny bile that, in the interest of preserving our friendship, has kept Scott and me from playing sets. It's not that we lack the competitive instinct, but rather that it is too strong in us.

Tennis Father looked down at me and cocked his head.

"I'd like to know what you're saying is all," I said, trying to dial it back a tad. "If you're going to be coaching her."

"I say to her you have the Federer game," he said. "She must learn to adapt."

After we'd had our turns at the net for volleys and over-heads, we agreed we were warm and that we should begin. We stood on either side of the net and I spun my racket, *M* or *W*. She chose correctly, but elected to return first, a ballsy show of confidence. Nerves got the better of me to begin and I started with two double faults, handing her a lead. Love–30. A service winner and an unforced error off my forehand wing made it 15–40. Overly cautious, not wanting to double-fault the game away, I hit a safe kick serve to her backhand, but she was all over it and torched the ball up the line to take the opening game.

On the changeover I tried to compose myself, told myself to calm down. Work the point. Wait for my opportunities. And the first point of her serve, I did precisely that. I put her on the defensive with a return to her backhand and peppered that wing twice more with inside-out forehands of increasing angle. It was then that she left a ball choicely short. I stepped in and put all my weight behind a crosscourt forehand winner that thudded against the backdrop. Though of course I didn't act on the impulse, I understood why Nadal, after hitting a twirling-undies forehand for a winner, may so often be found pumping a fist and making a thin innuendo of his hips and shouting "Vamos!" I'm embarrassed to admit how satisfying I found it, watching my opponent's narrow little-girl shoulders slump as she shuffled over to retrieve the ball. It's a common piece of tennis wisdom, almost a cliché, that it's only after you've been broken that you can begin to swing free. But it's one thing to hear this and an experience of an altogether different order to actually live it. If I was going to lose, so be it, but there was no way I was just going to roll over and let myself be taken at love.

Mysteries We Live With

I t's an experience that buffaloes my imagination: Ken-
neth Arnold alone in his small plane, flying from Cheha-
lis, Washington, to Yakima. Home. It's June 24, 1947, and
the sky's hallucinatory, a blue vastitude. Because he's in no
hurry, Arnold decides to spend some time searching for a
marine transport plane that had gone down in the area of
Mount Rainier. He's a citizen, will help if he can. After an
hour of fruitless circling he calls it quits and noses his plane
back toward home. He's on this course only a minute or two
when a tremendous pulse of light hits his cockpit. And again,
quick-like, another strobe flash, another retina-frying dose
of luminous energy. This time he catches where it's coming
from: the mountains east of him. He scans, squints, and there
against Rainier's stark-white snowfield he spots a chain of
nine peculiar aircraft careening southbound over the ridged,
rocky vertebrae of the Cascade Range.

They're semicircular, arranged in a geese's V, and appear
to be moving as though bound together somehow. He's never
seen anything quite like them. They dart in and out of the

valleys between the smaller mountain peaks. They're dark in profile and blade-thin, nearly invisible, but every so often one flips vertical and flashes against the snow and sky and when the sun hits their highly polished surfaces just right, his cockpit glows blindingly, like a revelation. Perhaps most astonishing, though, is their speed. Some fast math tells Arnold they're doing about 1,700 mph. That's almost two and a half times faster than any manned craft had gone in 1947—Chuck Yeager wouldn't break the sound barrier (an unspectacular 767 mph) until October, almost two months off. When asked later to describe their flight, Arnold will grasp after analogies. They looked like speedboats racing over rough water, he'll say. Like fish flipping in and out of the sun. But he'll forever embed a bogey into the public's imagination when he says, "They flew like a saucer would if you skipped it across the water."

"The UFO phenomenon comes in waves," Keith Rowell said. We were sitting on his back deck in West Linn, Oregon, a suburb of Portland. A short-haired dachshund lay mutely curled in his lap. I had a legal pad rolled open to the questions I wanted to cover—a standard fare of soft skepticism—and kept hoping I'd placed my old mini tape recorder close enough to catch everything Keith was saying. This was my first profile and I didn't want to fuck things up irrevocably from the get-go. "There's always a background of stuff going on, but there are peak times of activity. And the Roswell crash came more or less at the beginning of the 1947 wave."

Keith's a retired technical writer and has been studying UFOs since 1974. He now serves as assistant state director of the Oregon chapter of MUFON, the Mutual UFO Network, an international organization whose mission is "the scientific study of UFOs for the benefit of humanity." His hair is wispy white and cropped close to his head and he has a well-kept, matching mustache. If he needed to, he could earn easy extra scratch doubling as a late-career Richard Dreyfuss, at car dealerships or insurance stores or whatever. In the way I badly want Ohio to be a palindrome, I'm teased, tortured by how close Keith Rowell's name comes to being a perfect aptronym. Like Ms. Booker, the librarian, or Dr. Fingers, the gynecologist, he is one letter short of being Mr. Roswell, the UFOlogist.

According to Keith, still very little is known about what (literally, figuratively) went down at Roswell. And much of the event's intrigue lies in the persistent mystery that surrounds its most basic facts. In the course of my research, I'd come to learn that reading about Roswell (and about UFOs more generally) can be like finding yourself in a narrow, smoke-filled hall of mirrors so mind-bending that you're sure it must debouch in a nuthouse somewhere. It's a melodrama that spares not a trapping or trimming—posthumous affidavits, sworn denials, government cover-ups, supposed character assassinations. Faced with all the contradictory reports, all the he-said-she-said back-and-forth, factual truth can seem to hinge on what side your gut tells you to trust, that is, in whom you choose to place your faith.

"There were one, possibly two crash sites within a fifty-to seventy-mile radius of town," Keith continued. "And we still don't know the exact date of the crash. If you decided to grind through all the books about Roswell—and it'd take you about a year—you'd find that people report it as happening sometime between July second and July fifth."

The story's beginning, by now, is well known. A rancher named Mac Brazel found some debris from a crash on his farm. He moseyed into town the next day to alert the sheriff, who in turn told military personnel—concerned parties relish pointing out that the only atomic bomb unit in America at the time was stationed in Roswell. Lesser known, perhaps, is what followed. News traveled up the chain of command that too many civilians had caught wind of the crash. Questions needed answering. General Roger Ramey approved a press release written by Walter Haut, the public information officer.

"The press release is short," Keith said, dispensing these names and the sequence of events with the studied ease of a history professor. "Just around a hundred words or so. And it begins something like, 'A flying disc was captured today outside of Roswell and it was sent to higher headquarters.' This is big. It's the only time in history that any government agency—the air force, CIA, NSA, DIA, whatever—has ever issued an official document that acts as if the flying-saucer stuff is real."

It's hard to believe that we didn't have a working definition of "delusion" until 1913. But that's when the record shows

Karl Jaspers, the psychiatrist-philosopher, set down a checklist of sorts—guidelines that a medical professional could use during diagnosis. For a belief to be considered delusional, Jaspers wrote, the patient must first believe it with the utmost certainty. He went so far as to reject the idea that a delusion simply consisted of a patient's false beliefs. No. Delusions are, for those who hold them, true. They grow out of and are confirmed by experience. The second point echoes the first: the patient is incorrigible. He or she will remain unconvinced by even the most compelling counterargument. Finally, and most important, there's the impossibility, bizarreness, or flat-out falsity of the belief itself.

The first two qualities are self-evident, but words like "impossible" and "bizarre" introduce an element of doubt. "Impossible" and "bizarre" to whom? Because what about spirituality? What about the entire spectrum of suprascientific phenomena? Among the qualities William James attributes to mysticism, for example, are ineffability and what he calls a "noetic quality." "Mystical states seem to those who experience them to be also states of knowledge," he writes. And by "ineffability," of course, he means that that knowledge defies communicability and exchange. It's a ticket stamped for one ride only: "Mystical truth exists for the individual who has the transport, but for no one else." That James's mystical experience sounds a lot like Jaspers's delusion begs the question: along what lines can faith be considered delusional?

This is a question I've been circling, on and off and in one form or another, since I was a teenager and began to peel away from the religion I'd inherited from my parents. I grew up going to youth groups and Young Life, prayer breakfasts and "retreats." I once attended a happening called Promise Keepers—tens of thousands of men gathered in a stadium in Philly to pray and sing worship songs and weep and wave their arms together like reefs of sea anemones and share agapic embraces. We got hats. On the rare Sunday that my family didn't attend church, Dad would gather my brothers and me in the living room for an ad hoc Bible study—memory outfits him exclusively in the cotton kimono he'd picked up on a mission trip to Japan, a soutane that often failed to fully conceal his inguinal hinterlands, parting instead upon an eyeful of tighty-whities and a most profane moose knuckle. But for all this activity, I never had what I conceived of as "an experience," which is to say that a Whitmanesque God had never peeled back the corner of the universe to make moon eyes at me. That's how I'd come to conceive of the count-less conversion stories and testimonies I'd heard in church basements and on retreats, how I imagined my folks' own experiences of being blessed by the Spirit. Mediation had been billed as a fundamental part of the deal: at some point He popped in unannounced to rescue you from a life of paltry to middling significance. Mom had spoken in tongues. Dad talked about hearing the voice of God. I didn't merely hope to have a similar experience, I expected to.

I also knew that to expect or, worse, to demand such an experience amounted to a sin. It was with experience, after all, that the Devil had tempted Jesus in the desert. (Hence Matthew 4:4: "One does not live by bread alone, but by every word that comes from the mouth of God.") But I was a teenager and was having trouble setting the rudder of belief. Doubts as aggressive as kudzu crept in. Was I wired weird? Had my DNA shipped out before being fitted with the emotional modality that allowed for religious experience? Or was it that I'd been trying to access an ambient field of significance that didn't exist? Maybe the grand mysterious meaning I'd been longing for was a sham. Because wasn't doing the same thing over and over and expecting a different result also a working definition of insanity? Of being delusional?

My doubts were as shallow and limited then as my conception of faith. It'd still be years before I accepted that faith, by definition, meant living with uncertainty, that uncertainty was faith's lining. Years before I understood that chief among the things I should be doubting is personal experience. But the message had come down loud and clear: doubts were not to be dwelled on but gotten over, like a mean stomach flu or a broken heart. "Lord, I believe," I was taught to pray. "Help my unbelief."

There's one event from this time, in particular, that has its brights on in my rearview. Dad and I were driving home from some gathering downtown. I was in my middle teens, which puts Dad in his early forties. We soon found ourselves in dangerous conversational waters: lay theology, amateur metaphysics. The dread sharks of opinion and speculation were about. I asked a handful of questions and managed to cause offense. Things escalated, voices were raised. My general thrust wasn't much thrustier than a Mormon soaking: there are parts of the Bible that might be best understood figuratively, as a metaphor. Dad pulled us over for gas at the Village Exxon, a few miles from our house.

"The thing you have to understand," he said as he got out of the car, "is that every word in there is literally true."

Because it's so absurd, I'd like to remember laughing here. On the evangelical doily it's only the outermost lace that believes everything in the Bible is literally true. Was Dad really hanging all the way out at the fringe? Regardless of what he believed, it was abundantly clear that he was fed up with my probing and wanted to shut the conversation down.

How much can be said to hang on one conversation? Because I want to say that after this one, I knew in an unspeakable place down inside me that whatever was going to come of my faith wouldn't involve him. Whatever ideological umbilical cord had bound us was swiftly and summarily snipped. Instead of indulging my questions and doubts, instead of "meeting me where I was," as they said in the church basements of my adolescence, he'd chosen to wall himself up inside a tower of certitude. And there, warmly immured, I'm sure he thought I'd betrayed and abandoned him, that I was another in a long line of sons who fail to honor their fathers. But out on the gusty moor of religious mystery, I, too, felt betrayed and abandoned. It seemed that Dad was more interested in maintaining the infallibility of his belief than in fostering a conversation with his son about the very nature of ultimate concern. Point is, both of us were left to stew in resentment, to think, finally, "I am a man more sinned against than sinning." But more than confusion or frustration or anger, I remember, in the end, feeling just plain old sad.

Sad for him, sad for me—sad for us. It was as if all at once, Babel-like, we started speaking different languages.

There'd been chatter about a recent sighting outside Portland, an unearthly polygon spotted in the night sky. It'd made the news. In my search for more information, I stumbled upon the website Keith runs for the Oregon chapter of MUFON. There I found a treasure chest of info about UFOs: logs of reported sightings, an extensive annotated bibliography of books, a glossary of key terms and ideas, and more. I'd never been big on sci-fi growing up and if I'd thought about UFOs at all, it was to dismiss them out of hand. The prejudicial wordcloud that popped to mind when I thought about UFO enthusiasts included things like: Mom's basement, obesity or asthenia, Mylar-covered comic books, Twinkies, *Star Trek*, RPGs, pink eye, panniculus, old toys still in their boxes, retainer/inhaler, koro, Taco Bell specialty menu, heliophobia/scotophilia, cartoon porn, Asian fetish, impetigo, etc. But the hours of study and meticulous research the site represented confounded my expectations, scrambled my preconceptions. It was staggering and impressive, so methodical and patient and seemingly scientific, and I wanted an excuse to meet the man behind it. At the time I occasionally wrote for a little magazine and while I'd never done a profile before, I thought Keith might make for a good one.

He was game, but in our early correspondence, he also cautioned me: "I think I would be remiss if I didn't remind you that UFOs are thin-ice material. Don't fall in. To maintain your reputation in establishment circles, standard practice says you should maintain a studied distance from the subject. The reality aspects are to be avoided or at most treated in a very circumspect way. Writing about what the culture of UFO 'believers' is like is just fine. 'Looky, here! This is what the freaks are like. How amusing!' That tone is just fine, but not the tone and style of a person who takes the subject seriously as if it should be treated by academia as a normal part of human experience and the world. Just be careful. A Pulitzer Prize–winning Harvard professor of psychiatry (John Mack) almost lost his tenure while in his sixties for treating UFOs seriously."

The Oregon chapter of MUFON meets on the second Tuesday of every month. They rent a conference room from Mount Tabor Presbyterian Church in southeast Portland. To help pay for Muir Hall and other group needs, MUFON asks for a three-dollar donation to attend its meetings. But twenty-one dollars buys you a full membership, including a subscription to the organization's monthly journal.

Keith sat behind a table at the front of the room, beside our leader, State Director Tom. On the night's agenda was a MUFON-produced movie presentation, but the schedule first allowed for an open roundtable discussion. The vibe was awkward at first, with the fifteen of us unsure of exactly how to proceed, but the mood was broken by an Italian man in a baseball hat, who said, "I can just feel it. The world is uniting under the banner of antidebunkerism."

The room relaxed and a communal spirit bloomed and soon folks were engaged in a spirited crossfire, such that it grew difficult to follow the most intriguing threads of conversation.

"We can't destroy consciousness," said a man wearing a camouflage Hawaiian shirt. "Not even in chickens." He could prove chickens have souls, he continued. Take a chicken, any chicken, and cut off its head. If you point it to the south, it will flap about wildly. But point it north and it'll go calmly about its headless business. Try it.

"Suppose humanity has an expiration date?" a guy in sweatpants asked. And when no one answered, he added, "I think it's time for the bees to take over. The honeybees."

"Are you farsighted?"

"Of course."

"I'm trying to secure ten thousand debunker-buster bombs from the Pentagon! Who's with me?"

"Do you know the role of bismuth in antigravity?"

Chicken Guy addressed the group: were we aware that when we die our bodies become lighter? that something measurable escapes us? "And it's not just like a fart, either."

The woman next to me called down to a man across the table, "But you might not have any conscious memory of being abducted."

"True enough," he replied, and they both went silent, appearing to ruminate on that epistemological chestnut.

State Director Tom soon called the meeting to attention. Before starting the movie presentation, he encouraged people to watch the premiere of a television show called *The Event* on NBC, which used UFOs as a narrative device. A flutter of excited assent rippled through the room. He reminded everyone, though, to maintain their healthy skepticism of the mainstream media, which had burned them over and over in the past. Did anyone recall the hatchet job Peter Jennings did back in '05? Yes. Almost everyone did.

The lights were then turned off for the movie, a two-hour documentary lecture that recounted the eerie goings-on of late December 1980, at RAF Bentwaters, the air force base in England's Rendlesham Forest. Tom had described this as England's Roswell, and maybe a bigger deal in the grand scheme of things. It was the movie's intention to debunk the debunkers' explanations (or "explanations") of the strange, mysterious lights that appeared in the sky and the top secret cover-up that immediately ensued.

By way of a preface let it be known that the great and sworn enemy of the UFOlogist is the debunker, the person who entirely discounts the world of the paranormal. "His extreme skepticism is used as a protective mechanism so that certain subjects are never looked into," Keith told me. Debunkers are as invested in bankrupting the legitimacy of the paranormal as the UFOlogists and their ilk are on establishing that same legitimacy—they're on opposite sides of the same coin. And this struck me as odd: why such strident and unrelenting dissent? If the debunkers think the UFOlogists are incorrigibly batty, then why not leave them be? What is it about UFOs that inspires such passionate reactions, pro and con?

The documentary was based on such careful and exacting investigation, such thoroughgoing attention to detail, to minutiae really, that for many of the MUFONites there in the dark of Muir Hall the effect was largely just soporific. About thirty minutes in, I looked across the room and by the screen's glow could make out the Italian antidebunker, who had his arms crossed, his chin in his chest, and his eyes closed. Two others at the end of his table had their heads resting in their crossed arms. There was deep mouth breathing coming from someone on my side of the room I couldn't see. At a little over an hour, we lost radio contact with our leader, State Director Tom, whose head had been moving like one of those water-sipping birds you find in joke shops. Through it all, though, Keith was a wide-eyed hoot owl.

When the movie ended and the credits rolled, a handful of people clapped. Someone flipped the lights on and there was the nervous, startled rustle of stretching and eye rubbing and seat adjusting.

"So," Tom said as he stood, "any questions?"

The room erupted in gleeful laughter.

The first people to pipe up asked about plot details, as though trying to piece together a thriller's twists and turns. "What happened to the camera?" "Did he ever get to see the pictures he took?" "How long was he unconscious?"

Deeper speculation began when someone brought up the topic of time travel. The events in Rendlesham Forest, as well as those at Roswell, presented a knotty nexus of past, present, and future. UFOs must have the ability to tap into whatever it is we understand as time and manipulate it, or themselves within it. The knot-of-time analogy provoked questions about memory retrieval and hypnosis. Could memory blocks be implanted in us, preventing us from accessing certain parts of our own histories? With every question, it seemed like we were being asked to solve an equation that had one too many variables.

"No one knows how it's done," Keith said. "But it is."

"This is strange beyond the limits of imagination," Chicken Guy said.

"We'll never know what's real," said someone down the table.

"Zhey dezide vhat's rill vhor us," said a Russian lady in back who'd come in late.

Keith agreed: the intelligence and security around these occurrences were airtight and strictly need-to-know. He said the government ran "deep black projects," about which we'll likely never get a full accounting, the whole truth.

"Man," bemoaned the guy in sweatpants. "It's just gonna be a headbanger's ball till the end of eternity."

"This goes deep," Keith said, drawing the meeting to a close. "So deep that it's really about consciousness. There are no so-called answers."

Martha's Vineyard. Summer 2002.

There were other disagreements, other run-ins with Dad and members of my extended family, but still I couldn't manage a clean break from the church. The possibility of having an experience of divine significance, and of finding fellowship, a group of like-minded questers and an uncomplicated sense of belonging, continued to haunt me on into college. I dabbled in fraternity life and in the faith-based equivalents of frats (Cru, FCA), but came away from both feeling equally dissatisfied and no less alone. Chalk it up to my Protestantism, but I believed that my failure to have a bona fide religious experience was the result of my never having been sufficiently *serious* about my faith. Maybe I'd never worked hard enough at it? I mean, didn't the promised land lie at the end of forty years of toil? And so my spiritual whatever became a problem for me to solve. I'd give it the old college try.

There were nine of us students in the house—five girls, four boys. It's the closest I'll ever come to being part of a montage, imagining the midtwenties married couple assembling us on the merit of our application essays. They were pursuing graduate degrees in theology and were our leaders, but mostly by example. Imagine *The Real World*, only ditch the drunken antics for daily quiet times, swap the routine roomie diddling for weekly Bible studies. Aware of the temptations that a coed house could foment, our counselor-chaperones laid out two rules at the summer's start: "dating," by even the loosest of definitions, perhaps especially by the loosest of definitions, was verboten, as was drinking. And while not a rule, the guys agreed to shower pretty much exclusively outdoors—this was billed as a courtesy, a piece of chivalry, but I think it masked a deeper fear: that a glimpse of the girls' exotic wash stuffs, a mere whiff of their aftersteam, might trigger a catastrophic backslide. A chore chart was posted in the kitchen. Every evening a couple was responsible for dinner and another for dishes, and the housecleaning duties, like bathrooms and vacuuming and the lawn, were broken out by week. Periodically throughout the summer we helped administer camps for middle and high schoolers at our host organization's HQ, the Study Center, a compound of bunks and offices and assorted sanctuaries on a wooded knoll in West Tisbury. My most common job was to stand with the other guitarists and strum through the one-four-five chord progression that comprises like ninety percent of worship songs. With an eye to evangelizing (and making the rent), we all worked real jobs on the island, too. We were sandwich artists and traffic attendants and retail workers. As a clerk at Brickman's department store in Vineyard Haven, I sold a sweater to Ted Danson and some beach amusements to Marty McFly, but wussed out when it came time to invite them to our weekly small group. I'd always been a half-assed apologist, mostly because I had so little sense of what it was that I was supposed to be selling. The only person I invited from the outside was an au pair from Colgate I was briefly interested in dating (though only by the loosest of definitions), and by summer's end my tally of souls remained a dispiriting null set.

I can't say I didn't try, though. What I lacked in natural aptitude I compensated for with old-fashioned stick-to-itiveness, by applying the elbow grease of earnestness. When tasked with strumming one-four-fives, I strummed with all the passion I could muster. Verily I played my infarcted heart out. And I prayed. All throughout the day I prayed. In the morning over coffee. Before breakfast, lunch, dinner. Before bedding down in what was, indisputably, the crappiest room in the house, a room I shared with a guy who suffered from allergies all summer and kept a growing stack of used tissues by his twin bed, which I christened, privately, Booger Hill. I read the Bible, too, memorized verses and discussed Paul's epistles with my housemates. And yet still nothing, religious experience–wise. I was not flooded by sudden euphoria. My mind's eye did not open upon supernal vistas. There were no gleeful fits of glossolalia. And so I feared I was doomed to become an aspirant manqué, barred forever from firsthand knowledge of the numinous. Left to live out my days in the wan half-light of the merely human.

But if my time on the island was an effort to redeem or resuscitate my religiospiritual past, it was also part of an awakening to other possible experiences of significance and meaning. This was the summer after my sophomore year, during which I'd started to read deliberately, with intent. It'd been the Year of the Library, when I'd haunted the stacks like Banquo's ghost, when the chair at my favorite carrel practically became a mold of my ass. And I rode this new passion on into the summer. Our morning quiet times were supposed to be given over to reading the Bible and praying, and the journal I kept shows I was doing some of that, but it also shows that I was just as often thinking about Rilke and Eliot, Kierkegaard and Camus. I remember reading *Fear and Trembling* out on the weathered shingles of our house's roof, remember getting a tenacious sunburn reading *The Stranger* on, fittingly, a small beach between Vineyard Haven and Oak Bluffs. And before I'd head down the road to work, Chris, the male half of the married couple, would give me a note card chicken-scratched on either side with quotes he'd come across in his reading, lines plucked from folks like Coleridge and Schelling, Hegel and Arendt. While pretending to refold stacks of Nantucket reds, I'd study the cards, wearing them halfway back to pulp with my handling. The ink often bled, too, the words smudging so badly that it became as much an act of memory as reading when I'd make out, for example: "The primary IMAGINATION I hold to be the living Power and prime Agent of all human Perception, and as a repetition in the finite mind of the eternal act of creation in the infinite I AM." And nights after work, sitting on the house's big front porch and smoking, no shit, pipes, we'd discuss the quotes.

I would struggle to articulate this for years to come, but it was through these nightly chats that I first intuited a fundamental datum of my spiritual whatever: my experiences of profundity would likely be more literary than literal. The sudden eclipse of small concerns, the sweeping eradication of ephemera, the ecstasy of insight—these would be the product, most often, of language. For me language, in one form or another, would be the catalyst and coefficient of the spirit. Looking back, I sense that this was obvious to the others, who even then were up on their Luther, but for me it landed with the freshness of an epiphany. And that it serves as the soil out of which this realization grew has made it hard for me not to understand this house and my time in it as an allegory, like something from *The Pilgrim's Progress*. An allegory for what, exactly, remains forever on the tip of my tongue, but our little community encouraged me in this in everything down to its name. Christians love them a ponderous handle and our program was no different. It was called, simply, Cornerstone. *Was* because it no longer exists. And all irony aside, I was surprised to discover how much it disturbed me, when I learned recently that Cornerstone had been pulled. Its total absence on the organization's website suggested an erasure of a deeper and more metaphorical sort. Which is of course to say that it suggested an absence or erasure in me.

In 1974, having finished a degree in library science, Keith was working as a clerk for the Portland public school system. That's where several books about UFOs came across his desk. "It turns out that 1973 was a huge year. Lots of activity," he said. "So in '74 the publishers were responding to the public's interest." He took the books home and started reading. "Unfortunately for me, I kept reading."

We'd met at his home, in part so he could give me a tour of his library. The shelves that lined his entire basement held over fifteen hundred books. The lion's share were about UFOs, but almost all of them covered one of many topics that fall under the organizational golf umbrella of the paranormal. Telepathy, ghosts, out-of-body experiences, clairvoyance, etc. By his reckoning, fewer than thirty people in the world could rival his collection. (Of those thirty, it was my guess that somewhere in the ballpark of zero had been at the MUFON meeting.)

"I'm not an experiencer-type person. For me it's all up here," he continued. "I want to figure it all out from a rational point of view."

According to Keith, upwards of ninety-five percent of UFO sightings can be explained away by simple scientific means, but those that tease and tantalize him are the remaining five percent. The truly mysterious ones. The ones he feels mainstream science throws out with the bathwater.

"They've shipped us to the intellectual ghetto," he said.

He writes on his website, "UFOs have *not* been proved beyond a reasonable *scientific* doubt to exist. The scientific establishment must engage in serious, long-term study of UFOs to prove this one way or the other. Sadly, the scientific establishment has decided to be intellectually dishonest and avoid this study." Keith is delighted to point out that there's a rich history of such scientific disregard, of discoveries or breakthroughs that, when first presented, were overlooked by the scientific community of their time, and remained so in some cases for as long as a century. That, in this way, scientific truth can hang on human (read: flawed) consensus as much as the work itself.

Official scientific studies have been done, though. The most famous is probably Project Blue Book, which was run by the air force. But they've all ended badly, and none worse than Blue Book, which in over twenty years rolled through director after director. With each bringing a different degree of interest and commitment, rigor varied—to say the least. And in 1969, after receiving the results of a review led by a nuclear physicist named Edward Condon, the government closed it down. The Condon Report, which ran over fourteen hundred pages, concluded, once and for all: "Nothing has come from the study of UFOs in the past 21 years that has added to scientific knowledge . . . Further extensive study of UFOs probably cannot be justified in the expectation that science will be advanced thereby."

The government's investigation is, of course, shrouded in controversy—the UFO phenomenon, according to Keith & co., is bound by a slipknot of the paranormal and government's involvement. That equivocating "probably" screams out to them. The study's methodology begs many questions, is fodder for doubt.

"If you read the Condon Report closely," Keith said, "you discover that it contradicts many of Project Blue Book's own findings, set out in special report number fourteen."

Regardless of the counterarguments against it, the Condon Report sounded a death knell for official government participation in researching UFOs and therewith shattered UFOlogists' hope for mainstream scientific acceptance and legitimacy. Since then, all serious study of UFOs has been driven underground, and is pursued only by maverick scientists, who in so doing risk societal stigma and even their careers.

What knowledge there is about UFOs, then, is a mixed bag of accurate information, misinformation, and what Keith & co. call *dis*information, which is false information spread by the government and other powerful organizations, like Hollywood, to deliberately mislead. Things get a little tricky here, because in order to be more readily believed, disinformation is spun out of partially true and patently false information. Take the *Men in Black* franchise, for example, which has its roots in the actual reported appearances of such mysterious men at or just after supposed sightings. The idea here is that as long as the public associates these stories with fiction, with make-believe—and note the sinister overtones of that phrase—there's less of a chance that they'll take them seriously. In the eyes of the government, in other words, these phenomena are acceptable as objects of entertainment, but not of serious study. It's also common knowledge among UFOlogists that the government employs debunkers. Debunking itself has roots in a 1953 study commissioned by the CIA, the Robertson Panel, which concluded that a public relations campaign should be undertaken to "debunk" UFOs in order to reduce public interest in them.

Cutting through the blubber-like buildup, unraveling the truth from all the lies, can take years and years of intense investigation. Years of believing that your study, all your patient effort and sustained concern, will end in some meaningful insight or discovery, a Eureka moment.

When I asked Keith how he thought things would change if UFOlogy were granted the merit badge of science, he still landed on a note of skepticism, of uncertainty.

"I don't think rationality is ultimately up to the task of giving us a full understanding of the UFO or paranormal phenomena. But we're very far from knowing that. I can tell you what, though, it's amazing what you won't know if you don't ask."

The sky watch run by Keith's friend Randy was scheduled to meet at 4:00 p.m. in Nansen Summit Park, located on the small, flattened top of a dormant shield volcano in Lake Oswego, Oregon. It's less a park than a scenic viewpoint, really. I'd read enough by then not to be surprised by much of anything relating to UFOs, including the fact that we were to meet during the day.

I was the first to arrive. The park has one bench and I stood on it and took in the view. I could see almost all of Portland, out to the Cascade and Coast mountain ranges in either direction. The sky felt high up and was quite blue and seemed to go on forever. Only a little haze hung out around the mountains. Keith had told me to bring a camera, so I'd toted along my wallet-size point-and-shoot.

Going in, I didn't know what to expect from the sky watch. Would I see something? Something like what Arnold had seen in his plane? Something spectacular and conclusive? And more to the point: Would I believe it if I did? And if not, why? "Some persons," William James writes, "never are, and possibly never under any circumstances could be, converted."

I sat down on the bench and scanned the sky and, sure enough, there was something hovering out to the west. I literally sat on the edge of my seat. Squinted. A bubble rose in my chest. I got my camera out and switched it on and made small adjustments to my position in an attempt to bring the object into sharper relief. The object grew larger in the sky, drew closer. The bubble further rose. Before I could take the shot, though, the thrill of the moment passed. I burped. It was just a helicopter.

Keith arrived with his camera hung around his neck,

his hand out to support its two-foot telephoto lens. He had a camera bag slung from his shoulder and wore a vest and a sunhat. He looked like he was ready for a safari or, I don't know, a dinner theater adaptation of *Jumanji*.

"You the only one here?" he asked when he made it to the top.

"Yeah," I said, sheepishly tucking my camera back in my bag.

"A couple months ago there were almost thirty of us." Keith had talked about this, how people flow through organizations like MUFON, how public interest comes and goes. He seemed accustomed to the ups and downs and didn't dwell on the absence of other stratosphere hunters. He got going about how Randy had a psychic connection to UFOs. They seemed to materialize whenever he was around. And it was only a matter of time before more people figured that out. Although hopefully not the *wrong* people, if I caught his drift.

"Here he comes." Keith nodded toward a middle-aged man wearing a black T-shirt. On it was a squiggly lined representation of the Eiffel Tower, done in silver, and was that glitter?

"Where is everyone?" Randy asked.

"Looks like it'll just be the three of us," Keith said, and made the introductions.

I told them about my experience with the helicopter and they laughed.

"Don't worry," Randy said. "Last time we were out here we got blimped."

Randy hails from Tennessee and has a lacquerous southern accent. UFOs were a relatively new fascination of his. A few years back he'd had a close encounter: while out on a routine walk around the neighborhood, a UFO had buzzed him. He wasn't as shaken as you might assume, though—he's got a storied history with all things mystical and occult. He talked for a while about something called a kundalini experience and the fire snake that sits coiled at the bottom of his spine and the opening of his third eye—all of which well predated his study of UFOs. And he's seen auras since he was a young boy. "I saw a red one around my nephew," he said, but broke off in the middle of that thought and hoisted his bazooka lens to the sky and, according to an unknowable logic, fired off a scad of shots. Keith followed suit. Their shutters sounded like automatic weapons built for Lilliputians. What was happening? Was this my moment? What did they see? They stopped before I could zero in on what they were shooting and Randy resumed as though nothing had happened: "And he turned out to be a pretty famous artist."

"Hold up a sec. Whoa," I said. "What was that all about?"

Randy explained that he doesn't actually *see* many of the UFOs he captures on his camera. They're either too small for the naked eye or too fast. In order to observe them he relies on a deeper mode of vision, one that, when pressed, he couldn't get too specific about. In practice, though, his methodology involves "banging away at the sky" with his camera and then checking out later what he'd caught. But although I knew this, I was still never able to accustom my-self to the abruptness with which the conversation would break and the bazooka lenses would be hoisted skyward. I always got swept up into the dialectic of excitement and disappointment, a bummer of a seesaw to find yourself on.

"We're gonna ask to see a UFO here today," Randy said, more than once. He sounded a lot like charismatic preachers I'd heard, petitioning God for some minor miracle.

"I'm sick of the round ones," Keith said. "I want to see a triangle."

I asked them what their families thought of their interest in UFOs, of the sky watches and the MUFON meetings, of all the books and conferences.

"Just a weirdo thing Dad's into," Keith said.

"Mine just thinks I'm delusional," Randy echoed.

After an hour and a half without seeing anything promising on his camera's miniscreen, Randy suggested we go back to his place to check out some recent photos, including ones that Keith hadn't seen yet. His house was a ten-minute drive from the park and when we arrived, Randy had us take off our shoes before we headed upstairs to his office. His house smelled of stale potpourri and I wondered whether Randy had left all the lights off by accident or if maybe I'd missed something and it was significant somehow. Keith and I took our spots on a small couch in the dark office and Randy booted up his computer. We then watched as he scrolled through thousands and thousands of pictures of the sky. As thumbnails, they looked like pieces of a jigsaw puzzle from hell. But when they were resized to fit the screen, you could see little flaws in each image. Randy would then use a magnifying feature to make the flaw larger and larger. In some you could make out a semicircular shape surrounded by explosions of color or light. Some had distinctly nipple-like excrescences about their centers. Others still were little more than smudges of color, like a rainbow imprecisely remembered. For the next twenty minutes or so, Randy continued to show us strange picture after strange picture. And when he said he wanted to show me "the armada," Keith practically cooed. It was on another flash drive, though, and he had to dig through a plastic bag full of them to find it. He finally did and pulled up a picture of eleven black circles in front of a wall of clouds. Through the series he had captured the unbelievable movement of these circles. The pictures were literally incredible. Some appeared to hover as though stationary, while others skipped around to different parts of the sky, as though part of some four-dimensional game of Whac-A-Mole.

I looked over at Keith, who said, matter-of-factly and without taking his eyes off the screen, "Out of this world."

And yet as I left Randy's house and made my way home, I couldn't shake my uncertainty, my doubt. I'd been shown something, something compelling, but what had that really been? The pictures opened a new line of questioning in me. What happens to a digital camera's sensor when you fire off fifty-some-odd shots while swiftly arcing the lens across the sky? Couldn't that account for the smudges? The flaws? The nipple-like excrescences? Weren't Randy and Keith placing quite a bit of faith in their cameras? And wasn't there a deeper irony or antinomy at work here? Weren't they on a fool's errand, trying to prove the existence of something suprascientific through science's offspring, that is, technology?

Could it be that what I'd witnessed in Randy's small office was a textbook example of confirmation bias? That is, were they seeing exactly what they wanted to see? Or was the problem mine? Was I, as I'd worried in college, classed among James's unconvertible?

It's sort of like this: on Martha's Vineyard, I fished. A surprise, considering I hadn't been a keen or avid angler growing up. I'd never been able to manage the inlander's embrace of eddying rivers and boggy lakes. Their humid musk and the mysterious moss that lurks electric green alongshore, the sinister chirr of dragonflies and the neon whine of outboard motors: these were charms I was, and perhaps still am, too fussy to appreciate. Yet stand me up to my hammies in ocean chop or on craggy rocks seaside and hand me a ten-foot pole and I'm as happy as a clam in heat. The two-handed casting action was a lot like throwing a lacrosse ball, which I was skilled at then, and following the weighted tackle along its parabolic flight until it plooped far off and silently into the water satisfied a desire I didn't know existed inside me. There were days I woke before the sky to head up to the rocks at West Chop, and evenings after work that I'd drive out to the Chappy surf. I'd typically go alone, but every so often another house member would join me. I remember one evening in Menemsha with Grace in particular: she sat on the beach while I fished and we discussed Plato's ladder of love. Later we got clam chowder and watched on as the horizon drank the sun under.

The fish I caught that summer numbered precisely zero. No striper, no mackerel, and not a single blue. No bonito. I tried new lures; tried bait; tried lighter sinkers, then heavier ones, then lighter again. Still nothing. The internet existed in 2002, but I'm not sure the house had a connection and, regardless, those two and a half months yield no memories of my being online, where I might've gone to find out where and what fish were running. Instead I did things the old-fashioned way: I eavesdropped on the conversations I heard on my visits to Dick's Bait & Tackle. Glum poacher that I knew myself to be, I was too ashamed to ask outright, and so I seemed forever doomed to remain a step behind the fish. And while I once caught Chris's right thumb, the closest I came to landing an actual fish was a July afternoon at West Chop. There were a few of us out there, but no one was having any luck. After an hour or so, one of my comrades called it quits.

"You should've been here yesterday," he said in passing. "Could've fed the five thousand, the way we were reeling them in."

Given that I came away empty-handed every time, it's tempting to think that what I was up to all summer doesn't really qualify as fishing, or that it weighs in, at best, as a diminished form of the sport. But of course that's not right. A negative experience is still an experience nonetheless, isn't it? I might not have caught any fish, but I was still fishing, right? This is an idea that a fellow Cornerstoner, Simeon Zahl, has gone on to think long and hard about. In the time intervening he's become a respected theologian and specializes in the Holy Spirit, in pneumatology. When I recently asked him about self-deception and religious experience, he mentioned Christoph Blumhardt, a turn-of-the-century German preacher. Though a faith healer for much of his career and a firm believer in unmediated experiences of God, Blumhardt came to share Luther's fundamental distrust of human nature, a baseline suspicion of personal motives. But in a tidy rhetorical peripeteia, he ended up believing that "the reliable mark of the Holy Spirit at work is not so much divine peace as birth-pangs, the anxiety and unsettled feeling that accompanies profound change." Thomas Traherne, the seventeenth-century poet and theologian, puts it this way: "Be present with your want of a Deity, and you shall be present with the Deity." Maybe all along I'd been working with a narrow and naive conception of religious experience. Maybe all my experiences of absence and uncertainty, of doubt and anguish, all the clock time I've felt far from God, far from myself, maybe all of it, in the end, amounts to an experience of God. Maybe it'd been enough to have a line in the water. And what a mighty comforting thought I found this to be. It was a glorious eighteen seconds, after which I began to worry I was playing at word games here. Was my relief the result of nothing more than some fancy-pants brainifying? The comfort I experienced, how wasn't that just further evidence that I was *curvatus in se*, bent hopelessly inward upon myself? Because wasn't I using this theological insight to solve for a perceived personal lack? Simply calling my desire to have an experience of God an experience of God? "From wrong to wrong the exasperated spirit / Proceeds, unless restored by that refining fire," writes Eliot, portentously, in

"Little Gidding." Back then on my knees I found myself, bowed before a trough of doubt, nosing around in a slop of unknowing.

"Do you believe in pink elephants?" Keith asked, beginning a thought experiment. "Or unicorns? Do you believe in Superman?"

Of course not. No reasonable person would answer yes to these kinds of questions. But if he were to approach twenty strangers on the street and ask whether they'd had an experience with the paranormal—Had they seen a ghost? A UFO? Ever had an out-of-body experience?—he was sure a handful would say yes. And he bet they'd be eager to share their story.

The thought of polling strangers about their paranormal experiences cast me back to the MUFON meeting and the conversations that took place during the roundtable. "Freaks"—Keith's word—isn't quite right, even with how starkly some of their hypothesizing contrasted with Keith's own meticulous, scientific bent. What struck me in hindsight was the palpable desperation that lay behind all their speculation. No matter what form that speculation took—the indestructibility of consciousness (in chickens) or the role of bismuth in antigravity—it all amounted to a gesture toward, a grasping after something *more*. Something other than the plainly human.

"Paranormal or occult phenomena of the type I'm talking about are most like religious phenomena," Keith said.

"They're mostly ephemeral, hard to conceptualize. And the problem is they don't happen every day, so therefore don't have a close connection with ordinary human experience."

Keith asked me to imagine myself as a boat on an inconceivably vast ocean, a body of water that nowhere touches a shore. The water's color suggests a depth beyond reckoning. Every so often the boat will spring a leak. Water will rush in. The boat, he explained, is our incarnated body and everything that attends having a body. And the ocean is the transpersonal realm beyond us. The boat's job is to hold the water out. But sometimes it fails. And in those moments, we taste some part of our true potential for experience. William James put it this way: "Our normal waking consciousness is but one special type of consciousness, whilst all about it, parted from it by the filmiest of screens, there lie potential forms of consciousness entirely different."

This calls to mind Henri Bergson, who helped turn classical models of perception on their head when he argued that, rather than being productive, the brain's function, with respect to the nervous system and sensory organs, is largely eliminative. As an illustration, Bergson used movies, film. Film couldn't be counted on to depict a perfectly reliable picture of reality because of the spaces between frames. The metaphoric leap isn't hard to make: a person's mind is a projector's light, his perceptions the individual film stills. What escapes from between the frames as his brain creates the world?

When I asked whether a person, as a boat, could take on too much water and therefore surely sink, Keith said, "There are levels and layers of the other world. Multidimensions or however you want to say it." Metaphors mix and must all fail somewhere. Scuba divers sometimes talk about going so far down that their water world is all the same dark color, or of finding themselves caught up in a kelp bed surrounded by weedy green. In such moments they can become so disoriented that they're no longer able to discern up from down. The mind in such moments of crescendo-like panic must grasp after anything to settle its nauseating vertigo.

Feeling like I might have let the conversation stray too far afield, I asked Keith about the apparent intelligence that guides UFOs.

"The UFO phenomenon can't be completely explained in simple terms as 'space people' from outer space, very much like us, coming to visit Earth," he said. "It's much more than that. And maybe not even that at all."

"I guess I'm just trying to ground this in something concrete," I said.

Keith either laughed or scoffed, I couldn't tell.

"Good luck!"

I spent more time working on Keith's profile than I'd planned—the piece kept expanding, amoeba-like, to include more than I felt qualified to discuss. Much to the chagrin of my indoctrinators, Alexis and I had recently moved in together, and I know I taxed her patience with my underinformed talk about gestalt psychology and the phi phenomenon and many other brain busters re: the nature of perception.

My gut feeling was that what people see as UFOs could be explained away easily, with an appeal to psychology, to physiology. But there were also times I'd charge up the stairs and into her office to tell her about a sighting that strained my skepticism, that pushed it to its aphelion point. These reports eluded all the routine explanations (weather balloon, ball lightning, lenticular clouds, etc.) and weren't reported by trashy half-wits on meth but regular citizens, good tax-paying folks like Randy, and seemed to point to something legitimately unidentified. So while I could obviously draw a hard line at a coup d'honeybee, some of what I encountered remained confusing, hard to parse. I started sleeping like a maniac. Alexis told me I was grinding my teeth, said my side of the bed sounded like someone learning to drive stick. I went to the dentist and was set supine in a chair and as four latex-gloved hands palpated my mouth, with the drill's squeal and the nubby-tipped suction tube's gurgle-whoosh in my ear and the odd waffle iron of a light hovering above my eyes, I found myself thinking that maybe this was something like what abductees experience.

At times it seemed like writing this piece had exposed two opposite desires in me, both equally present and fundamental to who I am. On the one hand I want to maintain, at almost any cost, a reasonable, enlightenment-like skepticism; and on the other I deeply want to have that skepticism radically upended. Can one make it through the world as half believer, half debunker? Or is this a mark of cowardice? A wishy-washy unwillingness to commit to either side? This contradiction continued to hound me well after my deadline came and I was forced to file a simplified version of my essay about Keith. Parts of my past that'd sat long undisturbed—Alexis had heard about my Martha's Vineyard summer only in passing, for example—had been roiled, and every so often I would return to what I'd written and experience a deflating disappointment. There I'd find the naked frame of a house—no walls, no roof, a building fit only for squatters in a temperate clime. The piece failed, and spectacularly so, to address any of what I'd experienced in researching and writing it. And the amount of work left to be done seemed staggering, potentially never-ending. One's spiritual whatever consists of experiences so intimate and evanescent, so evasive and embarrassing, that ultimately no amount of reflection or examination is up to the task of fully unpacking their significance.

As I began to try to fill in the gaps, I was tempted by easy parallels. Weren't all of us—Keith, the MUFONites, and I—longing for "something more"? And wasn't this an ancient human yearning, one that'd led our troglodytic forbears to dream up the idea of religion in the first place? Wasn't the second Tuesday of every month an occasion for fellowship in much the same way Wednesday night Young Life, Friday morning Campaigners, and church on Sunday had been for me growing up? And couldn't patiently watching the sky be considered a form of prayer?

But late one night, as I lay awake vexed by metaphysical vagaries and hypnagogic visions of my teeth falling out, another correspondence emerged. Because wasn't grounding the mysterious in something concrete precisely what Keith hoped to accomplish? Wasn't that the point of his massive subterranean library and his routine sky watches? Didn't his line of inquiry end, like a crash test, in a brick wall of certainty? And in this way, wasn't his ambition more or less like Dad's, whose literal interpretation of the Bible had girded him in unassailable, unquestionable Truth? Though with time Dad's theology has only gotten harder for me to understand, I've found it equally difficult for me to fault him for it, to hold a grudge. Because hadn't I also been hoping to shore up my faith with a doubt-eradicating religious experience? Hadn't I also been looking for something that might absolve me of uncertainty and, at the same time, impart upon my life a purpose so grand that I'd no longer have to fear, at least not quite so fiercely, that life's end?

In revisiting this, I've come to believe that pining after the ineffable in the way I had as an adolescent and beyond was little more than thinly veiled narcissism. What was I really longing for but the simple feeling of having been chosen? Incontrovertible proof that I was special? And as I continued to think about Keith and UFOs and about the evolution of my own spiritual whatever, I was haunted by the parallel histories science and religion have spun for us on the loom of time, these epics of human ambition, of our undying quest to charm the fluid universe still. Sometimes I find it dumbly astounding, the imponderable amount of attention and energy and effort and care, the untold frustration and suffering, the head and tummy aches, the melancholy and mania, all the human ooze our scientific knowledge and religious literature represents. But in the face of these histories, I've kept returning to the idea that Kierkegaard pitied his professors, whether of science or philosophy or theology, sad men who together bewitched the world with their cleverness, their proficiency, but who never got to experience that critical point in themselves where everything flipped on its head. Because it's only after such an experience that you can begin to appreciate that there will always be something out there that you'll never understand.

Time has since worked its magic on my Martha's Vineyard experience and every so often a memory of that summer will return to me with the astonishing suddenness of a vision. The PG night with the girls from Ole Miss, sober and chaste, when we snuck onto a private beach near Gay Head to stargaze, the lighthouse off in the distance broadcasting its retarded Morse code. The time the guys stayed up all night watching the *Lonesome Dove* miniseries; how at dawn we went to get pastries for the girls and threw rocks into the Atlantic until our arms and shoulders went sore. The time two house members washed the rest of our feet—how odd and awkward I found that to be, but how disarming and moving, too. How after I suffered a bit of dental trauma (tennis racket, front teeth), a few folks went to the local library's annual sale and bought me boxes and boxes of books—never before had I felt so cared for by people who were not my family.

These memories and the many others like them seem to have been served an extra helping of significance, to exist on a mental plane closer to archetype than memory. Is this just nostalgia? Or is it rather that, by a strange lustration, a rock-tumbler-like refinement, the experiences have been allowed to make good on a potential that'd sat latent in them all along? Maybe these questions are asking the same thing, but whatever the case, the memories have acquired a quality that I do not find in others from the same period of my life. They have a weight and strangeness to them that I've always associated with religious experience, a depth beyond reckoning, but whether they count as religious, I'm not qualified to say.

I can say with certainty that I'd begun to notice a like quality in more recent memories, ones involving Alexis. Although we'd only been together a couple years, our earliest experiences were already boomeranging back to me. The first time I saw her, a comet smudge of blond walking up the stairs in my office—she was interviewing for an internship. The respect and humility and incipient pride I experienced when, after I found out who she was, I pulled her application to the writing camp I ran then and read her work—the essay ended on an image of her riding a horse across a Tunisian desert and it's at once innocent and erotic and it made me feel more alive and after the final period I'm pretty sure I was well on my way to being in love. After we kissed for the first time, months later outside a bar in Northwest Portland, she said, "You just kissed me," which delighted me more than the kiss itself: it was as though the experience wasn't quite real, for either of us, until she articulated it. I could go on, but like my memories of Martha's Vineyard, there's something paltry and even sad about trotting these out like this, as a shorthand for what they've come to mean to me. It's almost like the event specifics cannot displace the shared imaginary landscape they're a part of, a horizon of concern that is as much communal and shared as it is personal and private.

In the end, maybe what I'd been looking for all along was one dramatic experience of capital-*M* Mystery that might contain or explain all the daily small ones I cannot comprehend and before which language palls. I'd found myself wandering around our place, a little Tudor in Northeast Portland we almost didn't get, wondering whether it would one day assume the significance that the Martha's Vineyard house has for me. I'd caught myself trying to commit to memory its floor plan and various architectural quiddities (the corner fireplace in our bedroom, the odd built-in bookshelf in my office), in the hopes that I might more easily summon them to mind in the future, which you would think might dull its strangeness. But no, the house only grew more mysterious. Aside from the XX Cornerstoners, Alexis was the first woman I'd lived with, the first woman I'd really loved, and every so often I'd hear her reading aloud to herself upstairs, working out the rhythm of one of her sentences, or I'd step into the richly fragrant fog of her aftersteam, and I'd wonder at her presence in my life, at the inexplicable source of my good fortune. Who was this being who seemed so glassily limpid at the surface, but so brumous and befogged at any depth? This alpine lake of a woman? She was on a Dickinson jag in those days and in bed, from time to time, she would read me whatever had recently excited her. I remember this:

> Elder, Today, and a session wiser
> And fainter, too, as Wiseness is—

I find myself still softly searching
For my Delinquent Palaces—

And a Suspicion, like a Finger—
Touches my Forehead now and then
That I am looking oppositely
For the Site of the Kingdom of Heaven—

This is about what I think Dickinson means: soon after
we moved in I headed down into our house's unfinished basement, where the washer and dryer had grown old together. I
turned the corner at the foot of the stairs and there, hanging
like bats from the clotheslines strung between the floor's
beams, were Alexis's delicate underthings. Diaphanous, ever
so thrillingly see-through, they were all different shades of
pastel, the soft reds and purples and yellows of Lucky Charms.
And though I could name the colors, could describe the lace
that lined the waistband and leg holes, could render the
way they hung from the wooden clothespins, curled slightly
in on themselves like chrysalises, still there was something
irreducibly strange about the scene, something that eluded
definition, that slipped right through the sieve of my mind.
It was, somehow, more. So whatever time or fate or God has
in store for Alexis and me, whether what we've built so far
has been built to last, I am coming to learn, day by day, that
there are entire orders of mystery with which I'll be more
than happy to live.

Neighborhood Watch

Maybe it's just me, some personal or spiritual failing, but so little of my life feels like it's lived in the warm groove of scene. Seems I'm always getting caught in the sticky wicket of self-consciousness, overaware of how the story's being told. Overaware *that* a story's being told. My default mode tends to be this one of narration, meaning, roughly, that an experience doesn't really become "real" for me until it's prosed. Put under the hitchhiker's thumb of words, all dolled up in the dinner jacket of syntax. During broodier jags, I suspect this inability to "live in the present" has robbed me of experiential richness, kept me from partaking in the full range of emotion available to me as a human being. Are my joys as joyous as they can be? My griefs as grievous? Am I experiencing love as deeply as I'm able? At a full-force level ten? But every now and again it's like the gears of life will move in such a way as to force me out of myself and into the story. So then, action—

Home sick and I heard the first sirens around one in the afternoon. This was a Tuesday in March, some months back.

Although my neighborhood in North Portland is changing, caught up in the tidal shift of gentrification, its soundtrack still includes the high whine and squeal of emergency vehicles, the call and response of crisis. But a strange thing had happened to me in the three-plus years I'd lived here: the sirens had stopped registering with the urgency of alarms. Instead, when I heard them, I'd started to feel weirdly secure. On a handful of occasions, in fact, beset by a low-level suspicion or frustration or fear, I'd summoned the sirens myself. I know now that not everyone in my community feels the same way, shares this faith in how justice is meted out and by whom, and that I didn't question this faith then was thanks to embarrassing historical ignorance of nearly epic proportions. Among the many examples? I didn't know that my neighborhood had been redlined, and not all that long ago. But see, here I am, already impeding the action, contextualizing, betraying the way the event was lived.

I was lying on the love seat that looks out my house's old picture window, reading, and noticed that the sirens didn't pass by as they typically did, on their way to other, presumably less rehabilitated parts of the neighborhood. Their sound waves didn't elongate with Doppler predictability, but beat a steady and strident pulse. I pulled on some shoes and walked outside and found a fire truck, an ambulance, and several police cars gathered in front of Peter's house—he's three doors down and across the street. This wasn't itself surprising either, not really. For the months foregoing, Peter'd been spending more nights on his unlit porch, hanging out with shadowy characters, guys whose faces I could never quite make out in the darkness, staying up later and playing his music even louder than usual. His wife, Linda, had at some point moved out and was off living elsewhere with their two silken windhounds. Our walks to Peninsula Park had long since dropped off and though I'd given him an old racket of mine, I couldn't tell you the last time I'd seen him on a tennis court, let alone hit with him. His howls, what he'd probably call "yawps," had gone from being an occasional and endearing nuisance to a near nightly production, an unholy evensong, and they'd acquired a certain edge, too, were serrated with something like desperation or anguish or dread. They unsettled Alexis and me. And we couldn't have been the only neighbors who took all this as evidence that Peter was courting a minor disaster.

I made it to the corner, where a woman wearing a TriMet uniform was talking to a police officer. I'd never seen her before—was she my neighbor, too?

"I was walking by and saw the dog run off," she kept repeating. She must've meant Boo, the white pit bull Peter adopted after Linda left. "Just wanted to make sure the dog was okay."

Somehow I knew that what she was giving was a *statement*, that what she was was a *witness*.

Ernie, who lives across the alley behind me, emerged from Peter's house, and I waved him over. He's a light-skinned black man of around sixty, with a high forehead and a long braided ponytail. Soap-opera handsome and affably chatty, he's the type of guy who'll tell you his life story if you give him the time.

I asked him what was going on, was everything okay.

"Someone's been stabbed," he said. Just like that. Eerily vague and passive. Flat and far-off.

And Peter? What about Peter?

"Peter's dead." The words had a tried-on feeling to them, lacked the conviction of the fact they conveyed, and I almost didn't believe him. He said them the way an actor might deliver new lines, lines from the script of a cheap melodrama, something straight to streaming. "I tried to give him CPR. It was a deep gash, though. Nothing we could do."

His face went into a distant stare and I didn't know what to do or say and had already begun to calculate all the ways I was failing to live up to this moment when, without realizing it, I had taken Ernie into my arms and was hugging him tight. He was quivering, his body a kind of tuning fork, vibrating like it was trying to find life's frequency again. I raised my hand and held it to the back of his head, cupped the nidus where the ropy tether of his braid roots, and, to be honest, I don't know whether I made this gesture out of genuine human sympathy and solicitude or because making the gesture created an image, better yet a *tableau*, that would fit the story I already knew, someplace deep down, I'd tell about this experience later.

We broke and I held Ernie by the shoulders. He was still fuzzy and uncertain about the eyes. I asked what I could do to help. He told me to go into his house, into his kitchen, and see if he'd left the oven on. If he had, he said, I could turn it off.

Mine's not a memory that regularly date-stamps what it stores away so I can't remember exactly when I met Peter. Seven, eight years ago now? Looking back, he begins for me as a vague presence, ghostly and out of focus. The setting would've been the tennis courts at Irving Park, which is in one of the bougiest neighborhoods in Portland, a neighborhood much farther out on the gentrification spectrum than our own. He would've ridden up on his bike, his ashy hair emerging out from under his black, brimmed hat that was straight out of *Crocodile Dundee*. The Beatles or the Grateful Dead or the Doors would've been blaring from the boom box he always kept in his handlebar basket. After riding in circles on the blacktop outside the fence, he may have parked his ride and begun to blow soap bubbles. He had a largish plastic wand that he'd slip into a scabbard of bubble juice and then he'd arc it through the air as though part of an interpretive dance—he often looked like he was trying to catch imaginary butterflies. I would've noted his height (news stories after his death listed him as six-seven and one neighbor he hadn't alienated described him as a "gentle giant") and chances are he was barefoot. But really I'm just speculating here. Truth is I probably wrote him off as another of this city's many hippie holdovers, another Elder Dreamer, an archetype my generation tends to look on with a strange mix of respect and pity. What I'm sure of is that Peter didn't come out onto the courts and play—that wasn't until some time later.

Another reason he might not jump out in my memory is that he was but one of a whole crew of characters who hung out at Irving then. I was in my midtwenties, renting a house with Alexis a few blocks away, and whenever I passed by I'd find that they'd colonized a court or two. And they always appeared to be having so much fun, laughing and hooting during points, ribbing one another jocosely after. Their interactions were unscripted and unedited, governed above all else by spontaneity and wit. They seemed so free with themselves, with one another. It's worth noting that most of these guys were black and I'd be lying if I didn't admit that this was a large part of what appealed to me, why I wanted in. I'd rather lie, to be honest. Play it like it wasn't a thing. Because while it's true what they say about this city and its appalling lack of diversity, it's not entirely uncomplicated, either, is it? addressing the lack of diversity in one's life? There's the squirmy notion of tokenism—you know, "Some of my best friends. . ."—and the icky tendency to romanticize difference, to apply a filmy whitewash to an entire group of people. It's a real question, though: How can we honor the desire to expand the range and timbre of our experience without turning that desire into a microaggression? some iffy form of social cred? Without all the smug self-satisfaction? How can we acknowledge, accept, and celebrate difference, but not too much? Is there an alternative path to the patronizing PC bullshit that proliferates online? These are knotty questions that occurred to me only later, ones for which I still don't have satisfying answers. At the time I wanted no more than to pledge this fraternity of tennis players, a group of dudes who yucked it up—*communed*—in a way that appealed directly to my herniated soul.

There was John, he of the scoriated voice and shimmery metallic grille, who liked to get a little stoned ("take his medicine") before playing. He'd worked tanks in Vietnam and loved storying, shooting the shit, and he sat around watching other folks play, calling foot faults from two courts over and laughing at his joke, just as often as he played himself. And look, I know how this might sound, but Fred really did look a touch like Michael Jordan, and he greeted you with a chill upright–hand clap–chest bump production that I found thrilling and even vaguely exculpatory, and he was basketball tall with a wingspan that made him a nightmare at net. Ronnie's wardrobe was generously stocked with argyle sweaters and those that weren't vests he often wore in the French way, tied over his shoulders. He had an air of hardness about him, though, that broadcast the message loud and clear: Fuck not with Ronnie. Tony, who grew up in a town house across from the courts, had some form of martial arts under his belt and practiced an obscure sciamachy between points, fending off imaginary assailants by chopping and punching the air in front of him.

The list could go on but no matter how long it got, it'd have to end with Lawrence. Lawrence acted as the unofficial (and unelected) president of the Irving Park Crew, strutted around all cock-of-the-walkish. Come fall, it was Lawrence who brought a leaf blower and push broom to clear debris from the courts, but he had a way of turning this courtesy into an assertion of power and ownership so that you actually ended up resenting him for it. He had long dreads and always played in sagging warm-up pants and what you'd probably call an athletic sunhat. Rumor had it that he'd been a star fullback in college, but rumor it was doomed to remain because it was nigh on impossible to get anything in the way of personal info out of Lawrence. If he was there as much to socialize as to play, like the rest of us, he had a strange way of showing it. He must've thought that because he had some of the better strokes out there he was justified in going around telling everyone else what was wrong with theirs. But such gratis instruction was almost always unwelcome and tended only to piss folks off. A few times during sets of doubles against him, after hitting a winner, he clutched his crotch and waggled that fisted gnarl at me. That so many years passed without a serious incident is, in hindsight, miraculous.

The story's still told in the hushed tones reserved for major family fallouts. And like those stories, it's come to be told mostly in shorthand: the time Lawrence and Tony fought. I wasn't there when it happened and there are conflicting reports about what started it, but all the tributaries converge in the mighty ancient river of human violence. After a kerfuffle over a line call or a score escalated, all that pent-up ill will and frustration was released. Lawrence, so it goes, left the courts only to promptly return with a knife, intending harm of a Renaissance drama sort. He approached Tony, blade dancing ready at his side, talking his brand of incendiary and instigative shit. I imagine there was a tense pause before Lawrence made his play, at which point Tony proved the usefulness of his kung fu shadowboxing, disarming and dispatching him with frightening ease. Embarrassing ease. As though all along he'd been practicing for this very moment. And when Lawrence left the courts for the second time that day, he appeared to do so for good.

Point is, memory-wise, this is what Peter was competing with. He only begins to shore up in my mind, to emerge and materialize as Peter, when he steps onto the court, which he does like something out of *Field of Dreams*. You see, the quality of tennis at Irving wasn't great and at times it was almost laughably bad. Most of these guys had picked the game up later in life, were self-schooled and choked up on their grips and hit everything way short and with a maddening amount of back- or sidespin. They played a devious and wily Old Man game. Now, as something of an aesthete when it comes to tennis, I'll sometimes claim to value hitting pretty shots more than the end result, than winning. But still there were times I left the park so frustrated, having lost, that I swore I'd never come back. So then I invite you to imagine my surprise when one afternoon, after months of going to Irving, I watched Peter trade his bubble wand for a racket and step on the court and start hitting with long and fluid strokes, strokes as graceful as they were anachronistic. They might as well have been taken from a time capsule, come down from when courts were predominantly grass and rackets were wood and players wore pants and spikes and drank cocktails on changeovers. Sometimes, when he was so moved and wanted to goof off a little, he'd hit a lob fifty, sixty feet in the air, so high you nearly lost sight of the ball, and it'd make its meteoric return to earth and land six inches or a foot inside the baseline, throwing the opposing team into a tizzy, a wry half smile on his face. That he could exercise such control, that he was capable of producing such beauty, given how large and tall he was, how very barefoot—it didn't add up. Turns out he'd played in college, that he had a PhD in history and used to be a professor, that he'd written a book about Wittgenstein. Turns out he had all kinds of stories to tell.

After seeing to Ernie's oven, I wandered back out into the midday sun of March 4, 2014, the day Peter died, was killed, murdered. What had started as just another Tuesday in March was now a point on a timeline, part of a plot. A false spring was on—local knowledge has it that you can expect rain here until July 4—and the light and the warmth made it seem like time itself was somehow out of joint, like God was scratching on the ones and twos. Before that week we hadn't seen the denuded sun since I couldn't remember when and it seemed that even the weather was contributing to the afternoon's irreality.

An old Crown Vic pulled up as I came to the corner. A woman in the passenger seat hailed me over. She was unhealthily thin and her blondish hair was on the last legs of an already shitty dye job. The driver leaned way over and, state I was in, it looked a little like he'd emerged from her chest.

"You know what's going on here?" he asked, and nodded to the cop cars. His body was electrically restless in a way that suggested doings unsavory. There was a compact video camera in the woman's lap, a small screen open at its side, and between them a police scanner crackled with staticky voices.

"No clue," I said. "Was just out to see for myself."

"Cool, thanks," he said, and pulled off, the words hanging momentarily behind the vanished car like this was a cartoon.

I looked around, confused, and spotted my across-the-street neighbor standing in the road. He's a youngish Latino hipster-looking guy who can often be found in his front yard with his cat on a leash. Alexis and I met him and his girlfriend/wife/partner back when we moved in, but hadn't acted on any of that new-neighborly goodwill, and very soon after found we'd forgotten their names. Consensus was we'd passed the point that it'd be cool to admit this, so now we waved to them and exchanged the occasional, rudderless small talk, content to live in this bizarre social penumbra between knowing them and not. We talked often about how convenient it would be for one of their monthly bills to show up in our mailbox, then at least, at last, we'd have one of their names. As I approached Luis or Juan or John or Louis or Brad, a realization came over me with a shameful terror: I didn't know Peter's last name.

"Peter was murdered," I said. "It's crazy."

I felt cheap, relating it like this, like it was no more than some dirty laundry I'd spotted, a gripping piece of gossip I hadn't been told directly but picked up while eavesdropping, and I immediately regretted it. Can an event like this be told in such a way that the words don't so apparently and so thoroughly fail the story? That doesn't level it into the voluptuous sensationalism of local news? Or is it that something essential about an experience is always lost when it's compressed into a story, like what happens to music when you convert it into a shareable audio file? In any case, the little info I'd related seemed to fully satisfy _____'s curiosity, and he headed back into his house without asking anything further. Had he, like me, watched Peter walk by every morning, to and from the store on the corner, one of the many convenience stores around here that, owing to crimes past, is sometimes referred to as a "murder mart," to pick up the day's domestic tallboys, one by one? Had he also measured his morning's progress by these walks? Were they now forever lost from his daily routine, too?

There was a separate hub of police cruisers down the block and I couldn't make out whether they were working this same incident or whether something else had gone down yonder, some unfortunate coincidence of misfortune. Ernie was talking to a pair of uniformed officers near where I'd left him. Caprice, his wife, a short white woman with curly, astonished blond hair, had joined him. She'd been Peter's closest friend, at times what you could maybe call his ally. Other uniformed officers had started to square off the intersection with yellow police tape, turning this part of my neighborhood into a *crime scene*. These cops, they appeared to be almost giddy with purpose—one was literally whistling while he worked.

Maybe it was shock that had caused the oversight, but it hadn't yet occurred to me to wonder who'd done it, who'd *committed murder*. And did the police have the *perp* in *custody*? *Downtown*? Or was *the suspect* still out there, still *on the loose*? All these clichéd words and phrases, bearers of cheap tension, it was a relief, electrifying even, to have reason to resort to them. This was the language of action, of story, was it not? And though I tried, I couldn't stop myself from imagining a chase, a frenzied search through my neighbors' backyards, the K-9 unit nosing shrubbery, hot on the trail, maybe a *Cool Hand Luke*–ish captain looming large somewhere in the background.

I walked up to the officer working the tape who wasn't whistling. I'd intended to have a simple conversation, see if I could get a handle on where things stood with *the investigation* and whether we had to worry about a criminal being *at large* in the neighborhood, but realized at once that we were working at cross-purposes. I, a civilian, was simply talking, chatting, but he, an officer of the city, was "communicating," abiding by some preordained set of rules for dealing with the public that he'd probably picked up in a Saturday seminar on crisis management. He could traffic only in facts, couldn't tolerate or indulge any uncertainty or speculation. This made any vagueness seem excessively, almost preposterously, vague.

"I can't say for certain we have the guy," the officer said.

"What does that mean, exactly? Like, you have a guy and you aren't a hundred percent it's *the* guy? Or you're not sure you even have a guy?"

"Yes," he said.

"Yes, you have a guy? Or yes, you don't have a guy?"

"Yes, the first one."

"Okay, so I don't necessarily have to hurry back inside and lock all my doors, is what you're saying."

"No, that's not what I'm saying at all. I can't say that's not a good idea. It's a good idea actually. Regardless."

Trying to imagine the protocol he had to follow, all the cogs of bureaucracy his uniform represented, was like trying to hold my entire family tree in mind. It just kept going back, back, back, back, back. I decided to cut my losses, thanked him for his time, and headed for home.

By now the first reporters had arrived, ageless men and women in civvies holding spiral notebooks and little electronic voice recorders. It was mesmerizing, watching them bop around like pollinators, bystander to bystander, as they tried to catch up to the story, a story that'd started as all stories do for them, in medias res. A few of these reporters approached me for information, but I begged off, claiming I knew only as much as they did, which was next to nothing, and mostly true. Being approached in this way unsettled me—I'd been unwittingly cast as a minor character here. Plus I couldn't shake the thought that we, Peter's neighbors, were entitled to a knowledge that they, the reporters, and by extension the public, were not. At least not so soon.

A woman reporter wearing a no-nonsense pantsuit pressed me after I played dumb. But had I known the man who was murdered? The *victim*, what was he like?

No, I said. I hadn't. He was just my neighbor. And as I walked away, resentment burbled in my gut. Gone pugnacious now, I wished I'd known something real juicy, if for no other reason than to feel like I was withholding something from her.

Back inside my house, a new urgency gripped me. I knew I had to *break the news* to Alexis. As I took the stairs up toward her office, I debated how to phrase it. Died? Was killed? Murdered? Died? Was killed? Murdered? My resentment of the reporters grew more pointed and intense. I held them responsible for my feeling like I'd been turned into the bearer of information, a data delivery system, and decidedly not a storyteller, or at least not the kind I was comfortable with. The story here was related to this news, of course, but wasn't exhausted by it. There would be excess, ragged edges. I mean, this was Peter's story after all, wasn't it?

When Alexis and I were looking at what would become our first house, in 2010, near the bottom of the most recent financial crisis, our Realtor talked a lot about this neighborhood's potential. She emphasized this word, "potential," in such a way that you knew it existed somewhere as a bullet point. Worse, you knew it existed there for buyers like us, a couple of young white DINCs with more future ahead of them than past behind. And we felt full of this potential ourselves, full of the very power that lives inside that word. There seemed to be no difference between our lives and how we'd choose to tell the story of them, no need to alter or amend. We'd gotten engaged not long before—and in Paris. I'd planned things for the story I thought Alexis would want to tell, hopefully, for the rest of her life, so the bridge we stopped on afforded an unobstructed view of the Eiffel Tower, which glittered bedazzlingly behind me as I proposed. And now we were planning a wedding. We'd settled on a location, an idyllic farm outside Portland. In their pitch the owners told us that, on a clear day, you could see the four ghostly mountain peaks of Hood, Adams, Saint Helens, and Rainier. The prospect of buying a house (we were preapproved!) had only kicked our imaginations into overdrive. How easy it was to cast ourselves ahead in time. How wondrously did the future shimmer! We populated that future with children, a whole passel of towheaded and cheeky little cherubs, so adorbs that people flagged us down on the street to tell us so, children born so painlessly and inconsequentially that they didn't disrupt our lives, not a smidgen. Experience after experience unfolded in the crystal balls of our dinner conversations—holidays, sure, birthdays and other special occasions, but summer BBQs and routine pizza Fridays, too, the predictable rhythms of a Tuesday afternoon—experiences that brimmed with significance, that were so loamy rich with meaning that they'd continue to feed us well into our dotage. All these future memories, would they begin in this house? In this neighborhood? The stock here was among the city's best, after all, block after tree-lined block of handsome old Foursquares and Craftsmans, places with "good bones," a phrase I now understand to mean that they'll renovate nicely, which is really to say that it won't be too tough to erase what's currently there. And the cutesy knickknack shops and fancy restaurants that the city was (in)famous for? They were getting closer to us all the time. Had we read about the upcoming development on Williams? All the eco-friendly condos and their concomitant storefronts? Or about the projects the city had planned to beautify—or at least descarify—Killingsworth? She might as well have sparked some incense and taken us on a guided visualization that replaced the murder mart with a tasty brunch spot, the sketchy furniture outlet down the block with an industrial-chic cocktail bar. But go further still and imagine a street full of young families like ours, with kids of their own, kids who could play in the streets undaunted, crime having dropped to squat, who would attend the local schools that had, with time, improved beyond all recognition.

Obvious though it is, it bears stating: to imagine what a place can become is to dismiss or reject what is already there. "Imagination" of this sort really functions as an insidious and particular brand of arrogance, one that ignores all but economic forces. I understood this in an abstract way when we moved in and it gave me pause. I felt guilty. But this guilt didn't give way to historical inquisitiveness, to a desire or, better still, a duty to understand the social dynamics that had swirled through the area like pressure systems. No. My guilt was one fit for a venial sin, something mincing and pesky but that nonetheless called for forgiveness. It was like, growing up, having to apologize to and ask forgiveness from one of my younger brothers: I knew I'd done whatever wrong I'd done and felt ashamed for it but disliked having to apologize, because apologizing ratified the story of my wrongdoing, made it real and put it in the world, and of course that was the point but still. In any case, I understood all this had to do with community, a word I kept hearing tossed around. I no longer fully understood what people meant when they said it and it now put a question to me like a poke in the chest. At root it seemed to have something in common with the idea of family, to partake of the same sense of belonging, complicated and fraught as it may be, full of the same self-sacrifice and intimate fucked-upedness, fucked up because of the very nature and extent of that intimacy. But it was more casual than that, the way I was hearing it used. I kept wondering what community was supposed to mean in an age that also advocated such staunch and unremitting individualism, whose highest ideal is the turbidly vague state of authentic selfhood—a culture of you-do-you. Is it nothing more than social back-scratching, then, the orgy of mutual masturbation you find online? Follow-for-follow, like-for-like, etc.? Or, worse, was it simply economic symbiosis, as it seemed when my neighbor thanked Alexis and me for buying our house for what we bought it for because it allowed him to refinance his? What I knew for sure was that the chief downside of gentrification was the dissolution of community and I didn't want to feel responsible for that, for what amounts to arriving at a party and immediately changing the music. I didn't want to think of myself as that kind of character. So when I saw Peter walking down the sidewalk soon after we moved in, I experienced something like relief. Here was the agent of my absolution, just the man to sell me an indulgence of sorts and open the door to a form of membership, belonging. "Community." And all of this could happen below board, without anyone (possibly even me) being the wiser.

It so happened that Peter and Linda got their first silken windhound, Apollo, at about the same time Alexis and I got our dog, Percy. This was a couple months after we moved in and, sharing the giddy excitement of new parenthood, we formed a quick and easy bond. On walks with Percy, I'd first stop by Peter's house, a beautiful old Craftsman he'd been in since the eighties, with a yard he'd let go to seed and grow into a ready metaphor for madness, with a small rickety metal fence out front that kept the dog penned only when he didn't

feel like jumping over it. He'd suit Apollo up and we'd head
to Peninsula Park, less than half a mile away. A sunken rose
garden with manicured, rectilinear hedges and a century-old
fountain season the park with a distinctly continental flavor.
Down in among the roses, you might could be in a French or
Austrian or Danish city. This flare of foreignness, the way the
park can make you feel like you've been transported abroad,
was one of the things that finally sold Alexis and me on the
neighborhood. When there, we could easily imagine we were,
in fact, elsewhere, as though our lives together were nothing
but a permanent vacation, a sixty-year holiday before our second and final shift down in the mines; where, as on vacation,
we could easily overlook or ignore whatever at the time was
making our lives complicated and hard, whatever we might
choose to revise or edit out of our life story. And while it's not
a dog park, after we made sure no security was about, Peter
and I would let the dogs off their leashes and, as they chased
each other through the hedgerows or circled each other in
the field above, we'd stroll behind them and talk.

Peter was about as old as my dad and at the time, in my
late twenties, after a spate of father-son contretemps, banal
run-ins that left me feeling embarrassed about how much
pain they'd caused me, it seemed I couldn't meet a man of a
certain age without saddling him with filial baggage, great
bulging panniers of misapplied longing, thinking maybe
he could help me, give me some guidance. Of exactly what
sort, this guidance, I couldn't say. Might've been as simple as
wanting someone to demonstrate that life was possible, that
one could get accustomed to the fact that it went on, that is,

until it didn't. Something so straightforward, but it seemed impossible to me then, that one's life continued to happen, that the days and years and months and weeks kept coming. How did one countenance it? And what was one to do with the collateral damage of all that time: "experience"? It was in about here that I found myself walking around muttering this sound bite from Gertrude Stein like a sinister mantra: "Identity always worries me and memory and eternity."

Everything seemed so far away, maybe most of all myself, and I thought someone could or rather had to shepherd me out of this morass. Prima facie, sure, Peter made for an odd casting choice. Even when he had his shit together, when Linda was still living there and he had the dogs, his life, by any conventional marker, was a mess. He was no longer teaching and the reasons for this were cloudy and charged in a way that you knew not to ask after. I figured it had something to do with his drinking and that the drinking was related to unrest of a deeper, more unresolvable sort, an unrest that fed his wildness. And it was this wildness that first attracted me. There was something poetic to it, something that suggested the age-old binary star of madness and genius. He seemed, in short, to live closer to the sweet sour molten marrowy core of life and I envied that, idealized that way of being. It had a musk of authenticity I hoped would wear off on me. This musk, on Peter, had a whiff of failure freely embraced, of ambitions deferred or retrofitted or abandoned altogether. Not shamefully, but willingly, in a way that struck me as noble. In my work as an editor at the time, I seemed to be dealing exclusively with successes, with writers who'd just

sold—always "just"—X to Y for $Z00,000, who'd been nom-
inated for Important Prizes, who'd won them. MacArthur
Fellowships and National Book Awards and Pulitzers. I
worked on a story with one writer who, shortly after, won
the fucking Nobel. Being exposed to accomplishment on this
scale was obviously and rightly humbling, but it got to be
cloying, stultifying. It made it so easy for me to indulge the
worst and most facile sort of writerly kvetching. Perhaps I
would always only help others tell their stories, I'd bemoan,
my authorial jollies forever confined to having an image or
sentence of mine not accepted, exactly, just not stetted. How's
a little dinghy supposed to navigate waters crowded with
such tankers? Being around Peter eased the lamest of these
anxieties, and helped me recall why I'd started reading and
writing in the first place: for the fun of it, for the leagues-
deep sense of belonging.

And so we walked, talked.

These talks, they were the kind that almost erase themselves as they go, that follow digression after digression until
the starting point has long been lost, no Hansel and Gretel
trail of thought leading back to the beginning. Peter was
nothing if not a world-class talker and it's thanks in large
part to this that, rangy as they were, these conversations never
felt scattered or diffuse. He had a scholar's thoroughness and
attention to detail and a poet's gift for association, so that
each digression he introduced in some way augmented or
amplified what'd come before, no matter how big a leap it
seemed on the surface, from philosophy to poetry to music
of all genres to pop culture to painting to history. Big as he

was, I sometimes imagined he had more literal room to store knowledge, that his body was one great lumbering maze of learning. He often adopted a Socratic style, proceeding by interrogative feints and parries, so sure of himself, of all he did and did not know. And early on this frustrated me. I'd bristle when he introduced a new angle, a related topic, ask whether I'd considered things from this or that perspective, etc. I also thought of myself as something of a reader, fancied mine to be catholic tastes, book- and culture-wise, and while decidedly not a scholar, I was no sciolist either. But then I learned to give over to the experience of our conversations, let them grow into the untamable organic things they wanted to become, and began to understand that when Peter projected authority, it was not at the expense of his curiosity. He wasn't being pompous or dickish, but a teacher. He'd admit when he didn't know something and would really listen as you talked about it—you could practically see him rearranging his mental lumber to make room for the new knowledge. And as each day's walk came to an end, what we were left with, more than knowledge proper, was a sense of resonance, something akin to what exists in the air after a rung note stops ringing, a gentle disturbance in the fabric of shared space. So this is how I prefer to see us now, when I survey the past, as two men, neighbors, standing side by side in the field at Peninsula Park, the marked difference in our heights making us look like a bar graph of considerable loss, letting a break in our conversation extend and experiencing in the silence the tug of respect, the pleasure of it, of giving as much as receiving it, as we watched our dogs play.

Silken windhounds—I'd never heard of the breed before. They're sight hounds, like something straight out of the pages of Tolstoy. They have the lithe f-hole bodies of a borzoi or whippet and their long legs and flowing coat make them look ghostly and elemental when they run, which they were bred to do. And Percy? She is a silly small vehicle of hypoallergenic cuteness, imagineered for the dander-intolerant to cuddle, a breed whose name embarrasses me too much to set down here, but—hint, hint—it shares a suffix with a world-famous cookie. It was always impressive and entertaining to watch Apollo, hunched low, his paws appearing to barely touch the ground, looking not unlike a rhythmic gymnast's ribbon, run literal circles around Percy. A thing of wonder, to behold an animal in its element like that, unencumbered by questions of purpose or ends. Every so often Percy would get spooked and pull up short and Apollo would have to make a last-second adjustment, often leaping gracefully over her, and, skittish as she is, Percy would tuck her tail and cower and look back at me. How, she seemed to ask with those cartoonishly adorable eyes, how is he managing to be everywhere all at once?

By almost any standard you want to judge it, the chase that followed Peter's murder was tame, even dull, and as Caprice told me what'd happened (gave me *the scoop*), I found myself having to temper what I recognized immediately was a very shitty form of disappointment, a species of boredom brought on by life's having failed to live up to the expectations that stories had nurtured in me. There were no roadblocks or helicopters or K-9 squad. No standoff or hostages or demands. No. The action here had been far more ho-hum than that, actually almost Lynchian in its banality. After the stabbing, the suspect, Steve, one of the heretofore nameless figures Peter had sat with nightly on his shadowy porch, walked calmly up the block to the murder mart. There, according to Caprice, he bought a six-pack of beer, cracked and downed one can right away, and was at work on a second when the police picked him up, when they *apprehended* him.

"This was just there," she said, pointing down the way to nothing in particular at Williams and Jessup, where the second cluster of cop cars had been earlier.

Caprice was eager to relay these details when at last I got some time with her. I'd returned outside after Alexis and I shared our private moment and after talking to Scott and asking him to let the folks from Irving know what'd happened. I told myself it was important that our people find out from one of us, and imagined word racing like a lit fuse through the branches of a ramifying phone tree, trying to outpace all the other, less intimate media channels out there. The action outside continued as more officers showed up, suit-wearing homicide detectives now among them. But before I left the house for the second time, I grabbed my pocket notebook. It was a pathetic gesture of credibility, I knew, and there in my hand it seemed a cheap prop, an absurd affectation. Who was I hoping to fool with this act? With this performance of myself as "writer"? More than anyone, to be honest, probably myself. I hadn't written anything in months and had started to wonder whether I ever would again. It seemed recent life events had conspired to crowd me out, to deny me the space I needed to translate them, which is to say, tame or control them. And after all, couldn't I be happy with a life in literature lived offstage, gesturing directions inaudibly from the wings? Wasn't I already fluent in the passive-aggressive semaphore that editors employ? Guilty as it made me feel, though, even I, with my underdeveloped nose for narrative mojo, recognized that what was happening outside was material, the makings of a story.

From the elevated vantage of my front porch, I watched on as Caprice and Ernie circulated among the reporters and officers like the hosts of this demented cocktail party. My heart began to hurt for them and the friend they'd lost, for the grief that was stalking them, immense and relentless as hunger, as they talked to all these men and women whose concern was so manufactured and cynical it was practically coming off them in stink lines. By now the broadcast journalists had arrived—the heavies. Their crews had schlepped tripodal cameras around until they'd found the best angle of the scene, which the officers had boxed them out of. Between the officers and the journalists there seemed to be a flirty hostility reminiscent of middle school love affairs.

I stepped off my porch and made for Caprice and Ernie, trying to stay out of the cameras' sight lines because I couldn't stomach the thought of appearing on-screen later and being outed for what I was, but another supernumerary ogling on, a needless quidnunc cupping his pud. They were still occupied with reporters, so I hung in the background. Skulking about like this, I got a little spooked. Paranoia needled me. And for a spell there I pretty much just wigged out. Every stranger's eyeballs issued an indictment: Interloper! Buttinsky! Asshole! And were they not correct, after all, these eyeballs? Was I not a voyeur of a particular American stripe, having been seduced by the suffering of my neighbor? By the trauma he'd endured? How was I any different from the other journalists here? I had a GIF going in my head and that GIF was this: with both hands Peter clasps an absurdly spurting wound and exclaims, "O, I am slain!" before keeling over. Keeling over—Christ. All the language I had available seemed so callous, to lack the reserves of empathy I'd hoped to find in it, and only made me feel more fraudulent. But knowing no better course of action, I doubled down on language, hoping to ground myself by taking notes, hoping something fruitful would come of them. I scribbled in a frenzy, wanting to appear serious and studious, as committed to the story as a courtier, but probably looked a touch, well, touched. Through my thick skull I couldn't get it, the simple fact of Peter's murder, couldn't resolve its peculiar mix of momentousness and mundanity. Among so much else I noted that the fire truck and ambulance were now gone. They must've left while I'd been inside with Alexis, and again I had to check my crappy American disappointment, this time at having missed a good part, a climax. Surely a shrouded stretcher had been borne out of the house. My mind teemed with shameful morbid questions. Who'd hoisted Peter's tremendous body onto the gurney? Had it shown any signs of stress under the weight? How had they negotiated the stairs? Now dead, how much would the body continue to bleed? Had the sheet been stained a lurid incarnadine? Or had the situation demanded a body bag? And oh, what a horrible do-si-do those two words do: body bag, body bag, body bag. . .

Know this: Caprice is a real piston of a woman, a larger-than-life-of-the-party type. An ardent and longtime lover of cigs. When Alexis and I first toured our place, she was out on her back porch, tossing feed down to the chickens that have free range of her big backyard. "I'll sell you this place for three-fifty," she called across the alley, her voice as seasoned as cast iron. Once a cheeky blush-pink, their old Foursquare is now the worse for wear—think: sorority girl, out all night. "Chickens come with if you want 'em," she added, and laughed a laugh that was maybe as much a cough. She sometimes builds ziggurats of cubed white bread in the middle of our intersection to woo gulls over from the river. The commotion around us continued, but when she was free I stood and listened dutifully as she took me through a skeleton key of the incident. The basics. From her brief account, which she already told with the polished ease of multiple tellings, I put it together that Steve had been living with Peter. Apparently it'd been months. And before that, he'd lived with Caprice and Ernie, right behind me. For all that time he, too, had been my neighbor, and here, if asked, I couldn't pick him out of a lineup.

We were interrupted by the arrival of the Portland Police Bureau's Mobile Command Center, a twenty-plus-foot RV painted an official blue and white and emblazoned with the city's seal. Officers broke the yellow tape and allowed it to pass into the middle of the intersection. The RV had a handful of R2-D2 domes on the roof and I imagined they enabled a direct feed to headquarters downtown, allowing them to do remote forensic work, analyze evidence like fingerprints and DNA and ballistics. Somewhere inside the belly of the beast, a generator kicked on with the borborygmic vigor of a washing machine.

One of the suit-wearing homicide detectives called Caprice over for Official Business and I went and posted up next to a cruiser parked with its doors open in front of my house. Two officers were inside drinking Venti coffees, their job being, it seemed, just to be there. I'm still somewhat new to this, but I can't imagine I'll ever get over the astonishment of encountering state authorities who're younger than me.

All afternoon I'd been ping-ponging between competing thoughts. One was that I knew exactly what was going on here, from all the police procedurals I'd ever watched, and the second was that I didn't have the first clue. It was uncanny, that peculiar mix of the familiar and the utterly foreign. Hoping to clarify some of my impressions, and undeterred by my earlier failure, I asked these officers a few Qs. They were open and amiable, happy to help, probably because I wasn't asking about this case in particular.

We talked about violent crime in the neighborhood, how numbers were down here but well up in Gresham, the suburbs, where the gangs had been displaced. Then we got on about all the journalists, one of whom was practicing what he'd say on camera later. He sounded like a Gertrude Stein poem: "A witness witness? witnesses called police to this house house? home? to this home on North Haight Haight?

North Haight to say that a man was to say a man had been stabbed. . ."

"I got a buddy," one started. "He drives around getting video of scenes before we tape them off. Sells that to the networks, sometimes more than one. Makes pretty good money, too. More than you'd think, at least."

Eureka! Tweaker guy and the blondified ectomorph—vigilante videographers.

"In the footage the official media gets, we're always laughing in the background or something," the partner said. "But they show up like way later so what do they expect?"

I then inquired as to the forensic appurtenances one might expect to find inside the MCC. What manner of high-tech crime-solving gear was it packing? Could they do 3-D facial recognition? Alternate light photography? Was laser ablation inductively coupled plasma mass spectrometry an option?

"Oh, nah. It's mostly just a lounge," the first cop said. "There's a table and some chairs. Coffee. Snacks. Probably snacks."

"Well, that's disappointing," I said, before I could stop myself.

"We get that all the time," he said. "People seen too much TV."

I left them to their coffees and spent much of the rest of the afternoon sitting on my porch, taking in the scriptless drama from a distance. As I watched everyone go about their business, I felt like I was witnessing a holy rite of alien and opaque significance. It reminded me of attending my friends' bar and bat mitzvahs, when I'd listened to them perform their guttural, glottal passages from the Torah. There was something undeniably ritualistic to all the day's doings, something with the skin of the sacred. The crisis, the intercession, the working out of innocence or its opposite. The great profane paddle wheel of justice, churning us down the river time. Perhaps crime, and maybe especially violent crime, is the last way we feel comfortable addressing the ancient notion of sin, a notion gone nearly vestigial in us. Not to play loose with etymology here, but it's neat to note that many of the words we associate with crime—"incident" and "case" and "homicide" and "casualty" and "cadaver"—share a common root, *cadere*, which means "to fall." At some point during all this gummy and fruitless ruminating, I started to understand that no amount of journalistic diligence could possibly redress my confusion. Facts would not, really could not, resolve for me the primeval mystery of what'd gone down here on the __oo block of N. Haight Ave. Death had been here. Murder had left its sudden, inexpungible stain on the day.

The sky bruised up as the sun began to set and the journalists took off to meet their deadlines and the cruisers peeled off to pursue other urgencies. The MCC hung around until after it went dark and even from inside the house you could hear the dyspeptic chugging of its generator. Alexis and I missed the initial television reports but watched them online later. The anchors enthused while introducing the news. Their voices pitched, their manicured eyebrows lifted. Little windows floated on-screen beside their statuesque coifs: "Deadly Stabbing," "Fatal Stabbing," they read, and were accompanied by clip-art graphics of knives and police tape. Watching these reports, I experienced an almost cosmic echo of the day, like there'd been a hiccup in space-time. I saw my street teeming with life and light—there were my neighbors milling about and there was my car, my house—while out my window the same street was dark, the same houses featureless silhouettes. Sure enough, in a brief establishing shot of the neighborhood two cops stood in the background, laughing. "Witnesses called police to this home. . ." I heard, in a nauseating déjà vu. The night wore on and an eerie stillness bloomed outside and at first I couldn't place what was different, what'd changed. But then it hit me: the Mobile Command Center must've finally taken off. Now at last we were left to contend with the haunting hum of absence that had been at the heart of the day's noise.

The letter arrived in an unsealed, unaddressed, and unstamped envelope, a rogue missive slipped in with my other legit mail. I should clarify: a photocopy of the letter arrived thus, along with a copy of its first envelope, addressed to Linda Strauss, Peter's wife. It's postmarked 20 August 2012—more than a month before I got it, a year and a half before everything above went down. The return address is for "Percy Perwinkle" (Periwinkle?) at "__oo N. Haight Ave." No such street number exists and the only results I found online for Percy Per- or Periwinkle led me to a site that showcases amateur erotic fiction.

"Dear Laura," it begins, bafflingly.

I am a neighbor of yours and I want to bring some things to your attention concerning your husband (?) Peter. On Friday, Peter was outside yelling 'Woo!' and spraying water into the air. Inside the house, all people can hear is 'Woo!' However, outside of the house is a different story and I would like to let you know what he said. Peter yelled 'Woo! Fuck you! Fuck you! Fuck you all! Woo!' He kept this up several times until I heard him say 'Woo! Fuck you! I will KILL all of you! Woo!' I have been afraid ever since. This is illegal and I have seen 'Peter' do several illegal things over the past few years.

This is the first of eight single-spaced paragraphs that fill two typed pages. The work entire amounts to an impressive jeremiad, an impassioned rant in which the anonymous author ("I will not identify myself out of fear that Peter will kill me. . .") states the problem over and over: Peter is "terrorizing our neighborhood." He listens to his music at an "absurd and ILLEGAL level." He's lowering property values. He has prevented the author from getting a job and is responsible for untold hours of talk therapy. Among the illegal things he's been witnessed doing: he once cut a tree "down into the street without a proper permit." And now he has threatened to visit death upon the entire neighborhood. Quite simply: "He has made my life a living hell."

The writing throughout is unhinged and obsessive, its logic only loosely qualifying as such. For example, property values? The problem isn't that they're getting lower, of course, but too high, driving taxes up so that many folks who've been here for decades are having trouble paying them. It's this febrile and half-cocked quality that makes the letter so compelling. Paragraph to paragraph, often sentence to sentence, the tone varies wildly, cycling through concern for the community's and Linda's safety to exasperation with Peter's "antics" to anger of a rarefied sort. The author pleads with Linda to kick him out, to divorce him, and, anticipating the failure of these more reasonable forms of suasion, goes on to suggest menacing and portentous courses of action—e.g.: "I have homicide thoughts against your husband, daily . . . However, I do nothing illegal, but I do know Kerby Blocc Crips and this is their turf. In fact, I used to be one of them . . . And if they heard or knew about this threat, your husband would be put down like a dog." Threatening to fetch the gang should daunt us, but it doesn't. It reads as desperate, not to mention that it's a fundamental misapprehension of how things work now. My imagination can't get them out of Gresham, this crew of aging thuggards, dully peeved by proxy, arguing over which bus is best for the commute back to their turf. And of course, as all such letters must, this one includes an ultimatum: "I'm giving him a week to stop being a terrorist and respect his neighbors before I send out letters to fellow neighbors informing them of what he said." And later we get a wicked little addendum: "We may be sharing self-defense videos with our neighbors as well, so everyone knows how to kill him in a snap or at least paralyze him. Then you'd be forced to keep him in your life forever and feed him baby food." The letter goes on, but continues only to rest its restive case over and over again.

While it's abundantly clear that the author overreacted ("I don't care if he means no harm because I think he DOES."), that he or she got all hootered up on a beastly brew of enmity and pique, I'm sad to say I can sympathize. I'd been in the neighborhood for almost two years and my own patience with Peter had started to chafe. My house was far enough away that his music and hollerin' were muffled when I was inside, but I could imagine how frustrating it'd be if you lived next door, like Jim. Story goes that Jim and Peter had been tight, best friends, used to spend Thanksgivings and Christmases together, but, according to Caprice, the neighborhood's recording angel, they'd had a falling-out. Jim could no longer deal with how erratic Peter was, how downright mean he could be at times. Similar in kind, my grievances were fractional by degree. For example, on nice days Peter would often sit out on the corner improvising percussive travesties upon some bongo drums. Imagine an EKG of a cardiac arrest and you will have an idea of the rhythm of his beats. My solution? I'd visited my local Home Depot and splurged on a pair of commercial-grade, noise-canceling earmuffs—with them on, the only beat I could hear was the soothingly metronomic shloomp-shloomp of my heart. But on an afternoon when Peter was thus inspirited, sometime after I got the letter, Alexis had a migraine and was laid up downstairs with packages of frozen veggies over her eyes. Every high-pitched plinky-twongy thwack was for her a violent trepanation. I knew it was my husbandly duty to go out there and politely ask him to cool it awhile, but I kept putting it off. Instead I whipped myself into a rich and furious lather. The fuck are you thinking, carrying on like that? Don't you have a thought or care for anyone but yourself? And if play you must, couldn't you at least avail yourself of a recognizable rhythm? By the time I'd wound myself to a critical point and was about to go out there and further the ruckus, Peter stopped playing and went back inside his house. Alexis could've cried, so soothed was she by the relative quiet. And I was relieved, too, having dodged a confrontation with Peter.

But why? What had happened to make me want to avoid him?

The story had changed. I'd let it. As I settled in after the move, I started to collect fresh habits. Repetition tamed and automated my perception. The new route to work became my everyday commute and our new grocery store became just where we had to go to procure grub and bit by bit we filled our new old house with the warm safe security blanket of the Familiar and sure enough, as it happened, dailiness of this sort dulled me to Peter's charms. His wonderful whacked-out madness-genius modus came to seem a perpetual psychology experiment without a control. He'd become a burden, someone to deal with—by which I mean that he now sat on the same psychic shelf as Dad. Another quondam example turned cautionary tale. Soon enough Alexis and I had been in the house a year and it'd been months since Peter and I had taken the dogs to Peninsula and talked Auden, Benjamin, Caravaggio, et al. And with alarming ease those months became years. It was happening: I was aging. Linda left. Linda returned. They got a second silken windhound puppy and named it Pippin. Then Pippin was a dog and it was night and he and Apollo had together leapt the fence and fled the yard and were tear-assing around the neighborhood without a chaperone. I was coming home from the murder mart when I saw them on the corner across the street, smoky and apparitional. They came at me then, appearing to emanate more than properly move, closing the distance between us with frightening ease. Quick as pickpockets they were circling me, nipping at my ankles, and I started goose-stepping down the sidewalk, yelling "Peter! For fuck's sake! Peter!" as I went. Again Linda left with the dogs, but for good this time. And soon thereafter began the relative chaos of the late nights and the excruciating howls that no one could've imagined would end in his murder. Now on walks with Percy I stuck to my side of the street. If Peter happened to be out on his porch as I passed, I'd raise a hand across the way, a hand that said both "hi" and "stay."

When I first received the letter I assumed that the author had made good on the promise to alert the neighbors to what Peter had said, to his "threat." This seemed the easiest and most reasonable explanation, the one that required the least amount of mental gymnastics to figure. But there was a catch, a snag: the envelope. If it'd been the author, how to account for the photocopy of the opened, postmarked envelope? The longer I thought on it, the more I came to believe that it'd been Peter who'd made the copies, who'd slipped the letter in my mailbox. Maybe this was his way of reaching out, of asking for help. Or maybe it was his strange take on neighborhood watch, selling out the squares or narcing on the narcs or whatever. It's also entirely possible that he thought I'd find it funny. I can see him there, standing in the self-service copy shop up the street, laughing to himself as the pages multiplied in mysterious mechanical accouchement. But in the end, I can't say for sure one way or the other that it was or wasn't him. The only thing I can say with certainty is that no self-defense videos ever arrived. Had they, well, then we'd have a different story.

That Saturday night a handful of us gathered at Ernie and Caprice's for an impromptu and pretty half-assed wake. Their place is always murky dark and a little leaden and, as a result, entering presents a perceptual mindfuck, because while you walk up the porch to do so, it feels more like a descent, like surprise! you're spelunking! The decor inside appears to have sat undisturbed for ages, and Caprice smokes wherever she well pleases, so there's a pervasive and hearty musk of spent cigs. But I don't mean to suggest it's uninviting or cold. It's not. It's rather more ember-warm and homey, imbued with decades of coziness and conviviality. By now it should be apparent that Ernie and Caprice are party people, people people—tap their walls with your Moses staff and you'd drink a delicious eau-de-vie. In a way, to visit them is for one's spirit to slip into a pair of footie pajamas. Hospitable as they are, though, isn't it also always bizarre? going into a neighbor's house like this? It begins to dawn on you as you walk around, as you take in their choice of curtains and paw their gewgaws, the uncanny realization that life happens here. Life! A vital and vivifying mystery, this—all the meals made and eaten and the stacks of dirty dishes done, the routine maintenance of bodies (shit shower shave, lather rinse repeat, a whole kiddie pool's worth of fingernail clippings) and the innumerable loads of laundry (all those undies folded into drawers), the walls positively sponged up with scenes of sickness and sadness, anger and reconciliation, tenderness and care. Can it be? That all this is housed here? And so close to where the epic drama of your own life is set? It's almost too much to get your mind on the outside of.

Alexis and I added a bottle of wine to the smorgasbord of inebriants on offer and took our place on the barstools at the kitchen counter. The soft lighting felt fittingly lugubrious. Someone had brought one of those frozen pizzas with the laudable, leavening crust. A great tree of a woman, attractive in the mother goddess mode, was leaning on the end of the counter. When I asked her how she'd known Peter, she was bashful, even a little dodgy. In due time it became clear that things between them had been complicated, to use the parlance, that they'd been "involved." Visibly heartsore, she seemed confused as to what her role there was, how exactly she fit into the story. I could sympathize. In the far back corner, at a table in the breakfast nook we look out on from our kitchen window, a Native American man wearing a feathered fedora sat smoking, a blanket or shawl wrapped around his shoulders. With him was an older woman who appeared to be consoling him.

While Caprice fixed us drinks, she told us about the memorial service set for the next morning. It was to be a celebration of Peter's life and, as such, we were encouraged to bring music or poetry to share by way of a eulogy—this would be my first West Coast funeral. She handed us our glasses and raised hers. "To Peter," she said, and in kind we responded, "To Peter." And together we drank in remembrance of him. Full of an almost spritely energy, she left the room and returned in a trice with a CD and a number of articles she'd printed off local news sites.

"Did you see this one? About the song?" she asked, and laid an article before us. "Man wrote song just before he was stabbed to death, says friend," the headline ran. And of course I'd seen it—I'd read everything I could get my eyes on and in the process had learned that his last name was also that of an apostle: John. Story goes Peter had been sitting on the porch that morning, watching a bird lave gaily in the stone bowl on the ground, when inspiration had seized him. He strummed out chords on his guitar and jotted down a quatrain. "They weren't here for the Appalachian spring, / The sweet oboe solitary ring, / That small sparrow dipping wing, / Even frolicking."

"'Appalachian Spring,'" she said, and held up the case after she'd loaded the CD. "It was one of Peter's favorites."

The first measures of Copland's suite played so quietly you had to strain to hear. But this was disturbance enough for the two people in back, who stood and made for the front door.

"You know Chinook," Caprice said, and, in response to the silence that followed, "This is Chinook. And Marilyn."

To them she presented Alexis and me and we all greeted one another but Chinook made clear with his face that now was not the time for further niceties and continued on his way out the door. Marilyn and Peter's onetime inamorata followed him out.

"He's pretty shaken up," Caprice said, and then explained that he'd been there when it all went down, that he was an *eyewitness*. After Steve stabbed Peter, she went on with his story, he stood there blocking Chinook's path to the front door. Peter lay on the ground between them. A brief standoff ensued. "Are you gonna murder me, too?" Chinook asked, and Steve nodded, slowly, yes. In these moments he appeared to Chinook possessed, his eyes having gone frosty, vacant. Chinook then took up the fireplace screen and hurled it at Steve, buying himself enough time to bolt out the back door.

"Jesus," I said. "I can't imagine."

And none of the reports I'd read online had asked me to. The public story had been bowdlerized into a simpler, more digestible form, one related to the event in the way a blueprint is to a building. Given the bones, you had to picture the skin for yourself. Freed from the burden of specificity, the simple facts had been repeated until they wore a groove in the community's consciousness, a narrative path that would usher the incident, and so Peter, into the past, the rampant radio static of history. That Peter had been helping Steve, letting him crash at his place, made this a story of senseless betrayal, one that challenged our deepest beliefs—in the inviolability and sanctity of the Home and in the notion that we're duty-bound to care for those less fortunate than ourselves. No good deed goes unpunished, indeed. And from what we learn of him, Steve Kovacs makes for an easy Bad Guy, on par with such Disney villains as Maleficent or Jafar. He'd committed capitalism's cardinal sin, was unemployed, and, worse, he was homeless. His mug shot, featured online with most of the reports, shows the weatherworn mien of long, hard living, of bad decisions made daily. Beneath a dingy beard his washed-out face skin sags. Suspicious red-eyed sores spot his cheeks and forehead like someone's had at him with a tenderizer. And to his last name there cling little barnacles of xenophobia: "Kovacs, Kovacs. How are you supposed to pronounce *that*?" What's more—and this I had not known, because how would I have?—Peter had planned to leave town. Though there'd never been a sign out front, he'd actually arranged, with Caprice's help, to sell his house, and had gone so far as to put money down on a parcel of land upon a hill not far off, over the border in small-town Washington. There he would build a modest house where, rid of the stress of testy neighbors, he could play his guitar and his music as loud as he pleased and live again in peace with Linda and his dogs, looking out on a bucolic view of the river down below. In this way Peter's was a story that'd been interrupted at a turning point. It teases our desire for resolution, for redemption. An Oprah ending had been in the offing, the reports would have us believe, if only he'd been given the time. If only, if only, if only.

"That's when I ran into him," Ernie said. "He was out in the street saying his phone was dead, call 9-1-1. Then he said Peter'd been stabbed and I ran over to the house as fast as I could."

He went quiet. Ice tinkled in his glass and he replenished it with a four-finger whiskey. He took a long, measured look at the booze, as though the rest of the story lay in it.

"I'd lost my scarf," Caprice said, lifting an end of the one girding her neck. It'd been a gift from Ernie, who for the moment seemed happy to relinquish the story's reins, and it was among her most cherished possessions. High and wide they'd searched the house—no scarf. "I thought I might've left it in the car so I sent Ernie out to check."

The misplaced scarf was now a link in the great chain of cause and effect. Magical thinking had put it to work in the day's plot, transformed it into a horrific meet-cute. And many such details, things that'd gone from arbitrary to weighty and welling over with consequence, populated the day's growing matrix of meaning. Caprice took us through some of her favorites, but only after first refilling our drinks. The bird song, for one—his last poem and proof positive that, above all, Peter's had been a *creative* life. That he'd eaten what sounded like a kingly dinner the night before, prepared by an old friend, an accomplished chef, and that he'd remained sober, or at least relatively so, through it—a meal fit to serve as a last one. That he and Chinook had started to get serious about sobriety, had planned to attend AA meetings together, according to some as soon as that very day. That he'd been reading Proust and listening to *Concert for George* when Steve came into the room.

These details were meant to charm part of the chaos still, to capture some aspect of Peter's life worth memorializing, and, maybe most important, to direct our attention away from how it had ended. Caprice was wired as she related them, too, in a swoon of sorts. For the moment it seemed she might also be getting drunk on significance, on symbolizing. And while I hadn't been aware of it before going over to their place, I started to realize just how badly I'd wanted to hear this, the unexpurgated version of the story.

"Inside, the first thing I had to do was to roll him over," Ernie said, tapping back in. "He wasn't a small guy either, you know. Something like two-eighty or two-ninety or something. And there was blood everywhere."

And was this not also part of what I'd been hankering to hear? *The straight dope?* Was there not something sickly delicious about learning that the floor had been in such a state that Ernie's boots had trouble finding purchase? That as he attempted to administer CPR he was slip-sliding away like something from an SNL skit written by Cormac McCarthy? But beyond scratching an itch for morbidity, what purpose did such information serve? To what end were such details put? In order to understand what had happened to Peter, did I need to know that the knife Steve had used was a USMC KA-BAR, a fixed-blade, leather-handled combat weapon whose clip point gives it a sharklike profile? Did I need to watch as Ernie approximated the blade's length, measuring between his pointer fingers the size of a fish you'd keep? In what way was I edified by descriptions of the wound, by picturing a slot in his chest large enough to accept a silver dollar? Or by being asked to imagine his breathing, gone disturbingly audible? How necessary was it that I learn that Ernie thought he'd felt, between his compressions, the final beats of Peter's expiring heart? Did these details aid my efforts to understand what'd gone down?

My gut tells me that, at bottom, this has to do with empathy, with our ability to imagine ourselves into another person's situation and exercise deep care. This is an essential characteristic of our humanity, after all, isn't it? Part of what sets us apart from the lower order of beasts? My question then is something like: can so-called empathy coexist peaceably alongside the relief and gratitude we feel that what happened to someone else did not happen to us? Does pity preclude care? Can we learn so many details about a story that they cease to be empathically productive? At what point do horrific details begin to double back on themselves? To merely stoke the horror and so stultify any manner of healing? Like trying to extinguish a fire with gasoline? What do we say, for that matter, after we hear such horrible things? To my mind the most respectful, and so least pitying, thing we can say is "I can't imagine." But doesn't that seem to be the very opposite of empathy? Or maybe it's empathy's purest expression, in that it articulates our inability to comprehend the details, allows them to haunt and confound us, too, and therefore validate the sufferer's own confusion, the ineffability of his or her pain. And perhaps this is the final mystery at the bottom of all tragedy, the way life can scramble our greatest humanizing resource, the imagination.

"They say it's good to talk," Ernie said. "I grew up on farms and such, around animals. I've seen death before. I've seen dead babies. But never anything like this."

It nearly passed me right on by, so casually was the revelation made. Dead babies? What could have compelled him to offer up such an observation? I let it sit awhile and, sure enough, our drinks again revived, the conversation ended up providing an answer. I hadn't known this, but back in late May, early June, a dead baby had been found at a local recycling center. It'd rolled right out on the conveyor belt. This, too, had been a big story, local news–wise, full of brutal facts. The child was full-term, or very nearly so. A girl. Five pounds, four ounces. Her umbilical cord had been cut or torn, but was otherwise intact. A forensic pathologist confirmed that she'd been alive at birth, had breathed. From the evidence he'd gathered, he couldn't say for sure how long she'd been there. A day, maybe two. "One of our employees found human remains on the commercial sort line," the company's president offered in a statement. "We are saddened by these events."

That employee was Steve. He'd gone into work expecting another day of rote labor and walked out with a new ghost. And ever since he'd suffered a form of psychic torment that falls under the capacious diagnostic umbrella of PTSD. He'd ended up losing his job at the recycling center and hadn't been able to find another since. And according to Caprice, among the bad decisions he made was that he couldn't be bothered with unemployment or disability. What details from that day had been kept alive by the incubator of his memory? The imagination reels when it tries to re-create the moment of recognition. The foreign form on the conveyor belt resolving into limbs, a tiny body. The frayed end of a torn umbilical cord, affixed to the nameless baby's tummy like a Pull 'n' Peel Twizzler. It's almost too much, attempting to picture the condition of newborn skin that's been stewing in a slurry of beer cans and cardboard and backwash. To whom does such foul shit befall? And how would one begin to recover from it? I can't imagine.

The conversation moved mercifully on and we ended up discussing Ernie's family, his history. He took us through the house, pointing to portraits of his relatives on the walls. Our drinks were filled again and the photo albums brought out. Here were Ernie and Caprice at our age. Pictures of old neighbors, friends from community theater, adorable shots of their daughters from times bygone. Alexis and I finished our drinks for good and made an exaggerated show of needing to leave. It can be endearingly difficult to extract oneself from a hang with Ernie and Caprice.

"You know, I really needed that hug," Ernie said as he saw us to the door. "Just wanted to say thanks for that."

It was the least I could do, I assured him, and said we'd see them in the morning, at the service. We hugged again, this time more tentatively, bashfully, peppering the embrace with many manly backslaps. Tempted though I was to do it again, another tender cupping of his braid's nidus wasn't in the night's cards, not even with the aid of all the sauce. And as Alexis and I made the short commute across the alley to our house, I couldn't get over how caught up we all are in one another's stories, how much we happen to share what happens to us.

On this idea of community much academic ink has been spilled, a whole wine-dark sea's worth. And the curious autodidact, hoping only to glean some pointers for how to draw closer to the people he lives around, can find himself swiftly to the nostrils in jargon and charts, in schemas that smack of specialization and icy expertise. You've got your gemeinschaft vs. gesellschaft and your manifold forms of social capital, be they bridging or bonding or what. If you were of such a mind, you could freely brain yourself with a pallet of Bourdieu. Though at times enlightening, such reading can also make it seem so effortful and dull, this getting up with and going amongst other people, so much so that you can get to wondering how we ever manage to do it at all. And yet of course we do. Without ever really learning all the rules, we play the game. We get up with. We go amongst.

Reared as I was under the aegis of protestant faithfuls, I can trace my own most enduring and articulable notions about neighborliness and community to stuff I learned from the Bible. There are the basic Sunday school moral imperatives like "Love your neighbor as yourself" and the parable of the Good Samaritan, which ends with Jesus's simple and startling call to mercy, "Go and do likewise." Then we find this in Romans: "We, who are many, are one body in Christ, and individually we are members of one another." And what a phrase that is, how odd and poetically out of joint, "members of one another." With that sharpened clause Paul captures the sense of belonging and interdependence that a community is founded on, a sense of belonging that I'd experienced growing up, as an active member of my church's youth group and Young Life, not to mention as part of a large extended Christian family, a family that met for reunions not once but twice a year. And what about those times when a member of our community becomes difficult? When internecine conflict crops up? In *Life Together*, the theologian Dietrich Bonhoeffer writes, "It is only when he is a burden that another person is really a brother and not merely an object to be manipulated." I'd been assigned to read this book before arriving for that summer of intentional Christian living on Martha's Vineyard, an experience I still sometimes find hard to believe is part of my story. But I've strayed far less dramatically from this part of my history than I often like to think, and, consciously or not, I continue to try to act accordingly, to measure my behavior against it.

And so as Peter's behavior grew increasingly erratic, in the months before his death, I started to feel guilty, ashamed of how our friendship had failed to develop past its infancy. This failure seemed to echo my recent string of relational difficulties and disappointments with Dad. And when I found myself tucked up in the womb of resentment and frustration that I felt I'd let that relationship become, I tried to urge myself to think about all of Dad's positive character traits. Unlike me, for example, he's never been niggardly with his free time, never been so fiercely protective of his energy and attention. He used to enlist (compel?) my brothers and me in all manner of service activity, be it Saturday mornings swinging hammers for Habitat for Humanity or shuttling us of an evening to visit with a member of the church going through a rough patch. It was never a question of whether, but how he would help other people—"Let us love, not in word or speech, but in truth and action." He's always been a doer, almost restlessly so, and it seemed his faith manifested most in deeds of this sort. The frustrated and resentful cynic in me thinks that maybe he was so keen on service like this because it was visible, could be observed, and therefore end in praise. But it's wrong to scrutinize motives like this, wrong to judge. The point is that if I was indeed a member of this community, that is, if I wanted to go on thinking that I was different from the author of the irascible letter, then surely something more was demanded of me than the nothing I was doing.

On one of my walks with Percy during these last months, I saw a slick new Cadillac parked in front of Peter's house. I couldn't place it at first but I knew I knew that car. And sure enough, there he was as I passed by, visiting with Peter on the porch: Lawrence, shunned wielder of the blade. I hadn't seen him in ages, but that didn't mean a lot. I hadn't been around Irving much myself since the move. I waved my customary wave and Peter alone waved back—for Lawrence, the simplest human interaction is often cumbered with suspicion and distrust. But for days to come the image of them sitting together convicted me. It was something Dad would've done, come around to check up on Peter, see how he'd been doing. Sit, chat. Just be there.

A few days after I saw Lawrence on the porch, in a welter of nostalgia, I stopped at Peter's house on my way home from a run. He was outside, of course, with Boo, the white pit bull he'd adopted from a friend who couldn't care for him anymore. Peter came down his steps to meet me. And although I'd never been up there before, it seemed significant that he didn't invite me to come sit with him on his porch. We stood with the rickety fence between us and talked. The specter of our short former friendship seemed to haunt us, to imbue the conversation with cautiousness—perhaps he, too, preferred to think of us standing in the field at Peninsula Park watching our dogs play. We stuck mostly to tennis. He asked about "that backhand of yours" and said he hadn't been playing much lately. It couldn't have been the only reason, but he said he'd busted the strings in all his rackets. I jumped at the opportunity to be generous and offered him one of my old ones.

"They're just gathering dust in my closet," I said. "Hold tight."

Before he could say anything I jogged home. I fished the rackets out of the closet and hit them against one another, listening to the pitch of each string bed, and chose the one with the least amount of wear. I hustled back and when I presented the racket to Peter, he thanked me but insisted on paying something for it. No, no, I said, it was my pleasure, a gift. Some excessively polite dickering ensued before he caved and took it. Case might've been that in the end I was the more grateful, somehow.

We then got on about the guys at Irving and of course ended up talking about Lawrence.

"He's a good guy, really," Peter said. "Just a little pissed off at the world."

"Who? Lawrence? Nah. . ." The joke lamed about effetely at our ankles.

"He comes by every now and again. Knows I've got," he broke off, and his hands came alive, working through an inscrutable sign language before his words caught up to him: "Issues."

Though it was obvious to everyone in the neighborhood, this still seemed to qualify as a confession for Peter. Or if it wasn't a confession, it was something more than a simple acknowledgment. And his sincerity and vulnerability disarmed me. I didn't know how to respond. Did he mean this to be an invitation for further discussion about these issues? Or was it meant to be an apology? As if by reflex, I made noises of sympathy, ventured gestures of understanding, though in truth I didn't quite experience either just then. All I can be said to have experienced in the moment was awkwardness. This isn't uncommon for me, hyperaware as I am of social discomfort (And is not this self-consciousness de rigueur now? Do we not consider being alert to minor social hiccups a mark of sophistication and refinement?), but I often worry that I am also too intolerant of this awkwardness, too quick to turn my back on it. Sometimes, yes, an awkward moment simply needs to be gotten past, forgotten, erased as best as it can by some well-timed backchat. But sometimes awkwardness is only the first step on the way to something deeper. Intimacy or fellowship or whatever you want to call it. Community. Maybe the most evident and ancient example of this is grieving.

Sad as it makes me now, looking back, my talk with Peter more or less ended there, with his confession. And despite the semishaky way we left things, for some time to come I was flush with that particular pride that altruism brings on. I began to spin out clichéd sports narratives about Peter. His passion for tennis would be renewed. He'd soon start spending his copious free time giving lessons to underprivileged kids in the neighborhood, teaching a new generation his long and magnificent strokes. The community would take notice and he'd be honored with a service medal, an award of some sort. In his acceptance speech he'd quote the philosopher Martins, Buber and King Jr., and the poet Johns, Lennon and Donne. We'd share a knowing glance over the heads of the other crowd members; maybe he'd give me a slight head nod of gratitude. It was like I'd taken a time-release pill of bonhomie, so hopeful was I for his future.

But Peter must've sensed the undercurrent of selfishness in my gift—maybe he suspected me of merely fishing for praise—because one afternoon not long after I went out to get my mail and found, mingling with the envelopes and catalogs, a loose twenty-dollar bill. And even though there wasn't an envelope or a note, I knew exactly what it meant.

On the way to the funeral home Sunday morning, Alexis and I listened to the Dead's *American Beauty*. The sky had gone to pigeon shit–gray again and "Box of Rain" seemed a fitting theme song for the drive over—"Such a long long time to be gone / and a short time to be there." We arrived and made our way into the lobby, where we found a large wall-mounted TV playing a slide show. Against a stock image of an idyllic woodland river and to the accompaniment of a generic string quartet, pictures of Peter passed over the screen. Certain images kept recurring but at intervals irregular enough to make me think they'd been edited hastily, if at all. We found the programs in a wicker basket and both took one. They were just a piece of paper folded in half like it was touching its toes. On the front was a stick-figure sketch of Peter on his bike, black eighth notes coming from the basket in front. Behind him there trailed a solar system of bubbles, which were filled in with elaborate swirling patterns done with pastel colored pencils. Though it wasn't credited as one, I'd bet it was a self-portrait. Inside, on a vibrant watercolor background, printed in purple ink, was a short biography of Peter. I hadn't known he'd been born in England or that he'd shared a birthday with John Lennon or that he'd worked as a plumber before heading off to graduate school. I was suddenly ashamed, embarrassed, wearing a wrinkly suit and holding the book of poems I'd finally settled on. I'd known so little about Peter, had heard so few of his stories. And it seemed then like it would've taken so very little for me to have known more.

As we watched the pictures scroll across the screen and took in the program, Alexis began to weep. Her whole body got involved and we discreetly excused ourselves outside, to the parking lot, where we hugged and chatted until the fit passed.

"It's just so sad," she said.

We'd been married for years now and still the depth and clarity of Alexis's emotions routinely surprised me. It could still hit me with the force of a revelation, that she was a many-dimensional and, therefore, mysterious being, attuned to a situation in a way I couldn't fathom. I loved her sensitivity, her awareness of other people's needs and hurts. And most of all I envied her apparent ability to experience something without immediately spiraling away from it, wondering how that experience might work in words. Here, I envied her grief. Because the scene had failed to produce in me the same Wordsworthian surge of powerful emotions and I considered this to be another in a long line of my failures to meet life with the proper response. Again I understood this had to do with my overawareness of the story being told. What had seemed most sad to me were the pictures, the program—the absurd distance between these documents and Peter's life. I kept returning to the idea that there must be an irresolvable tension between life and stories. Life is lived and stories are told, after all, and to turn an event from life into a story, to pick and choose details and plug them into a symbolic system, to manipulate them in such a way as to make meaning, is to cheat life in some way. "The symbol is the murder of the thing," Lacan wrote, basically pointing out that a word is never the thing it names. I don't think he's being melodramatic here, either, when he suggests that violence is inherent in the naming process, that there's a strange betrayal in the house of experience. But then again, without stories, without that linguistic betrayal, how would we get at the stuff of life?

Back in the lobby we ran into John and some other guys I recognized from Irving but whose names had long since slipped my mind—had I ever really been part of that community? John was wearing a black suit with a shiny purple shirt open wide at the neck. No grille. We all shook hands and our heads as we expressed disbelief. We talked about how speechless we were.

"Can you imagine?" we asked.

"I can't imagine," we answered.

Given how little else any of them had to say, I suspected that they hadn't known Peter any better than I had, and in that moment it seemed as though we were all there to pay our respects to his tennis game. People had started to gather in the hall and we were directed in ourselves. At the front, artistically arranged with the flowers, were Peter's hat and guitar, relics of a sort, things invested with his presence. Alexis and I took seats in the middle of a row about halfway back. Around the hall I spotted many of my neighbors. Ernie and Caprice were up front, as was Linda, of course. Even Jim had come—he was sitting in the way back. I wondered whether the author of the letter was part of the crowd, basking in some sick sense of vindication. But not everyone was here. Not either of my next-door neighbors and not _____ from across the street. Perhaps the most noticeable absence, though, was Lawrence—I could've sworn he would've made this a priority. Before the service started, Boo walked around the hall off leash, sniffing people's feet and laps. A woman sitting up ahead of us hypothesized that he must be looking for Peter and the folks around her cooed sympathetically.

When everyone had settled in, a friend of Linda's, acting as the emcee or officiant, stood and offered some prefatory remarks. We'd gathered this morning to share stories about Peter, to celebrate his life. In his essay "The Storyteller," Walter Benjamin writes, "It is ... characteristic that not only a man's knowledge or wisdom, but above all his real life— and this is the stuff that stories are made of—first assumes transmissible form at the moment of his death." The program put this idea more succinctly with, "We are all stories in the end. . ." And the woman kicked things off by telling an anecdote about how Peter had helped her daughter learn the guitar. She then invited us, the crowd, up to tell our own stories. And for the next two and a half hours or so, if you count the intermission, that's what we did.

Former students talked about how instrumental Peter had been in their development, intellectual and personal. Friends lauded his passion for music, for both playing and listening to it, and his insatiable curiosity, his fierce devotion to beauty. A man with curly hair wearing great big clown shoes stood and stumbled through a speech about how much Peter had meant to him. At one point he looked at the ceiling and said, "I wore the shoes for you, man." A cigar box of snapshots was passed around. They were loose and unorganized and the color had started to fade out of some of the older ones, from when Peter and Linda were young. Each picture, like each eulogizer, told a sliver of the larger story, its truth or value not at all diminished for being partial, incomplete. Caprice got up there and mooned about all the times she and Peter had stayed up late chatting in his backyard. What she remembered most, she said, was laughing. There was a recklessness to the way she spoke, as if she wasn't entirely in control of what she was saying. She got on about how upset Linda used to get, how she'd ask them to keep it down or go to bed, badgering them as though they were teenagers, and I was thankful I could see only the back of Linda's head. No one was reading poems and with every new speaker it grew more and more clear that I wasn't going to get up there and read mine. I thought I'd call an audible and talk about his tennis game, how pretty it was to watch, how incongruous, but someone beat me to it. After a while I started to wonder what Peter's parents, elderly British expats, were making of this production. They were sitting in the front row, their four hands origamied together. What thoughts accompanied his father when during one of the speeches he excused himself to the bathroom? What was Peter's brother thinking, sitting next to his parents? He turned out to be the only family member who wanted to share something with us. He'd chosen a song—apparently he, too, had inherited the musical gene. "What a Shame," by the hard rock band Shinedown, includes the lines: "I knew him more than most / I saw a side of him he never showed."

The time between speakers continued to increase until it was clear that those people who wanted to share had shared, and then it was Linda's turn to speak. She talked about how Peter had been taken from us in a moment of darkness, about how his life had of late been shrouded in that darkness. But now we could all take comfort in knowing that he had moved on into the light. It was strange—had I encountered this line in a story, I would've found it hokey, forced, and not bought it whole cloth as I did in the moment. And Linda spared no details as she went on to detail that darkness, talking openly about Peter's struggles with bipolar disorder and his recent hospitalizations. About how they'd been living separately but together and how she'd been the one who found the property he was going to move to. Her tone throughout was calm and measured, almost clinical. And while it was oddly moving, her candor also felt strategic, like she was using these details to exert control over the story. Because it was clear that in telling it, she was also settling on a version of events that she could go on living with.

After she finished, miniature bottles of soap bubbles were handed around. We were instructed to blow them as we walked out of the hall, which would happen to the tune of "Give Me Love," by George Harrison. But first we'd sing through it once together. If you know the song, you know it's repetitive and incantatory and with it on repeat it was tough to discern when it ended and when it began again, so it wasn't until we were into maybe a third communal singing that we started to leave. And while some folks struggled to make any at all, what bubbles there were that floated and shimmered wet and oily and then blipped out of existence under the funeral parlor's fluorescent lights were really quite something to behold. I'm even tempted to go for the cliché here and say you couldn't have written it better, so well did the scene appear to encapsulate the end.

"The first symbol in which we recognize humanity in its vestiges is the burial," Lacan also wrote. And in an essay on memory and forgetting, Lewis Hyde offers a helpful gloss on this, explaining, "The grave marker is the symbol that recognizes that whatever has happened need not live forever. The symbol lives on but the real, once properly inscribed, is temporal and can be buried. Forgetting is the erasing angel that murders particularity so that concepts can be born, so that time can flow again."

And for a while after I finished a draft of the above, I thought I'd accomplished just this. Successfully translated and conjugated my experience, both of the afternoon and of my friendship, such as it was, with Peter. I thought I'd fixed things in such a way as to bury the tragedy. But the story hung around, wouldn't go away. In the weeks and months to come I couldn't turn off my awareness of things that could be put to use as details, invested with significance. After the murder, for example, I was alarmed to find Peter's porch light turned on. And it stayed that way, bracingly bright, for days. Coming home from Peninsula with Percy one afternoon, I walked up the front steps and, at long last, stood on the porch. I took in what had been Peter's view and then peered through the front window and thought I spotted, on the ground in front of the fireplace, a massive amoebic stain. I bought "Appalachian Spring" on vinyl and listened to it over and over, trying to develop a taste for it, an ear for what distinguished it from the soundtrack of, say, *Fievel Goes West.*

My cache of details about Peter continued to expand. Late one night and many clicks deep into a Google sesh, I stumbled upon his Rate My Professors page. It covered his time in the writing department at UC San Diego. Given my experience and what I'd heard at the service, I'd imagined Peter as a *Dead Poets*y teacher, beloved by his pupils for inspiring freethinking and resistance to sociocultural bullshit. The site, I was sorry to find, failed to confirm this story for me. He had fifty-six ratings and their mean, out of a possible 5.0, was a dispiriting 2.6. A pitiable score. And a lot of the comments, Christ, they stung. "His lectures are interesting, if your not falling asleep after the first 10 minutes of class." "Peter John, he is horrible . . . i guess some people like him . . . like 10 people that is out of almost 200 . . . His points are invalid and our topics of discussion are ridiculous." "No. No no no." It was hard to keep my mind from forming a narrative, reading through these responses. Peter struggling to get his students to care, losing interest, his patience. And finally maybe his mind. Because sure enough a few alluded to a rupture, a breakdown. The most succinct among them put it thus: "He mysteriously disappeared in the middle of the quarter, so I deduce he is unreliable."

At first this simply saddened me. Sad for all he'd had to put up with, sad he never figured out how to fit in. Also sad that I had access to these comments and lacked the willpower not to read them. But then a strange form of guilt began to court me, and this guilt only grew more dogged when, during another evening's Googling, I came across a site that suggested he'd left a different teaching job in the wake of a sexual harassment scandal. All at once my reading and research seemed excessive, borderline invasive.

I switched tacks, started to look into Steve. To hear Caprice tell it, Steve had looked up to Peter. She'd gone so far as to say that Steve had loved him, as one would a brother. And a capacity for or tendency toward violence? She never would've guessed it.

"He was just a Bubba," she said. "Just a beer drinker. A bump on a log."

In an effort to better understand his motives, I thought the police report might prove useful, so I filed a request. In return I received an official letter saying the case was still open and, therefore, the information I wanted was "exempt from disclosure." Other channels proved more fruitful, though, and soon I had in my possession a copy of all the classified documents relating to the case. That I could resort to "other channels" thrilled me, made me feel like I was a character in a spy story, engaging in a bit of tradecraft.

The day's events were recounted under a bold header: **FACTS**. I learned, among other things, that Steve had considered Peter his "last hope," which fit with Caprice's read on the situation, and that he'd had six beers that morning, not counting the one and change he had after the murder. Steve didn't consider that a lot, though, because he typically had twelve or more in a day. I also learned that he'd acted in a watery tunnel of unknowing—it was all a blur. I read: "He admitted that stabbing a person in their chest would 'probably kill 'em.' He admitted to Detective Michaels that he knew what he was doing was wrong and that he knew he'd be caught 'probably because I wanted to be.'"

"I'm very remorseful," Steve went on to tell the detectives. "I still have the fear but, for some reasons, I feel a little better because I know I'm gonna get three hots and a cot."

There's a word in German that is, well, germane here: *Torschlusspanik*. It translates literally to "gate-shut panic" and connotes that crazed anxiety we experience when we feel time is running out on us. Bets made to recoup losses, doubles ordered at last call, overbidding for items on eBay, etc. Steve seems to have succumbed to some limit case of this that morning. Faced with the tremendous uncertainty of his changing circumstances, "the fear," he'd snapped. Gone into a fugue-like state and murdered a man he'd looked up to, his "last hope." My neighbor.

But learning this was no salve. It only deepened the mystery for me. The story was incomplete, hadn't been put to rest. And maybe it never could be. I started to feel like I'd wasted my time. Soon I could be found luxuriating in the familiar bathwater of writerly insecurities. At my nadir I believed I was doomed to live out my days as an editor, as a top-hatted fuckwit who niggles with other folks' prose.

But it was a fraud, above all else, that I knew myself to be. All along I'd been working under the assumption, tacit though it was, that I could control the details of Peter's story in a way I couldn't control those of my own. I'd sought them out as a distraction, as a way to keep my mind actively off other things. Because in the months following Peter's murder, my parents finalized their divorce and my maternal grandmother, Mamaw, died. I didn't get back to Richmond for her funeral and because of this would every so often experience a haunting flutter of doubt. Could it be that she was still alive? One evening I found myself dialing her old phone number, my fingers working through the digits with startling ease. It was as though memory had stored them somewhere so accessible that in recalling them I bypassed conscious thought. I returned to my senses before placing the call but it was too late, that sequence of numbers had unlocked a trove of memories that left me sentimental and weepy. Nostalgic. During one of our conversations afterward, Mom told me my uncle, one of Dad's four brothers, had driven down from Connecticut to attend the funeral. Dad hadn't been there, she added. He'd been at the graveside service, though. Had apparently ridden his bike over—I didn't know his license was still suspended. And Jesus, the thought of him arriving to see Mamaw into her grave on some shitty ten-speed he'd bought at a yard sale or off Craigslist was almost too much for me to imagine. For the third time in her life, Mom got a boyfriend. She was always wanting to talk about him, too, and I twice had to ask her to stop coming to me for relationship advice. Dad left the country to be a gym teacher in Morocco and in a conversation we had before he left, he talked about how lonely he was. Later, from an internet café in Casablanca, he confessed to having a girlfriend himself. She lived in Florida and had retired early from her career as a flight attendant. She was "real attractive, a cheerleader type" and used to get busy with singer-songwriter Kenny Loggins. In his voice when he told me this, was that pride? Was Dad boasting about his new Eskimo brother? Bragging about having entered the danger zone? It was as though my past were eroding away, my history being rewritten. And the future? The stretch of time that'd opened so easily before Alexis and me? We lost our first pregnancy to miscarriage and the pain of that was ramifying and pervasive and so very adult. The doctor assured us we'd done nothing wrong, that these things sometimes just happen. But that it was random and out of our control wasn't the comfort she intended. It only intensified our confusion, contributed to the pain of our loss. This pain went all Whac-A-Mole on us soon after, as several of our closest friends announced, rapid-fire, that they were expecting. And what a fine expression that is, "expecting." How deftly and gracefully it involves you in your own future. We were no longer "expecting." And the powerlessness I experienced in the wake of this and all the other life experiences made me painfully aware of an obvious and basic existential truth: I could be the narrator of my life story, its hero or antihero depending on my mood, but I could never hope to be the author of my life. Shit now existed that I could never hope to pin down in prose. I'd gone in for some emotional sleight of hand, then, and ended up putting an inordinate amount of pressure on myself to articulate the senselessness of what'd happened to Peter.

A story is a residue. It's the moisture that remains in a sponge after it's been wrung out. And it's both a wager in and against time. We hope our preserved little packets of time, fixed between the bookends of beginning and end, will endure. That they'll float on over the prodigious and imponderable amount of time that flows us right on by, that does not get memorialized in writing or images.

My faith in narration had been shaken, the foundation now cracked and unsound, but time continued to flow just fine. Daffodils bloomed all over Peter's yard. Books and cassettes and miscellaneous furniture began to appear on the curb out front as Linda cleared out the house. I found a volume of Auden's poems but it'd gone fatly dropsical with rain so I left it behind. The buyers Peter had lined up for the house had apparently been undeterred by what'd gone down there—it had good bones, after all—and a woman in her twilight years soon moved in and started to renovate. The rickety fence out front was taken down, the yard tamed, largely cleared. The birdbath, site where inspiration once struck, was disposed of. A retaining wall was built out by the sidewalk and all around fresh beds were laid and planted with sensible, matchy-matchy flowers.

And before I knew it, it was summer again and at the tennis center in St. Johns one morning, I ran into Lawrence. While we waited to take our respective courts I mentioned, casually, offhandedly, that I'd been surprised not to see him at Peter's memorial service. They'd been close, after all. Hadn't they?

It's never taken much and I should've known better—this set him off.

"I was a friend to that man in life," he said, among many exaggerated gestures of aggression. "Any fool is welcome to be a friend in death."

I initially shrugged the encounter off—typical Lawrence. But what he said came to assume a new and startling significance after Alexis read an early draft of this essay. She said she hadn't realized I'd felt so close to Peter, seeing as we'd only gone on a handful of walks and played tennis a few times. This planted a seed of doubt in my mind. Had we been as close as I thought? Or had I merely suggested the closeness for the purposes of the essay, fudged things for effect? It brought to mind the famous last stanza of Elizabeth Bishop's poem "One Art," which was what I'd brought to share at the memorial service. "It's evident / the art of losing's not too hard to master / though it may look like (*Write* it!) like disaster." Among other things, Bishop is talking about how problematic it is that our loss is wrapped up in its articulation. Pointing out the tension that exists between what we experience and what we say (or *write*) that we experience.

And like Bishop, urging herself on to the end, I, too, was having trouble finishing. In the materials my source had retrieved for me there was a schedule for Steve's trial. I saw that he'd filed various motions and managed to postpone the proceedings. But the trial was scheduled to begin, finally, in August, a year and a half after the murder. I marked my calendar, sure at first that I wouldn't miss it. The journalist in me knew the story would continue in the courtroom and wouldn't be properly over until the judge's gavel sounded and Steve was pronounced guilty. Until the bailiff escorted him out a side door and into the relative stability of what would likely be the rest of his life. Before that happened, the story would, in a way, continue to live and breathe. Another type of storyteller, though, would've opted to end things with the image the memorial service provided: bubbles shimmering and blipping out of existence. It provided a ready metaphor— how fleeting our time together is!—and it happened in scene, and ending in scene is one of contemporary storytelling's many tenets. It's a tenet I often stress, to the authors I edit, the students I teach. Doing so leaves a reader with the fizzling menace of partial resolution, of consequences to come. But the longer I sat with that, the more it seemed just a trick of time, a contrivance. Deceptive and dishonest. In the end, what I was on the hunt for, and what I suspected I'd never find, was a way to express my astonishment at what remains, at the fact that time goes on and stories take shape. My abiding sense of wonder at how much of this living, in language and life both, is a living without.

Something's Gotta Stick

Should we have stayed at home and thought of here?
Where should we be today?

—Elizabeth Bishop

I.

Orientation. It's Sunday, June 16, 2013—Father's Day and the first of Windells's Summer Session 2. Late afternoon and the sun's out and the sky's a kid's picture of the sky, with great big cotton-ball clouds seemingly glued to a lucid blue. I'm sitting with the other skateboarders along the coping of a drained pool in the Concrete Jungle part of campus, which is tucked in the woods off Highway 26 in Welches, Oregon. My board is in my lap and my helmet's beside me and I'm wearing my favorite of the new T-shirts I bought for camp. It says RESEARCH across the chest. My legs are dangling beneath me with that pleasant sense of groundlessness I loved as a boy, perched in too-high chairs, and didn't know I missed. Until recently, I hadn't realized that it was possible for one's body to miss something that one's mind didn't also miss. That one's mind wasn't even actively aware of.

After a brief camp-wide introduction in B.O.B., the Building out Back, a hangar that houses the indoor skate park, the trampolines, and the pit of foam blocks, we were split off from the snowboarders and skiers for our sport-specific briefing. The facts here are simple enough: a month back I signed up to attend Windells's Adult Skateboard Camp. I paid online—a thousand bucks for the week seemed a steal at the time—and e-mailed over the twenty-page packet of waivers and my insurance information, as well as a physical form my doctor had to fill out. But like so much about my life these days, knowing these facts doesn't diminish a certain shimmery unreal quality that clings to them, and I almost feel like I need proof that I'm really here. The best I can find is the neon-yellow wristband I'm wearing, its adhesive so strong that it'll likely depilate my forearm for days to come. This takes me back about an hour, to when I checked in and learned, among other things, that to remove the wristband would bar me from all camp-related activities, including meals and the dodgeball tournament. The wristband is a small yet comforting reminder of where I am, but I'll take absolutely anything I can get in the way of continuity. Feeling lately's been that whatever ligatures were used to knit me together have stretched thin, if not snapped entirely.

Because I was going it alone, one of my unstated goals entering the week was to make a friend, a buddy. Best-case scenario, to get a nickname. I'd read about the Adult House's hot tub and had imagined having a soak and swapping stories with my fellow campers, slightly embellished tales of how we'd slain our local spots growing up, shredded ledges and conquered sets of stairs. I'm perhaps a skosh overeager to make this happen, which must be why I venture, to no one in particular, that we've all gathered here to get our "bearings." When no one laughs, I spin one of the wheels on my board in a schmucky hint-hint but don't even get a sympathetic titter. And for a moment I worry that I've inadvertently marked myself as a poser, what with my new T-shirt that still has its fold creases and my newish board and my shoes that are hardly scuffed and my lickspittling joke. I stop short of acknowledging the truth: that that's exactly what I am, and in ways far deeper than I'm willing to admit.

Jamie Weller, the head coach-counselor, starts to call roll. He's mid- to late thirties and his hair is close-cropped and so blond I can't tell whether he's maybe balding a little. He's short and stocky and looks like someone you'd encounter in a mosh pit. In response to their names, each camper raises a hand and says, "Here." As I watch on, a notion begins to take shape out on the edge of my mind. Most of the campers' faces are in varying stages of development, with disproportionate noses and ears and skin stretched like Silly Putty over still-growing bones. Their limbs are Muppet gangly and their feet almost clownishly oversize. There's also a coterie of prepubertal boys sitting together, a feral-looking crew that makes me nervous, they seem so unpredictable. After his name is called, one of these kids says, "Present," and all the boys around him laugh and dole out congratulatory dunches. I bristle inwardly at this rival jokester and fear that if things continue apace, I'm in for a long week, buddy-wise.

My mind wanders off in defeat. I work my wristband around and my arm hair prickles with pleasure-pain. Ever since I got married, I've fussed with my wedding ring in much the same way, mystified by its presence on my finger, wondering, at times, what it could possibly signify. I'll celebrate my two-year anniversary in a month and I'm still not a hundred percent on what it means to be a husband—that word seems to define a state of affairs that I haven't fully grasped as part of my identity. I focus on the pool. Although it is drained, it was never intended to hold water, and I'm having a little Wittgensteinian moment with that one when I hear my name.

"Here," I answer automatically, but it comes out sounding more like a question. The campers look at me like, finally, the solution to this riddle.

"Great. All right," Jamie says, and nods encouragingly. He checks his list. It seems mine is the last name on it. "There'll be another one of you, too. Maureen. She's on her way, just not here yet."

"Cool, thanks," I say.

The notion is fully articulable now: I am thus far the only adult to show up to Session 2's Adult Skateboard Camp. I am thirty-one years old and some fast math tells me I'm technically old enough to be every other skate camper's dad. It is then that I recognize the buffer of space they've left around me. There could be no congratulatory dunches for me after one of my jokes because I couldn't touch the closest person on either side of me if I leaned over.

I put it together that there's been a miscommunication

here. When I spoke with a camp representative last week, I asked how many other adults would be in attendance at Session 2. I was told there would be eight, a not unreasonable number. Enough folks to fill a hot tub. But what I didn't know to ask was how many of those eight would be skateboarding, not skiing or snowboarding. Had I, I would've learned only one. Some lady named Maureen.

"Okay," Jamie says, and turns to address the lot of us. "So who here loves skateboarding?!"

Everyone hoots and cheers. The campers standing poolside take their boards by the tails and knock the noses against the coping. One kid makes this whooping noise that probably qualifies as ululating.

"Nice!" Jamie says. "I can already tell this group's gonna be tons of fun." He then invites the four other coach-counselors to introduce themselves. They're all early twenties and stand with the same languorous cool-guy posture that skaters stood with back when I was growing up. After we go over the rules and the schedule, Jamie hints at the shindig that will end the week. In B.O.B. there will be tunes and dancing and skating and salty snacks and candy and soda and contests and raffles for free boards and other righteous gear. They've christened this sober bacchanal "Disorientation."

"This is your week," Jamie concludes. "You're in charge of how much fun you have."

There's still some time before I have to meet with the other adult campers and I need to unpack and do my Father's Day duty and call Dad, so I ride back toward the Adult House, a four-bedroom rancher across the five lanes of Highway 26, quarantined from all the other bunks.

Campus is an amoebic network of concrete ramps (bowls and quarter pipes and spines), manual pads, and stairs that have low rails and ledges—89,500 square feet of skateable terrain. Behind the dining hall there's a course for BMX bikes, big dirt jumps that lead to other big dirt jumps; I swear that if I listen really hard while looking at it I can hear the midi soundtrack to Nintendo's *California Games*. For the skiers and snowboarders, there are two sets of dry slopes, which are made of small interlocking sections of white plastic that have firm cilia protruding from them—up close, they look like reefs of sea anemones. In the woods there's a steep approach to two ramps from which campers may launch and land in a great inflatable bag like the water blobs you find on lakes, and in front of B.O.B. is the Ranch, a gentle declivity about a hundred yards long, dotted with jibs for campers to develop and refine their Slopestyle know-how. The way these areas sit in amid the pine and fir trees gives the few acres a distinct Fern Gully meets Neverland feel. And I understand it's all something of a wet dream for my fifteen-year-old self, with whom I've been in uneasy touch of late.

I make it to the highway and stand by the entrance. Cars whiz by in either direction. As I wait for my chance to Frogger across the five lanes, I regard the camp's sign and its curious punctuation. WINDELLS, it reads, after the founder, Tim Windell. And below, in big block letters, THE "FUNNEST" PLACE ON EARTH.

II.

On the drive out, I kept losing Mount Hood behind the trees, only to find it again when I came around a bend or crested a hill. Every time it reappeared, I felt a shudder of recognition, maybe even awe. I was trying hard not to make a sentimental metaphor out of this, which had become a problem, my meaning-making apparatus having been set to overdrive, investing almost everything around me with the ache of preciousness and fragility. I was trying, rather, to shake the idea that I'd made a mistake in signing up for skate camp in the first place, a miscalculation. In the week or so before, it had started to feel like a dare I couldn't go back on. Because fun wasn't exactly what I was going to Windells to have—I actually wasn't sure I was capable of having the kind of fun Windells promised anymore. I was going for more diffuse, nebulous reasons, reasons I hoped my time there would help me articulate.

The nub here is that for months I'd been having these vicious fits of nostalgia. Out of nowhere and of a sudden, a particular thing in the world would provoke an overwhelming experience of poignancy, in the full sense of that word that includes actual physical pain. Take, for instance, the dogwood tree out front. Looking at this tree—*my* dogwood tree, in *my* yard, seen from the big front window of *my* house, that *I* own, facts of propriety that, two years on, I still can't get my head around—would call to mind the one we had in front of the brick ranch house I grew up in. This would, in turn, rouse a slew of warm-fuzzy memories, real Hallmark-type shit, about my family, which had become unrecognizable to me after my parents' late-in-life divorce and seemed to exist only insofar as I was able to remember it. Chains of memories had been forming inside me in this way, growing organically, compounding into great crystalline structures. These diamonds of schmaltz imprisoned me. When finally released, I'd be nauseated, emotionally spent, my eyes often reddened from tears, and left in a mood equal parts wonder and wistfulness, longing and regret. Part of my discomfort with these episodes was that they exposed a flaw in who I thought I was, a contradiction in my identity. Despite overwhelming evidence to the contrary in the form of old journals, I didn't think of myself as a particularly sentimental person, and whatever, if I had been, once upon a time, I thought I'd trained it out of me by reading novels and poetry and philosophy, by a process of sophistication or refinement or whatever nonfussy word you want to use for the ability to appraise your emotions and deal with them accordingly. I've always figured that this stoic fortitude or sagacious moxie was a chief benchmark of adulthood, the implicit promised end of all my reading. And I know for sure I hadn't had any problem dismissing nostalgia in the recent past, writing it off as a second-rate emotion, maudlin and bathetic, born of self-pity and not fit for serious consideration.

But how could I argue with all the countervailing evidence now? The welling tears and the stifled blubbering and the dilly-dallying on Memory Lane? Is this just me? Or does time contain a pussifying reagent? As it accrues inside you, does it catalyze an effete sensitivity? How else could my interior landscape have come to be repainted by Thomas Kinkade?

As uncomfortable and claustrophobic as these spells made me, I actually found myself courting them. I surrounded myself with things that might serve as a trigger, that had a certain warmth or familiarity about them, realizing full well that they were siren songs of a sort. I pulled out old pictures, ones of my brothers and me as kids, of old friends and me at nostalgically charged locales, and framed them. I bought an old Mercedes similar to the ones Dad had driven when I was young, but mine was a roadster, a convertible, and I experienced a little patricidal tickle whenever I thought about how it was way nicer than any he'd ever owned. It was a great day when I discovered the existence of a Nintendo emulator online, a trove, a veritable goddamn Golconda, of video games I'd spent untold hours playing as a boy and that the site allowed me to play again for free. And because using the keyboard to play was like having becondomed sex, three-tenths as pleasurable as I knew it could be, I ordered a classic controller from another site online that plugged into my computer's USB port—my body had a certain way it needed to interact with the games in order to satisfy what I was craving. It'd been fifteen years or more since I'd seen these games and yet my body had retained a recondite knowledge of them: e.g., when I pulled up *Contra*, my hands mindlessly entered the code for ninety-nine lives that I'd have to think about in order to put into words. And I was having these long, weepy sessions listening to all the music I'd listened to in high school and sometimes I felt like I was the only person in the world who understood how *sophisticated* Emo music was.

What was becoming of me? Whence this sissified mushiness?

For Christmas I got on eBay and bought my brother a handful of the now "vintage" G.I. Joes we'd played with growing up, hoping that by sharing my nostalgia I could in some way manage or dilute it. But it didn't work. I could tell by the politely excited face he made when he opened them, the same fire had not been lit in him. And it was no wonder, because no matter how much it's tied to cultural history, nostalgia is a lonely emotion or mood, hermetic in some essential way. To talk about or expose the particulars of one's nostalgia is like relating a dream or a drug experience: one should do it sparingly, if at all. Like dreams and drug experiences, nostalgia entails a considerable amount of amplification, which is to say distortion. Faced with a time of our lives that we cannot return to, we manufacture ad hoc relics, invest things from that time with a significance and meaning that's peculiar to us, to our notions of home and who we are. "Nostalgia," after all, combines the Greek word for homecoming (*nostos*) with the one for pain or ache or longing (*algia*). The longing to return home, homesickness—or at least that's what it meant when it was first coined. As I lived with this nostalgia, though, I came to understand that as much as anything else it was wrapped up in who I once imagined I could become, how I had once imagined myself in the future, as an adult, that is, right now, in the present. Nostalgia can become a fun house–mirror mood in this way, reflecting all the potential future selves that once sat in us, future selves that time aborted, dreams we allowed to fall into desuetude as we settled into the reality of our identity. In this way it has as much to do with our full relationship to time as it does with any one place, with a literal "home." This might be related to the idea that we feel more alive, more ourselves somehow, when we're imagining what we could be than when we're reflecting on what we are, because it's in exercising this imaginative faculty that we get a taste of the eternal, whereas in reflection we're confronted over and over with the radical bummer of our finitude. Or I don't know, that's at least what Blake thought. I know that my relationship to time had gotten a lot more complicated. It had borne me forward for so long with the easy and soporific rhythms of an engine, a locomotive lullaby, sliding along rails that narrowed to an inconceivable vanishing point on the horizon, in the future. But all at once it'd become directionless and weird and dark, a *Back to the Future* train that could fly off the rails and that was fueled by fear and anxiety. The past was no longer simply the place I'd come from, the future no longer where I was headed. Up could be down—and in a sudden rush it returns to me, the beginning of the code for ninety-nine lives: "up up down down. . ."—and back forward and in this I lost touch with whatever had previously grounded me. A dizzying experience, a seasickness of the soul, that had me scrambling for a foothold, for something solid to stand on.

As it happens, I am not the first human to be existentially upended by such an experience and the internet abounds in options for adult fantasy camps, sanatoriums of a sort for the nostalgically afflicted. Had I banded together with friends growing up and chugged out power chords or beat inconsistent rhythms on a thirdhand drum set, I might have attended Rock and Roll Fantasy Camp in Vegas. Had I achieved distinction at baseball, I might've signed up for Adult Baseball Camp in Vero Beach, Florida, hosted by luminaries, past and present, of the LA Dodgers. If I'd been a dear bespectacled dweeb who'd lain awake nights, awed by stellar doings and visions of extraterrestrial travel, I might've gone in for Adult Space Academy in Huntsville, Alabama. But none of these describe my experience. I'd been haunted by skateboarding, which I remembered being very good at, once upon a time, and so it was on skateboarding that I landed.

III.

No one's in the Adult House when I return and the living room's vibe is one of latent depravity, the raunch manqué of an empty frat house. The floor's just the foundational concrete and the walls are exposed and painted-over cinder blocks and sheetrock and against them, lined up like day laborers, are the skis and the boards, both snow- and skate-. I figure that a few of the other adult campers, the skiers and snowboarders, must've brought skateboards, too, for night sessions in B.O.B., and I add mine to the bunch.

There's a run-down pool table in the middle of the room, its baize the sallow color of a malnourished lawn. Behind that is the lounge area, where a pair of wizened leather couches face a wall-mounted TV that's playing a muted snowboard video for an audience of ghosts, shredders from hangs past. I head through the Spartan kitchen and back toward the color-coded bedrooms. When I dropped my stuff before orientation, I chose the only room that appeared to be unoccupied, the orange room, because as much as I wanted a friend, I still valued my privacy more. And during a quick survey of the place, my self-preservation antennae noted that while the door to the bathroom in the hall will close, the latch doesn't catch, let alone lock, so heads-up. On a sliding scale of coziness, I'd say we've ticked past Ski Chalet, past Dorm Room, and that we're maybe one busted pipe or shat-up toilet short of Orphanage.

I unpack my extra shoes and jeans and my fifteen T-shirts. Why, pray tell, have I brought so many T-shirts? Because I am what you could call a sweater. My closest friends growing up, kids I skated with most often, sometimes called me "Sweatston." When comradely affection peaked or when I was particularly soaked after a long session, I was "Sweatston Knapsack." My hopes for getting a nickname this week are tinged with a fear that I will end up with this one again. My ibuprofen and Advanced Relief IcyHot go on the night table, along with my copy of *Thus Spoke Zarathustra*. For more than a decade I've been claiming I read this book when I was seventeen, while in fact I never have. But it's always sounded like something I wanted as part of my story, that I was the type of person who would've read Nietzsche in high school, on his own, unprompted. I can say I was a lot of things at seventeen—a semiserious skateboarder, the captain of my lacrosse team, an emotard who worked part-time at the Gap—but what I can't say is that I was a reader, not yet. I was envious of kids like that then, though, kids who had intellectual gumption and acted on their curiosity, who felt entitled to knowledge and not intimidated by it. That sort of freedom was still years off for me. To be curious means that you care about things and caring about these things, intellectual things, in the prevailing slacker aesthetic of the midnineties I grew up in, was to display a kind of sensitivity that opened you up to being called a pussy or, worse, gay, a faggot, and my sense of identity was way too fragile then to withstand charges like this, so I didn't flirt with them. I almost certainly would've pronounced Nietzsche's name as though it were an exotic martial art and paraded my ignorance around as something to be proud of. It's an abiding mystery of my life that this person ever existed, and it's even more baffling that this person was, and in irksome ways still is, me. No matter what I do to silence him—but it's stronger than that, to erase or exterminate him—there he remains, a cockroach of identity, a *Groundhog Day*–ish self I cannot wake all the way up from. (Evidence that this former self lives on in me? Time to time *The Gay Science* is still good for a fratty chuff. *Ecce Homo*, a Buttheady chortle.) In any case, I intend to make good on my claim during my time here, although, honestly, I still haven't decided whether I will come clean in the future or continue to say I read the book as a teen. Finally, as part of my campaign for friends, banking on junk food being an ageless staple of sleepaway camp, I've brought family-size packages of Double Stuf Oreos and Nutter Butters and Cheez-Its, which I drop on the cracked linoleum counter in the kitchen as I head outside to call Dad.

The boards on the porch have gone soft with rot and on one of the two picnic tables there's a large piece of plywood painted robin's egg blue with WINDELLS written in white on either side. It's for beer pong, I deduce from experience. And the hot tub? Nowhere to be found.

I catch Dad off a Father's Day golf outing with my youngest brother. When I tell him where I am, he laughs. In his version of the family mythos, Dad is responsible for getting me to stop skateboarding. So it goes, I was hanging out with a questionable crew in late middle and early high school and he stepped in and got me to play lacrosse, which he'd played D-1. But I skated all through high school, through my lacrosse days, and took a board to college. Strange as it is, given how often I've heard him tell this story, I've never corrected him. While I couldn't have said why until recently, I think I've always understood that he needed his version more than I needed him to know the correct one. No doubt the story's a product of his own nostalgia, his longing to return to what he must understand as his halcyon days, when he had three young boys and a wife, an intact family living in a house he owned, with a dogwood tree out front and a backyard that served as the setting for so much fun; when, I imagine, it wasn't quite so hard for him to feel full of purpose and meaning, days that must play in his mind now like a haunting phantasmagoria. On the flip side, I've also started to see that this nostalgia is responsible for a kind of arrested development. Because I'm not entirely convinced that Dad has known what to do with my brothers and me, since we became adults. The stories he tells of us are all taken from when we were young, when he fulfilled a more obvious "fatherly" role, and sometimes now when he looks at us he'll cock his head a little and on his face there'll appear something like confusion, something maybe like betrayal. But even he would have to admit that his presence in our lives started to fade after we entered college, as we drew closer to and then surpassed the age at which he had us. Given how little I feel he knows about me and my life now, I often wonder what he thinks of when he thinks of me. Does he see a young man all got up in a pair of billowy drawstring trousers from Structure and a black "ribbed" mock turtleneck he stole from his after-school job? Does he see a cloud of angst accessorized with a puka shell necklace and a hoop earring in each ear? More likely he sees me as a six- or seven- or nine-year-old boy, perhaps on my birthday, in our backyard, running an obstacle course that he set up for me and my twenty classmates, a steeplechase in the manner of *American Gladiators*, with different stations, different tests of strength and agility and speed, and which I continue to regard as a bellwether of my understanding of fun. Regardless, it makes me sad in an achy and emotardish way to think he sees someone who does not yet see himself.

I've been thinking a great deal about fatherhood these days, mostly because Alexis and I have been trying to start a family of our own. Still speculative, this desire of ours exists in that vague and dreamy realm of possibility. It lacks the pinch of imminence, is a tornado watch and not a warning. And after we discuss it, I often feel like we've just been talking about what might have been, and not what could be—a strange and disorienting confusion of tenses. The most material thing to come of our talks is a pet theory that some men are more naturally disposed to be a father to younger kids, while others don't really hit their stride until the kids get older. I place Dad squarely in the former group and believe I will fall into the latter. But I suspect this is a theory born of ignorance, however well intentioned it might be, and that, in truth, it isn't and won't be so black and white. Maybe it's at once simpler and more complicated. Maybe we've never been great communicators, Dad and I. While on the phone with him, for example, I don't know what he's doing for work or where he lives exactly, but I do know that to ask after either would be to bring us into a muddied fen of confusion and awkwardness and discomfort, a low-lying and murky zone we do our best to avoid. When we do talk, Dad will often ask after my memories from a certain time or place fertile with family lore, but the sense I get is that he's not interested in hearing my memories so much as he is in corroborating his own nostalgia—more than once he's asked for my memories of a time when I was too young to have them, e.g., of the house we lived in until I was four. In the end, maybe it's that we haven't yet acquired a language fit for adulthood, which I've found is nothing if not muddied and confusing, awkward and glutted with discomfort. Maybe time has relegated us to these separate but adjacent cells, where with our sporks we're doomed to spend our days tapping out a crude Morse code on the wall that divides us, hoping to recognize a pattern in the hollow clicks, grasping after anything that has an echo of previous meaning.

"You were good," Dad says, which brings inexplicable and frustrating tears to my eyes—not even my bitterness can be pure anymore. "I remember you were good at it."

IV.

Despite what its Greek roots suggest, "nostalgia" was actually coined by a Swiss doctor, Johannes Hofer, in 1688. Call it faux Greek, then, an antique reproduction. The experience the word's meant to define, though, existed previously. And there were words for it. The Germans had their *Heimweh*, the French their *maladie du pays*, and the English their "home-sickness." But Hofer was the first person to puzzle over it as a problem for medicine to solve. In his Enlightenment diligence, he recast the experience as an affliction. And in this new guise as a disease, the experience needed another name, something official sounding, decidedly less poetical and wishy-washy. With his neologism, his newly minted diagnosis of "nostalgia," he planted a seed in Western culture and a sensation was born. Historians talk about the time following its baptism as being filled with "outbreaks" and "epidemics," as though nostalgia were the plague or a case of crabs on a college campus. It's worth noting that these were particularly common during or right after revolutions. Periods of political or social upheaval. Great change.

For a long while doctors believed it could be treated and the cures they suggested read like a list of facepalms. Leeches, opium, stomach purges, and warm hypnotic emulsions. Leave it to a doctor during the French Revolution to venture that the only cure was pain and terror. Torture. As evidence, he cited the intimidating tactics of a Russian officer in 1733 who, as his army moved into Germany, threatened that the next soldier to "fall sick" would be buried alive—a threat, so it goes, he made good on. During the American Civil War, nostalgia was thought to be caused by a deficiency of manliness. The prescription? "The patient can often be laughed out of it by his comrades, or reasoned out of it by appeals to his manhood; but of all potent agents, an active campaign, with attendant marches and more particularly its battles is the best curative." Daydreaming about the verdant rolling hills of your home? Try some public ridicule. Mooning over a honey pie? Check where you last laid your nads, Mulva. Miss your mama? Help yourself to a serving of war.

Over time, doctors gave up trying to cure nostalgia—one finally called it a "hypochondria of the heart," fed by its own symptoms like some Ouroboros of the psyche—and they bequeathed the task of exploring it to poets and philosophers. But it wasn't until the 1950s that nostalgia fully shed its connotations of pathology, left the realm of psychology, and became a household word. This is due in large part to the fact that nostalgia also began to lose its strict meaning of "aggravated homesickness," largely thanks to the fact that the word "home" itself lost much of its vitality. And it was after this final instar that nostalgia achieved its broadest expression as a general longing for the past. It now connotes "childhood" and "warmth" and "good old days" more than it does "homesickness," and it's far more likely to be considered alongside emotions like love and fear and envy than disorders like depression and OCD, as it had been once, and not long ago.

Given this history, it's funny, or at least ironic, that nostalgia has piqued the interest of doctors again. Psychiatrists have been studying it more seriously these days and it seems like new reports are coming out all the time—though the joke among specialists is that nostalgia is always old news. Despite its wistful, bittersweet character, these reports claim that nostalgia is, on the whole, a positive emotion. It acts as a shield, a psychological buffer against the fear and anxiety and discontinuity that occur when one's identity is threatened by tumultuous changes, things like divorce or the death of a loved one. Sparked by experiences of loss or displacement, nostalgia provides a refuge from instability. One study went so far as to suggest that on a cold day, nostalgia can make you feel literally warmer.

But if anything, I felt like my nostalgia was deepening my feelings of discontinuity. How in the world could *I* have been all these other people? Has my life been nothing but a series of failed experiments in identity? And I didn't need the help of any theorist to figure out that my idea of home was fucked—it was like a crater left behind a pulled tooth that my tongue kept prodding, an absence that was more confounding than it was painful. I was waking from terrifyingly vivid dreams about skateboarding, my muscles still alive with the remnants of dream activity, as though my limbs had been twitching as I slept, like my dog's sometimes do. (I owned a dog?!) I'd see myself as though through a fish-eye lens, the chosen lens of almost every skate video I've ever seen, and I'd be putting together a run at any number of spots around Richmond. This wasn't memory of any sort I was familiar with. It was recollection with an attitude, that talked back. When things reached a certain pitch, a tinnitus of the soul, I bought a board. And not long after, I signed up for camp.

V.

Before dinner, our Adult Host, James, gathers us in the lounge area for intros. He has shoulder-length blond hair and snowboards semiprofessionally, although he's a little cagey when I ask him what that means. For the summer he's living in a shed behind the Adult House and his chief responsibilities appear to be waking us up every morning and ensuring we have fun.

We all follow his lead and go around the room saying our names and what we're here for. Zach and Ben are brothers and are here to ski. As is Facundo, who also attended Session 1, which ended yesterday. He's from Buenos Aires and works in the electronic music industry and I like him immediately—he strikes me as a person who's used to people liking him immediately. Having spent the previous week together, Facundo and James have developed a bro-closeness that I'm menvious of and want in on. Mitch and Garryl and Pat are here to snowboard. So's Caleb, who's from San Diego. Deeply tanned with sparse, piratical facial hair, Caleb is attractive in a very specific way, one maybe epitomized by the extras you find in the background of MTV Spring Break programs. He's wearing big designer sunglasses and an LA Dodgers cap with a level-flat brim and his long, dark hair is gathered into a strategically disheveled ponytail, which pushes his hat up off his head so it's perched there rather than properly worn. He's here as a chaperone-coach for one of the younger campers, and he goes on to say that if anybody else needs additional coaching up on the mountain, they can feel free to come to him, too. In the wake of that offer we're all quiet for a confused beat. Caleb then fills the silence by kindly asking that we all please call him "Sparrow."

Listening to all these introductions has gotten me almost giddy with possibility. As I was leaving town, I stopped at a friend's house to grab the extra T-shirts he'd picked up for me at a thrift store and to roll a few spliffs I thought might help facilitate Operation Buddy Munchies. We sat and talked about my week ahead.

"Have you decided what you're going to tell the others?" he asked. "You know. About yourself?" We share a thing for cons, for harmless little deceptions, ones that warp or blur reality if not change it outright. The table was littered with papers and tobacco and shake. I'd just finished an uneven and blimpish spliff that I decided to live with rather than reroll a fourth time. At this point in my life, I'll probably never be able to roll a remarkable joint and, in the moment, this realization landed with a disproportionate amount of failure.

"I hadn't thought that far ahead yet, honestly," I said.

We sat there for a while drumming up different stories, inventing alternate histories for myself. I could choose one depending on how I read the audience. Each story had its gestures of credibility and authenticity, small corroborating details that would withstand or discourage cross-examination. Or I could be coy, intriguingly vague about my profession and where I'm from. Cast an aura and let them fill in the blanks.

"You could be anything you want," my friend said, excited himself. And it was a dizzying idea, that reinvention could be so easy.

But when push comes to shove and it's my turn, I for some reason can't bring myself to tell them any of the stories we'd come up with. I tell them my name and what I really do for work and feel the familiar, mild disappointment in these plain facts of my existence. Do they really convey anything meaningful about my identity? Whatever it is I mean when I say "I"? Having entered early middle age and begun to live down decisions I made long ago, I've become increasingly aware of how contingent these things are, how easily they could be otherwise, and then also how little of my past I feel any ownership over. I've even started to think that contingency might well be one of our emotional life's governing forces, like electromagnetism is to physics. Gravity. Only this has served to weaken my connection to roles I play and once trusted to define me, and, worse, to ones I wanted and hoped one day would. Words like "editor" and "writer," "lover" and "husband," "son" and "father" cleaved from whatever relief they'd once delivered or promised to, peeled away like a Fruit Roll-Up from its cellophane, leaving only a cloudy square of silence where once there'd been something at least partially nourishing. But I don't get hung up in the moment and my delivery is as seamless as it is insipid. In fact, the ease with which I can deliver these details is one of the chief reasons I've come to distrust them.

James goes on to explain that we'll spend the first few nights of the week hanging around the house and skating B.O.B.—pros will probably join us at least one night, an intriguing prospect. Then on Thursday we'll head into Portland for a sushi dinner, camp's treat, and maybe follow that with a visit to Casa Diablo, which I know to be a vegan strip club of dubious repute. Facundo repeats the name, "Casa Diablo," and the grin that comes over his face then can only be described as devilish. He's printed the week's schedule of dancers from their website and it appears he's circled a few names in Thursday's column. Friday's the beer pong tourney and Saturday we'll hit "Disorientation."

At the Heshin' Delicatessen for Taco Night, I find myself sitting across from Mitch. He's thirty-two and his face is as bright and genially nondescript as one arranged with breakfast victuals. He's also married—in fact, his wife and some of her family are in town and he plans on heading back to Portland most evenings to be with them. Mitch is chatty and generous with himself and yet I find myself wanting to put some distance between us, almost by instinct. I fear if I'm not careful the other Adult Campers will lump us together, that we'll become the old, married guys. And so in a misguided effort to hide my wedding ring from view and thus take marriage off the conversational table, I hold my burrito with a contorted three-fingered grip that I believe is known colloquially as the Shocker.

"Remember when it was cool to have the bill of your hat folded?" Mitch asks.

And Jesus, while of course I remember, distinctly remember spending hours removing the mesh lining from my hats and working their bills into perfect upside-down parabolas that would, when worn as low as I wore them, give me a partial case of tunnel vision, I pretend I didn't hear the question. Two tables over I see Facundo and James are trying to put their fingers in each other's burrito, which I know I could play for an easy double entendre, maybe get a congratulatory dunch or a "Hey-oh!"

The most basic criticism I can level against Mitch is that he looks his age. And by that I mean to say he looks *our* age. He has a receding hairline that he's maturely accepted and his jeans are baggy in a midwestern way and he's wearing a predistressed polo shirt and business casual shoes. I am acutely aware of all the ways his appearance betrays his age because I've gone to pains to avoid outing myself likewise. In advance of camp I let my hair grow shaggier than I typically keep it, hoping some solid wings would extrude from the sides and back of my new trucker hat. I acquired my cache of T-shirts because at some point in time, likely during my frat phase, I'd become a collar guy and all the T-shirts I owned were used pretty much exclusively for running or trips to the gym and their pits were jaundiced and crusted up with precipitate of stank. I picked up two new pairs of shoes, one for skating and the other for an activity that in my head I was referring to as chillin', though I couldn't quite bring myself to say that out loud. When I came downstairs to leave for camp, wearing my "Research" shirt and new hunting-orange trucker hat, its brim left unmolested, and my new skating shoes, Alexis looked at me and said, "I don't even recognize you." And so proud was I of my transformation—of my resurrection, really—that I didn't stop to question whether this was indeed a good thing.

Mitch and I find acceptable common ground when we get on the topic of what we'd like to achieve at camp. In addition to the many waivers we had to sign before arriving, we had to fill out a piece of paper that asked us to list three goals for Session 2. I name a number of tricks that I'd like to get back, ones I used to land all the time. The 360-kickflip in particular—that'd been my favorite growing up.

"That's cool. I remember those," Mitch says. "Or a couple at least. What I'd really like to do is land a backflip." And just to look at him, I know he might as well have said he'd like to colonize Mars or make love on 1962 Catherine Deneuve. He talks about how he feels his time is running out and how he and his wife plan on having kids soon, at which point sayonara backflips while strapped to a pliable plank of wood. And though I understand this motivation deep in my bones, I don't offer word one of sympathy. I don't say that one of the main reasons I'm here is to get some footage of me doing my tricks because I want evidence for a posterity of my own. On a recent trip home, I searched the house my parents moved to after I graduated college, a large idyllic place in the central Virginia countryside with a view of the Blue Ridge Mountains, a house Mom designed and that now bears Dad's absence like a suppurating wound, looking for tapes I was sure I had of me skating when I was younger. In the upstairs closet, amid other family detritus, much of which I recognized from the hall closet in our old ranch house, I found a handful of familiar-looking VHS-C cartridges, those dwarfish cassettes. As a kid I used them over and over, trying to get the best stuff I could, turning the cartridges into late-modern palimpsests. As I watched them, I was disappointed to find that much of the footage was distorted, likely from overuse. A fuzzy bar played across the top or middle or bottom of the screen. Or odd, blurry boxes corrupted the picture, the inscrutable pixelation of scrambled XXX flicks. Even in the good footage, though, everything seemed to be happening slower than it should've been. But you could still get a handle on what was going on. And I was dismayed to find that I'm younger than I was when I was at my best and nowhere near as good as I remember myself being. The footage I was looking for, what I remember having seen and been proud of and ridiculously considered editing into a Sponsor Me video, was most likely shot with a friend's mom's camera. I haven't spoken to that friend in more than a decade and the cartridges I remember were probably cluttering up whatever closet his family used to store crap like that. I tried to convince myself of this, that there was good footage of me, that is, footage of me as good, somewhere, but still the movies I had were disconcerting. I started to doubt myself. Had I been as good as I remember myself being? Or had I embellished my skills? In the absence of ready evidence, and in the more regrettable absence of friends from that time to reminisce with, friends who could confirm or deny my talent, put things in perspective like a form of social autocorrect, had my memory and imagination colluded to make a myth of this part of my past? When I name the tricks I want to get back, do I sound like Mitch? Like I want to make love on 1962 Catherine Deneuve?

Sitting at the picnic table, I don't tell Mitch any of this, don't indulge these anxieties and self-doubt. I nod my head in polite approval of his ambition.

"But really I just want to have some fun without getting hurt too bad," he concludes.

And this is too much for me to hold back my sympathetic laughter. For my third goal on the questionnaire, I wrote "Not get hurt." Alexis, too, has been vocal about my being extra careful. We have a trip to Europe planned for later in the summer and if I am to break anything, she's said, it is to be an arm or a wrist. She's been having nightmares that involve me Tiny Timming around Paris or cruising the streets of Copenhagen on one of those knee scooters. After Mitch and I stop laughing and collect ourselves, he nods to my palsied burrito hand and says, "Hey, so how long you been married?"

VI.

It's dark by the time Maureen arrives at the Adult House. We're all playing pool and putzing around on our computers and half watching *Billy Madison* on TV. She takes a seat on the couch and introduces herself. Maureen goes by Mo. She has the laid-back good looks of skater and snowboarder chicks the world over. Long, thick auburn hair, a slim but not boyish body, a smile off a real estate bus bench, and a pert nose whose left nostril has a tiny, beacon-like stud in it. She's driven over ten hours to get here, all the way from Kalispell, Montana.

Now, the interaction that follows her introduction could've been ripped right out of some Italian movie. Or it's more like a hipster reenactment of a scene from an Italian movie, with all of us vying for her attention while trying desperately not to appear to be vying for her attention. Our excitement is muted, our flirtatious gestures made as though underwater. There's some restrained hot-dogging around the pool table. Sparrow, still wearing his sunglasses, peacocks a little by putting on some sensitive-sounding club music that he calls his "new jam," the vocals of which are so heavily mixed they sound like they've been crooned by animatronic parakeets. Facundo plays possum, looking up only now and then from his computer, a display of confidence that's as intimidating as it is charming.

When Mo gets up and grabs her gear, knowing I've taken the last open bedroom, I offer to move so that she might have her own space, one unsullied by a Y chromosome. This confuses her. She says not to worry about it, assures me it's cool, encourages me to stay. She smiles in a way that both confuses and intrigues me. Oodles of fetchingly crude scenarios irrupt in my mind before I insist on moving into the Yellow Room, where Pat has posted up.

For a good while there I hoped marriage would issue in a new order, one in which I'd be able to kick my reflexive habit, when I meet a woman, of conjuring extravagant libidinal *tableaux vivants*, these set pieces of bucknasty congress, full of Cirque du Soleil acrobatics and heroic feats of strength and stamina. I'd grown tired of them, of always rooting around these routine social situations for some scant trace of sexual tension. I thought that under the sway of a deeper love I'd be able to slough them off, trade them in for more productive fantasies, maybe ones that involved me changing my car's oil or learning to use a saber saw. And as I continue to wait for that change, just as a certain breed of religious folk continues to refine the date of the apocalypse, I've been forced to content myself with altered expectations. So instead I brim with chipper husbandly pride as I carry my clothes from one closet to the other, feeling like I've passed a test in resisting Mo's offer. Maybe on some level this is what marriage is about, this reification of our superegos. Are not spouses there to help us realize our best selves, after all? Or is this another damning manifestation of my self-centeredness? Has the nostalgia made me even more self-involved than I already was? Absurd as it is, I wish Alexis could've been there to witness my minor victory, to congratulate me, though of course I know her presence would've asterisked the win in a Heisenbergian way. Worse, I know that had she been present she wouldn't have seen the temptation resisted, as I did, but only the temptation itself, and that seems an unhusbandly emotional car wash to run her through.

Mo and I return to the lounge area where the other guys look at me like I've just handed away a winning lottery ticket.

En masse we make for B.O.B. Upon arrival, James plugs in his phone and as we spread out around the hangar, tunes of a distinct Jack Johnson mold pour out of speakers mounted high up on the walls. I run a few steps, dragging the tail of my board on the ground a little before jumping on, and cruise to the far end of the space, past manual pads and flat rails that sit on the ground like metal lizards, estivating under the industrial fluorescence. I ride up the six-foot quarter pipe and turn lazily at the top and head back toward where I came from.

Growing up, whenever I got to a spot, I'd first ride around like this, taking a lay of the land before starting to skate in earnest. This would open a part of the world to me. There'd be this phenomenological shift whereby everything at the spot became the pieces of a puzzle. A ledge, a curb, a sidewalk, a set of stairs, a handrail. What could I do with each one? How did they all fit together? Could I stitch them up with a run, a line? I know this might sound new-agey, like some strange urban pantheism, but to skate a spot is to commune with it in a way that your normal city dweller does not. It is to respond to and unlock that place, to be surrounded by potential. Possibilities. And often, the tricks I'd end up choosing to do at a spot weren't the product of my will alone. They seemed to emerge out of the terrain. In some mystical sense, some very peculiar form of entelechy, when you do a trick it's almost like you're giving the trick back to the spot, literally expressing it. I think this is more or less what people mean when you hear them talking about a skater's vision. The best skaters show us this hidden potential of the world around us. And this is a revelatory and poetic and radical action.

As I now stand on the large platform by the entrance, though, I feel as impaired as a man with cataracts. I hear Alexis's voice in my head and decide to take it easy tonight, not go for too much, nothing crazy, and head over to spend some time in the miniramps with Pat. He's doing proficient blunt stalls over the center spine and small frontside disasters and long fifty-fifties across the coping, but everything looks labored and is a little hard to watch. For me, skating is nothing without style, which is to say, in most cases, an air of effortlessness. Grace. It's been a part of skating's code since its inception: that you can do a trick has never mattered quite as much as how you look doing it. This is one of the first lessons about art I ever internalized, long before I knew I'd apply it to pursuits other than skateboarding: style is inextricable from content. One skater can be less technically accomplished than another and still be more interesting to watch.

I turn away from Pat and look up to find Facundo on one of the rectangular trampolines on the platform above me. He's jumping so high he can touch the ceiling, maybe nine or ten feet above. The springs sigh metallically each time he lands. Once he's reached peak height he launches away from the pad and does some crazy combination of spins and flips and lands in the pit of foam blocks. On the other trampoline Mitch is practicing his backflips, confirming the absurdity of his ambition—picture a lawn chaise being upended by a stiff wind and you will hold in your mind an image of his form. Mo has joined them. She hops on where Facundo has left off and simply jumps.

I watch. There's something mesmerizing about the way her long hair, cinched into a loose ponytail, hangs momentarily above her head as she comes down. It's like a charmed snake. At one point she drifts away from the trampoline's center square and lands awkwardly on the padded plywood that covers the springs. She swallows a small cry that maybe only I hear and steps off the trampoline and slides down to sit against the wall. Facundo takes her place on the trampoline and pumps himself higher and higher, loading up for another aerial whathaveyou. When Mo tries to get up, she cannot bear her weight and stumbles and catches herself against the wall. I hop up on the platform and help her down the steps.

"Fuck, fuck, fuck, fuck, fuck," she says.

James decides she should go to Urgent Care and skates off to get one of the camp's large vans. He leaves his phone behind, so the music continues to play loudly over the speakers. I help Mo hobble to a bench outside of B.O.B., where she lies back and props the ankle up on her knee and sobs. The sky is so full of stars it looks like freshly laid asphalt, and there's a *Twin Peaks* eeriness to the brooding outline of the woods on the edge of campus, where the dry slopes radiate a ghostly glow.

"It's broken. I know it's broken," she says. "I heard a pop."

Below the hem of her jeans, which have been rolled to her calf, is a globular mass, the size of something citrusy. Even if the ankle's not broken, her time here at skateboard camp is up, of that much I'm sure. In an effort to get her mind off the situation, I ask what else she has planned for the summer. She tells me that she recently broke up with her longtime boyfriend. She clarifies "longtime" by saying they'd been dating for thirteen years. I do the math: they've been together since seventh grade, when they were twelve. The list of life events they've been through together likely includes puberty. Other than my family, there's not one person still in my life that I've known that long.

"I was just really looking forward to spending some time away from him, from home," she says, and chokes back something different now, something more profound and nuanced than bodily pain or the simple fear that accompanies it. She breathes deep breaths that carry her off somewhere inside herself. A silence gathers between us like a long yawn. Whatever Mo's thinking about, I understand, involves an adjustment of her expectations, a reorientation of her relationship to her future. I feel close to her somehow, and try to imagine what this future of hers might entail, the particulars of her ex-boyfriend and their impossibly long relationship in Kalispell, Montana, with its enchanting, fairy-tale name, surrounded by a mountainous landscape like a castle's battlements. But I come up short. Her life there eludes me. Already I can feel this moment receding from us, bound for the back of both of our minds, taking with it the peculiar intimacy that has arisen here between us. And as we wait for James to arrive and as our eyes allow us to see more of the dark, I wonder whether she, too, can hear the muffled chill beach music from inside B.O.B., whether she, too, will remember it sounding like it was coming from someplace far away.

VII.

After breakfast the next morning the skaters are milling about outside the Hesh, waiting for the coach-counselors to bring the vans around. I'm not fully awake yet and go back for another cup of coffee. The kitchen and its crew operate under the watchful eye of Tom Inouye, a bona fide OG from the Dogtown days, who collective consciousness has it invented the wall-ride and was among the first people to skate a drained pool. Like, ever. He's in his midfifties now and still skates and his left arm is bent crooked, akimbo even at rest, from an injury I'm too bashful to ask about. I know it's ridiculous but in my mind I equate asking him about his arm to asking Jesus what up with his palms. Everyone here calls him "Wally" with the same jovial tone that the cast of *Cheers* said "Norm!" and he always has a smile on his face and his attitude is infectiously good and so I feel rather dickish when he walks by me with a tub of dirty plates and I start wondering about the retirement plans available to the pioneers of this sport. Wally and the other crew members are cleaning to Sublime's self-titled album and though I haven't heard it in years, I'm surprised to find I know almost all the words to the song that's on.

Back outside I stand near a huddle of the cooler-seeming teenagers but not so close that I'll appear too eager to stand with them. They have names like Boston and Scotland and I can't tell whether those are nicknames or what. Their hoodies are pulled up over their heads and their postures are almost competitively slouched.

As we load into the vans, I tell Jamie what's happened to Mo.

"Bummer," he says, and shakes his head. He holds eye contact to show he really means it and then makes a mark on his roster. "That's a bummer."

"I know, right?" I say, slipping back into speech patterns that had been freeze-dried inside me. "Bummer."

When we get back this afternoon, Mo will be gone. On my way out of the Adult House that morning, after all the other guys had loaded into the van and made for the mountain, she was sitting alone in the lounge area, her crutches leaning against the pool table. Her ex-boyfriend was coming to get her—her car's a stick and she needed someone to drive her home. In my bunk last night, as I stared at the slats above me, one of which bore a sticker that said I ♥ TRAMPS, I could hear her across the hall, making these plans, her voice a steady, smoky whisper. Pat was playing a first-person shooter on his computer and the tinny sound of small-arms fire chirruped from his headphones and his face was lit by the chaos on his screen and I know it wasn't me ripping the SBDs and I wondered how things would be playing out now had I taken Mo up on her offer to stay. No grand visions of funny business this time, but the mild intimacy of a late-night heart-to-heart, that weird honesty that can arise between relative strangers. The ex-boyfriend was on a flight that left before six this morning and was taking a cab from the airport. I have not and likely won't ever meet this guy, yet I feel like he's managed to teach me something about commitment by example. Because if that's not one husband-ass move he's pulling for her, I don't know what is.

"Well, have a safe trip home," I said, and waved a wave I immediately regretted. I held my hand out straight and made a so-so motion and waggled my fingers as though I were playing air piano. It was Dad's wave, emerged from somewhere inside me.

"Yeah, thanks. Have a fun week, I guess," she said. "A nice life." And her flippancy sent a shiver of sadness and loneliness through me. I understood in that moment that I would, in fact, be the only adult at skateboard camp this week. Only the sadness and loneliness were too rich to be explained away by that alone.

The day's park is about an hour away. When we arrive, we pour out of the vans and make for a large concrete area sitting like a mirage in the middle of a field. When I was growing up, I rarely ever went to parks. There weren't many around, first off, and those we had certainly weren't as well appointed as the area I'm standing on the edge of. The terrain here is expansive and impressively variegated, a muckle of possibilities. There's a large wall of a quarter-pipe at one end and at the other are the bowls, one of which even has some vert. In the space between them are wax-darkened ledges of the sort my friends and I used to search Richmond high and wide for. Step-ups and boxes and little hips. Sets of stairs to nowhere and their concomitant handrails, which are perfect, low and mellow and smooth. It's a dream of a place and my cohort is eager to explore it. As they push off, a few of them emit little squeals of delight. I try to recall the last time I squealed likewise but draw a blank.

I wait a moment and watch the others. There's an unspoken

hypothesis among skaters, at least there was when I was younger, that you can gauge how good a person is by how he pushes, how he simply rides. This most rudimentary action says something about one's general comportment to the craft and can reveal talent of a deeper sort. If this hypothesis holds, I'm happy to discover that the situation isn't as bad as I'd feared: I will not be the worst skater at Session 2. A few guys use their front foot to push, which is called mongo footing and is amateurish and clumsy and looks like a move from the hokey pokey. Many of the younger kids hunch over their boards and employ a frenetic stomping motion, as though the ground were on fire or covered in bugs. Then there are the counselors and the cooler-seeming teenagers, whose feet barely seem to touch the ground, whose long, pendular strides suggest gravity's gone slack. Their motions are so fluid that the board more or less disappears underneath them as they cruise through the different areas of the park.

I drop my backpack at a picnic table on the concrete's edge and join them.

VIII.

And it's here that I start to fear a breakdown in communication. I'd like to write what I'm up to out there but know that doing so would obscure more than it would explain. Because in order to talk about skateboarding in any meaningful way one has to use its language, and if you don't know this language, then encountering it here will be like eavesdropping on a conversation between lovers in a foreign country. This is the maddening and deeply alienating experience I have when I watch, say, ice-skating on TV. I'll sit and listen as the announcers say the names of different jumps, but the jumps themselves look *exactly the same*. Without the language to appreciate it, I watch ice-skating as though through a veil, in a state of mildly awed boredom, shamefully hoping the skaters will fall, because, ironically, it's only when they fall that I can appreciate how hard the jump is. I'm sure this is what happens when non-skateboarders flip on the X Games or Street League series and see a cluster of bros waiting to take their turn leaping down a set of stairs to nowhere or flinging themselves skyward from a huge wooden U. And I think this points to the magical poetic naming power all languages share: to learn to say something is to learn to see it.

To wit: skateboarding's language is a concrete poetry of action, in which all the nouns are also verbs. There's no distance between the thing said and the thing intended, no connotative flimflam. You do a kickflip, you kickflip, and vice versa. Its grammar is radically aware of one's orientation, both with respect to the board, on which your stance can be regular, switch, nollie, or fakie, and to the world, in that tricks and obstacles are either frontside or backside. And while some tricks have special names, most are formed from simpler component tricks. After the ollie, you have the 180s and shove-its and kickflips and heelflips. You stack these together like atoms to create a new trick. So a backside 180 kickflip is a backside 180 and a kickflip, a varial heelflip is a frontside shove-it with a heelflip. Because the tricks can quickly grow cumbersome to say, you get the slangy shorthand that non-skaters often make fun of with a stonery drawl. Backside flip, varial heel, tre-flip, front heel, etcetera, etc., &c. As a general rule, the more tricks you stack together, the more "technical" they are, the more difficult they are to pull off. And when you start adding manuals and grinds to the mix, you can end up with a concatenation of words worthy of the German Idealists: hardflip-to-backside-nosegrind-to-nose-manual-to-nollie-backside-180-flip-out.

Half the fun of watching skateboard videos growing up was naming the tricks the pros had done, letting the language catch up to what we'd just seen, or, as was the case when you watched a true genius like Rodney Mullen, the quasi-mystical experience of not yet having the words to name what'd played on-screen. Skateboarders are hyper-aware of this language, too, because while simple and strictly denotative, the language has some wrinkles that novitiates don't want to get wrong. E.g., there's no such thing as switch nollie or an inward kickflip and while a nollie halfcab would convey the trick you've done, saying it that way will get you laughed at—skateboarders have no truck, as it were, with descriptivism. This language barrier, a shibboleth of sorts, is one of the prevailing reasons why the sport or art or life-style or whatever you want to call it (a spart?) has been able to retain its aura of edginess while having been so widely accepted as a part of the culture at large.

And this language was one of the things that first attracted me to skateboarding in the early to midnineties, when it was on the rise and going through an adolescence of its own, moving away from vert ramps and toward the street skating we recognize as the dominant form of the spart today. The language seemed a strange code, a jumbled signal I felt I heard louder than other kids because I thought cracking it would unlock the safe that held a better, more authentic version of myself, an identity I could live with. Before I started skating I'd dreamed of being a professional athlete. But throughout middle school I was cut, over and over, from the basketball, soccer, football, and tennis teams. I can still summon the tearful shame and existential terror of running my finger down the rosters posted on the brick wall outside the Tuckahoe Middle School gym, the sky gone to gloaming and Mom or Dad sitting in the car around the corner, and reading name after name of kids who were not me. It should go without saying that there were consequences to being so roundly rejected. At a time when confidence is a hard commodity to come by, when identity is a particularly fluid and vexing problem, not making these teams seemed to ratify all my self-doubt, to confirm my pervasive feelings of worthlessness. It was in skateboarding, then, that I found a whole new way to engage with the world, an identity to slip on like a suit of armor, one that would transform me, *Mask*-like, from the outside in. Most important, though, skating opened an avenue for me to imagine myself into the future. I was going to be a pro skateboarder.

As I improved, the language nourished this illusion that my identity could be mastered or resolved. The way I understood it, I was no more or less than the tricks I could do. They were like the axioms of a personal *tractatus*. To learn a new trick was to broaden your ability to express yourself and, therefore, increase the ease with which you moved through the world. And I obsessed over them, over learning new ones, worked on them for hours a day. If I couldn't skate with friends, I practiced on the brick walkway in front of our house. If it was raining, I practiced in our carpeted basement, where I occasionally knocked the fiberglass panels of our drop ceiling out of joint as my hands rose above my head for balance. I know I once used an old tabletop as a ramp down there but, given the restricted space, cannot remember or fathom how that worked. To this day, hour-wise, I still don't think I've done anything as much as I've skateboarded. And I don't mean this to sound boastful, but Dad's right. I was good, had talent. Probably tops in my school and among the best in the area of Richmond where I grew up. I didn't do the biggest gaps or rails or stairs, but I could do more tricks than most kids and had "style." In seventh and eighth grade, when someone found out you skated, their first question was typically, "What tricks can you do?" And I remember answering by naming every single one I had down, including the stance, so that many tricks became quartets, even octets (shove-it, fakie, switch, nollie shove-it, frontside, fakie frontside, switch frontside, nollie frontside shove-it, *ad absurdum*), feeling a sick and demented but overwhelming pride in this list, which acted like a force field as it filled the space between me and whoever had asked the question. And later, in high school, at my remembered best, I would take to the blacktop at Tuckahoe Elementary while a crew of kids thirty or forty deep sat by and watched me lay down a run, feeling in such moments like there were no limits to who I could be. Behold the man, bitches. Ecce fucking homo.

IX.

What I'm trying to do on the concrete, then, is rebuild my vocabulary, to get back the words of a language in which I was once fluent. For the first hour or so, I chip away at the basics, my 180s and shove-its. It's not long before I find I can do a few fakie and nollie and switch. While I'm working on these, one of the younger kids rides up to me and asks whether he can eat his lunch now. It's ten thirty in the morning. He's maybe eight years old. When I tell him I'm not a counselor, but a camper, too, like him, he rides off haughtily. I move on and do some short noseslides on a modest ledge, but one I have to ollie into nonetheless. A measure of the old wonder comes back as memory pulls these tricks up from inside me with the ecstatic surge of remembering a word that was on the tip of my tongue. My feet know precisely where to go, what to do. The board conforms to my wishes for it. But how? In what basement or attic of my self had this fugitive knowledge hidden? Pride of a sort I haven't experienced in years floods through me. I do backside 180s and switch frontside 180s in quick succession and I must look like a ballet dancer gone loopy on the pirouette but I'm too enthralled to think about what I might look like. Why had I ever stopped? Wouldn't my life be more fulfilling had I stuck with it? Less confusing? The harder tricks will return, I'm sure. With a little time and work I'll find everything I came to camp looking for. I imagine myself as some late-modern Odysseus, out to prove myself in order to be welcomed home.

Sometime before noon I get my kickflips back. The first of them flip under my feet like a dog rolling over. Clumsily, inexpertly. But soon I'm popping them off the ground and catching them in the air, landing on the bolts and riding along as though nothing happened. There are exceptions that prove the rule but I think this might be the truest measure of style in skateboarding, when a trick is performed so smoothly that when it's landed it seems like nothing happened. Like a shooting star, it's alive only in the minds of those people who witnessed it, who continue to witness it when they tell others about it later.

I break for lunch then and sit at a table with three younger campers and eat my sandwich. While I do, I pull out the Nietzsche and read, trying to track and parse Zarathustra's speechifying over the chatter of the three kids and the park's noise. It sounds like a construction site, what with the constant hammering of all the boards on the concrete and the clunk and sputter of missed tricks and the rock-tumbler churn of the grinds. More than anything else I ever listened to, any hardcore or emo or hip-hop, this is the music of my youth. After lunch I start going for tricks that are a little more technical. A few times I land on the board and it shoots out from under my feet and my stomach drops and fear flashes through me. Then I have to go running after it like I've seen fathers at the park hurry after their truant toddlers. After one such instance, my board rolls into the grass off the far edge of the park. I retrieve it and stand there a second, collecting myself.

I watch two of the better kids, Boston and Christian, launching from a concrete ramp. They're clearing a gap with harder tricks than I'm trying, and with maybe three or four feet of air. The camp's videographer keeps changing his angle, crouching low to ensure the tricks look as big as possible. We've been told that they'll make an edit of this footage later and post it to the Windells site. There it will serve as both a keepsake, for campers to remember what they did during their time here, and as an advertisement, for potential campers to get a feel for what goes on at Windells. After the videographer gets into his crouch, Boston pushes off and gathers speed and heads up the ramp. At the top he does a hardflip—imagine the board doing a gainer—that travels between his scissored legs so perfectly it seems to happen in slow motion. As he floats through the air he looks like a deft puppeteer, his arms Karate Kidded above his head, the board flipping as though controlled by strings. It breaks my heart a little, witnessing this, but not because I envy his skill or youth or anything like that. It breaks my heart in a purer way, in the way certain sentences or poems or paintings can break my heart; it seems to satisfy a craving in me that I didn't know existed before I saw it. It wounds and heals me at once. It is, simply, beautiful. His feet catch the board as it flattens out underneath him and he lands lightly even as his body gives a little with the impact and he rides off like nothing to see here.

"Fuck yeah," the videographer says after Boston's out of the frame. He runs over and gives him a high five and those of us who saw it knock our boards against the ground, clacking out "Sick!"s and "Tight!"s and "Dope!"s as though we were sending them by telegraph. Then the two of them huddle over the camera's small screen. The videographer shields it from the sun in a way that looks like he's maybe trying to warm his hand by its weak light. And as they watch the footage of the hardflip together, all the air whoopee cushions out of the moment for me.

I'm tempted to espouse an atavistic belief here and say that some portion of the hardflip's beauty is diminished by it having been recorded. Captured on camera, it has already become just another hardflip. There's no time for the trick to chafe against language, to spread around the park, or beyond, and achieve a certain mythic status, as tricks could and did when I was younger. You'd hear that so-and-so had kickflipped over the five-stair rail at Tuckahoe Elementary or finally stuck an ollie down the huge ten-set in back or 360-flipped the six-set at the Church and reports like this would live in your imagination with a potency that video evidence can't touch. These tricks would become part of the lore of that spot, part of its history. "Heard melodies are sweet but those unheard are sweeter," Keats famously wrote, and likewise some of the best tricks I ever witnessed were ones I never saw. And this is how kids I grew up skating with continue to live on in my mind alongside the Gonz and Rodney Mullen and other skate legends, how the spots we skated still retain their charge, why they continue to show up in my dreams all these years later. Boston's hardflip was good, in other words, but there on film it can't ever become something maybe ever-so-slightly *more*.

It's more complicated than that, though, what's happening here.

Now that every smartphone has a built-in video camera, for which you can buy fisheye lenses, and now that practically every crew of skaters has at least one GoPro (those small, rugged handheld cameras), it seems like every trick gets recorded. And there's no question that ready access to creating these clips and sharing them online has revolutionized the way skaters interact. Given how deeply time-bound an art form it is, skating has probably benefited from developments in digital technology as much as, if not more than, any other subculture, aside from maybe porn. The most popular sites, like TransWorld and Thrasher and the Berrics and Hellaclips, post fresh content a few times a day. Then of course there's the labyrinth of YouTube and skaters' Instagram accounts, which are all full of clips, mostly shot at their local skateparks. And while on the whole this technology is probably a good thing—one could even argue that skating couldn't have progressed as quickly as it has without it—I'm still deeply ambivalent about it. I don't believe it's unimpeachably good. If a company has to post more and more clips to stay relevant and alive, I worry, isn't the skating itself in danger of becoming just another form of advertising? "Content"? Maybe not. Maybe I'm being oversensitive and geezerish. Nostalgic.

This wouldn't be a question or problem at all had skateboarding's relationship to the market not always been riddled with tensions. There's a long and knotty history here, one that goes back to the late seventies and early eighties, to Fausto Vitello and Stacy Peralta and Craig Stecyk, et al., and their somewhat contradictory goal of wanting to popularize skateboarding while also maintaining its antiestablishment and anarchic aura. They're the guys who came up with the slogan "Skate and Destroy." What this history boils down to is that the spart doesn't cotton all that well to the notion of a bottom line. You'll very rarely hear the owners of skateboarding companies talk openly or directly about the products they sell, for example. (After a couple frenzied periods of innovation, the products themselves, the durable goods, have become more or less standardized, and what innovation still goes on is often gimmicky. Soft goods like clothes and shoes, of course, follow the logic of fashion.) Instead, they'll promote their team, the skaters they've "sponsored."

I think this misdirection has everything to do with the fact that skating is founded on a rigorous notion of authenticity. Applied here, authenticity means something like putting your body on the line in order to reveal and enact beauty, to say something truthful in the language of skateboarding. It means prioritizing actual skating over all other cultural noise, perhaps most of all the noise that surrounds the skateboarding industry. (Think of the spart's heightened sensitivity to posers, who pull on the accessories of its culture—that is, the products skateboarding companies sell—and act as though they were one of the tribe.) By dint of the transitive property, then, a company is only as authentic as the skaters who ride for them. And in focusing on their team, by celebrating the skating it has made possible, a company can deflect or mask its need to sell products—without doing any research on this, I'd bet that shoes and clothing and other soft goods sell more than any skate-specific hardware, and, furthermore, my guess would be that a good chunk of these sales, especially as skating continues to enjoy more and more acceptance by the culture at large, are to people who don't skate, who admire the "skater" look and lifestyle, which is to say, posers. In this arrangement, the skaters themselves don't have to feel like they've whored themselves out, because all they're doing is skating, being real, living the dream. It's like that little bit of cognitive dissonance that allows you to live with yourself.

This comes down to the fact that skateboarding, at bottom, is a symbolic form of protest, a way of saying no while making it sound like a resounding and joyous yes. "Skaters by their very nature are urban guerrillas," Stecyk wrote. "They make everyday use of the useless artifacts of the technological burden, and employ the handiwork of the government/corporate structure in a thousand ways that the original architects could never dream of." Here Stecyk is echoing the radical political philosophy that came out of the Lettrist and Situationist movements in France in the fifties and sixties, strands of which philosophy have Plinkoed through time to inspire, among other things, the punk movement. Behind the impressive thinking (and drinking) of folks like Guy Debord and Raoul Vaneigem, the Situationists were looking for ways to live freer, more authentic everyday lives, ones that promoted creative intuition and passion and a sense of play, in the Nietzschean and capital-*R* Romantic sense of that word, and that were not so indebted to and controlled by capitalism and the mass media, what they called "the spectacle."

That's a drastically simplified précis, but here's roughly what I think they mean: summer nights growing up, my friends and I would sometimes skate at a branch of a national bank in downtown Richmond. It had these perfect knee-high marble benches out front that you could thread together with runs. The air would be balmy and electric, alive with an ambient rebellious power. Turn your nose the right way and you might catch a whiff of significance as we threw down our tailslides and crooked grinds and 5-os, a meaning whetted by danger, by the possibility of coming face-to-face with the human representatives of the power we were protesting, the "authorities," building security or the actual cops.

In this way, skating can be said to complicate one's relationship to the notions of property and ownership. It asks questions, probes. It's the performance art equivalent of graffiti. If someone had a particularly good session at the financial institutions and schools and corporations we skated, we'd say, "You owned it." Through vision and an execution of it, that spot was yours. I don't think I'm being idealistic or too Pollyannaish when I say that, in its purest form, skateboarding isn't only subcultural, it's countercultural.

So call me a pessimist or an alarmist or a theory monger, but watching Boston watch his hardflip right after he lands it feeds all my suspicions that the spectacle has fully infiltrated skateboarding.

There's another wrinkle here, because videos have played an important and integral role in skateboarding from the get-go. My friends and I treated one's release like it was a dispatch from the front lines, like it contained vital news about our comrades in arms. There was an easy balance at work here, though, because of how long they took to produce and distribute. They were able to serve as a company's chief marketing strategy and still exist as messages to be studied, communiqués. And we shared them like samizdat, which allowed us to nurture that special sense of belonging reserved for the excluded or exiled. They had a decidedly amateur or DIY aura that lent them a flavor of authenticity, an aura that was, for the most part, lacking in the videos I was watching online. Most of these new videos existed in the hyperreality of high definition and had adopted the pace and glam of music videos. And to watch them you first had to sit through short commercials, which seemed to set a contextual tone for everything that followed. Furthermore, most of these videos had been shot in skateparks, places where local governments have sanctioned skateboarding. If you think about it, skateparks aren't that different from reservations, a lame offering of appeasement. What's for sure is that a skatepark can never be a spot. A spot, like a person or an idea, bears its history into the future—so we can talk about Tom Penny's frontside flip at the Carlsbad Gap or Eric Koston's backside noseblunt at Hubba Hideout and for some of us that calls to mind a collective cultural memory, a form of belonging in time, of placing oneself in history. Anything can happen at a skatepark, it doesn't matter. Because skating a skatepark doesn't require vision, at least not vision of a sort that *means*—everything there was built to be skated. It's like fat-free treats or e-cigarettes or climbing a rock wall in some suburban gym: a form of the original stripped of what made it dangerous and indulgent and so worth doing in the first place. A recent contest I watched on TV featured an exact replica of Hubba Hideout, which when it was torn down in 2011 inspired an outpouring online of what can only be described as grief. Grief as real and as poignant as if a person had died. Same thing happened when they closed the Brooklyn banks and tore down the Carlsbad Gap. For a while some fellow nostalgist from Richmond ran a Facebook page for Tuckahoe Elementary School, whose blacktop had been annexed by auxiliary classrooms. The Hubba Hideout replica, then, was like a tombstone: it honored what was gone, sure, but it also confirmed it as dead.

With that all said, I'm ashamed to admit that after my short time out on the concrete, I'm also secretly hoping that I'll get good enough this week to earn a few meager seconds of footage in the promotional video. Maybe do a little run, string three or four tricks together through a park's terrain. I imagine watching a screen in the not-so-distant future, progeny in my lap, and saying, "Yes, young son and/or daughter Knapp, apple(s) of my eye, product(s) of my loins, that is Daddy. Daddy did do that. Isn't it fucking dope?" I guess I also have to admit that I've been harboring an irrational Lamarckian hope here: not only do I want them to witness me doing these tricks, I want to pass them down. Though I know better, I don't yet believe that I can't. And if not the tricks themselves, then some measure of authenticity I take them to represent. As I stand there mooning over all this, disturbed by the damning narcissism this line of thought ends in, thinking I may be no different than Dad trying to triangulate his nostalgia and might actually be worse, Jamie rides up. He's been taking it easy today, not skating too much, riding around helping some of the younger kids.

"What are you doing here?" he asks, only emphasizing the "here," and not the "you," so I know he's not trying to be snide. I know I have, in part, paid him for this solicitude, but it feels genuine nonetheless, like it comes from Jamie's abiding love for skateboarding.

"Fakie frontside flips," I say.

"Sick! I love that trick. Let me know if you need any help."

And as he rides off to help other campers, I understand the inadequacy of my response—I know I've only partially answered his question.

X.

Because but really, what am I doing here? While I know Jamie didn't mean it to, his question pops something of a bubble in me. It calls back that agenbite of inwit, the stab of self-consciousness. When I signed up for camp, I believed that this little bit of adventure tourism would prove abreactive. Confronting what had been making me nostalgic would help me shore up my shaky sense of self, clarify my relationship to my past, and, in so doing, help me lean into the future as if it were a headwind. Of all the identities I've ever assumed— basketball-tennis-soccer kid, lax bro, son, brother, Christian, emotard, Virginian, frat boy, poet (briefly), lover (often *very* briefly), editor, husband, writer, etc.—that of skater said the most about me. By that I think I mean that it created the least amount of dissonance between how other people knew me and how I knew myself. Call me naive or fatuous but I wanted a taste of that simplicity again. To cut through my life's noise and live more authentically. Except as the heady thrill of meeting a few new people and getting some tricks back wears off, the specter of irreality I was trying to escape begins to edge back in, to stalk the back alleys of my brain like the noirish and ghostly clouds of fog you find pouring from city manholes. The possibilities for the week begin to settle into the reality of it and I grow less and less sure of myself as it wears on. And this lends to the rest of my time at Session 2 the experiential quality of my nostalgia, that is, the aqueous wash of dreams.

Routine takes swift and firm hold of our days, blurring them into a running stock ticker of experience. In the morning, James barges into our rooms to wake us, a deranged muezzin, heavy metal playing at full blast in the lounge. This is meant to amp us up, I know, to get us stoked for the day ahead, but I find it much darker and more menacing than that. I am generally so sore upon waking that my body feels alien to me. My back and quads sing out like rusty hinges. And my groin—it's like I've given birth in the night. I take ibuprofen and apply liberal palmfuls of IcyHot jelly and yet still I have to take little Andre Agassi steps to avoid the pain. Every morning I'm convinced the other campers figure me for the source of the mentholated cloud hovering in the Hesh.

At brekkie one morning, I find the table of adults full and take a seat at an empty four-top whose red-checkered vinyl tablecloth is sticky and flecked with other campers' fugitive food. Three kids promptly join me. They're maybe seven or eight years old and each presents an adorable sleepy mien. Their hair is mussed into cute cowlicks. Crusty patches of dried drool spot their cheeks like wadis. Their feet dangle from the chairs and I almost encourage them to remember how that feels. One of them props himself up on his elbows and sits on his knees. This is something, I think. But what, I don't know. Maybe it's an amuse-bouche of fatherly delights to come, part of some as-yet-inscrutable typology of my life. Will I one day take a like and simple pleasure in the residue of sleep on the faces of my wee tykes? Did Dad delight in such residues when my brothers and I were wee, when we were all a we? After a moment a fourth kid appears at the table's side, by my chair. His face is a command phrased as a question and I understand he's shaking me down. "Oh, did you want to sit here?" I ask, and he nods his head, slowly, yes. And although this fourth kid is the least cute of the bunch, his hair a shade of blond that time will surely turn dark, I laugh and give up my seat and finish my powder eggs and Cheerios standing by the bus tub Wally will gather later.

Because of the soreness, I tend to take a pass on the day's first skatepark and spend my a.m. time on the sidelines, alternately watching the others and reading. "Are you a man *entitled* to wish for a child? Are you the victorious one, the self-conqueror, the commander of your senses, the master of your virtues? This I ask you. Or is it the animal and need that speak out of your wish? Or loneliness? Or lack of peace with yourself?" Most of the teens skate with earbuds in, listening to music, sealed off in their private worlds. If we'd had the option, I'm sure my friends and I would've done the same when we were growing up, but we didn't, which qualifies me to judge this as a lesser way of engaging with the spart. It cheats the communal aspect of skateboarding. Why not bring a boom box? Have everyone listen to the same tunes? But what it practically amounts to is that I'm really only able to get any social traction with Jamie. I sit shotgun as he ferries us from campus to park to park and back again. Our conversations build upon one another, the next broader and deeper than the last, and it comes to seem like an organic thing is emerging between us, a fragile little shoot of a friendship maybe.

By day two the olfactory situation in the Yellow Room is positively fugged up. So quickly does it achieve peak dankness that I'm convinced it must live in the walls in some diluted form, a spider cell of noxiousness, years of fart-stink and foot-stink and behind-the-ears-on-a-hot-day stink waiting to be released or activated by some sympathetic agent. One evening early on Pat enters limping, an ice pack wrapped around his right knee. After it becomes clear he's not going to offer up any information gratis, I ask what happened. He says he tweaked it that afternoon on his way to winning the camp-wide rail jam and that he's going to get it checked out in the morning. There hangs about Pat that modality of loneliness peculiar to late teens, an air of mild dejection and confusion that makes you want to care for them in exactly the sorts of ways they'd resent. I come to think of him as a representative of my younger self, a Scrooge-like vision of Cheston Past. Maybe he is here to help me learn to accept and even love those parts of myself that I've been trying so hard to annihilate. It comes out that this is not Pat's first time at Windells. It's not his second, either, but his third. His first two trips were cut short by injuries. Last year, right after orientation, but two hours into the first day, he took a hard fall while dicking around on the Ranch and broke a leg.

"Those dry slopes are gnarly," he says with the affectless air of a stoic. "I mean it. They'll fuck you up."

"This place is snakebit for you," I say.

"I guess," he says. "We read some of that for school," he adds, pointing to my book.

I clam up.

Is this what's commonly referred to as a "teaching moment"? Should I be giving him some pointers, other philosophers to read? He's read more Nietzsche than I had at his age, after all. In my Christian days, I would've referred to this as witnessing. "Have you heard about this pretty tight philosopher named Camus? Nothing's sicker than *The Plague*." But the silence goes on too long for me to say anything else and if there has been a moment here, I miss it. He pulls out his computer and puts on headphones that soon begin their noise-canceling tintinnabulation. By the time I return to campus the next afternoon, he is gone. Thrice booted early from this cursed place.

After dodgeball, our nights in the lounge area take on the texture of time-lapse footage. People switch positions on the couches or stand to play pool or leave to piss or get another drink. It's been so long since I've hung out in quite this way that I often wonder whether I'm doing it right.

"Who brought the Cheez-Its?" Mitch asks the one night he stays in the house. Thanks to a miscue on my part, we're sitting next to each other on the couch.

"That was me," I say, a little bashfully. I've been secretly hoping Facundo or James would be the first to remark upon the booty I've brought.

Sparrow introduces the house to booty of a different sort, a new dating app called Tinder. When housebound, Sparrow is more or less always shirtless. Following the arc of his rib cage is the word "Nesta," which a quick search, refined for relevance, tells me was Bob Marley's real first name. It means "messenger." In the flats below the Jockey's Ridges of his obliques, he has tattoos of the Volcom diamond. To clarify, there is one on either side. Two Volcom diamond tattoos. The genius of the app, so far as I can discern from his description, is that it adopts the compulsive fuckability-indexing of Hot or Not and makes it actionable. In preparation for Thursday's night out in Portland, Sparrow has set the radar's range to max and established connections with over fifty girls. How has he managed to write so many messages? Easy. He's written one flirty note and copied and pasted it to every single girl like it's some heat-seeking missile. We're all a little awed by this. I'm overcome with a combination of respect and revulsion. The self-assured grin on his face says it all: "Don't hate the player, hate the game."

Mitch turns to me and shares an app he likes and finds useful. Maybe I'll like it and find it useful, too? It organizes your grocery shopping.

"See, your wife can put something in on the computer

or her phone and you see that here," he says. He indicates a checklist on his screen. The first item is "Nausea Pops" and I quickly avert my eyes, wishing I could unsee that, and try to change the subject.

The night we're ousted from the dodgeball tournament by a cabin of teenagers, we watch a documentary called *Bones Brigade: An Autobiography*. It's about the eponymous skate team, history's most famous—Tommy Guerrero, Mike McGill, Lance Mountain, Steve Caballero, Rodney Mullen, and, of course, Tony Hawk. Directed by Stacy Peralta, the team's manager (and he's superkeen on reminding you of that), the movie is gooey thick with nostalgia and unabashedly so. As the story of the team's dissolution approaches, some of the skaters start wiping tears from their eyes. Lance Mountain up and weeps. And despite Peralta's self-aggrandizing and smarmy direction, this is enough to sink a fellow nostalgist. I excuse myself to the kitchen under the auspices of getting another beer. I cool myself in the open fridge and try to stifle my tears, chiding myself for being such a big softie.

Wednesday morning Jamie shows up outside the Hesh, limping. After yesterday's session, he woke up with such terrible pain in his feet that he's going to see a doctor.

"It's a bummer," he says. "But I'll be all right. Rip it up today!"

Without him there, I'm bumped to the back of the van. We're going to a park over the mountain. I've made a judgment call and have not told the two coach-counselors that I sometimes get carsick. They play Black Sabbath and The Cramps so loud that even the teenagers behind me start to complain. "Can you turn it down a little?" they ask. "I can't hear my music through my headphones," one says. They either don't hear them or else act like they don't—either way the music stays. It starts to feel like it's coming from under my skin, peeling me away from myself from the inside out. When we finally arrive at the park I'm dizzy and my proprioception is off in such a way that my body feels like it was drawn by a five-year-old. I ride around the park, trying to warm up my legs, fully convinced that the week has conspired to isolate me, that it has systematically removed the people I could talk to and therefore forced me to talk only to myself. I start to think that maybe the punctuation on the Windells sign isn't wrong after all. Maybe this is the quote-unquote funnest place on earth.

XI.

Rain Thursday disrupts the routine. The sky's tenebrous and spooky ectoplasmic clouds are caught in the trees behind campus. Highway 26 appears to be boiling. Scuttlebutt at breakfast among the winter-garbed is that the mountain's a mess. The slope cams relay shrouded views and you can't see shit. Jamie is on crutches—doctor says it's bone spurs, that he'll need surgery to fix them. There won't be any skating today, either, he says. It's raining the state over—on Doppler radar, Oregon looks like it's been colonized by moss. Camp has contingency plans in place for situations like this, though, and I return to the Adult House to help decide on ours.

We sit around the lounge and enact an experiment in true

democracy. Options are presented, pros and cons debated. We vote. In the end, votes for the indoor water park in McMinnville come out six to one. James says we'll head right into Portland from there, so we should be packing for the night, too.

Eighty-five percent of our crew is practically agog, while I, the remaining fifteen percent, am hesitant, a little skeptical. I get to wondering whether my suspicion of fun has been learned, a leeriness adopted as a defense mechanism against a culture in which those people who seem to be having the most fun are the same people who are always trying to sell me some version of it; or whether, as I've feared since I learned the word, I actually suffer from anhedonia, which is the inability to find pleasure in typically pleasurable things. This is a thought that keeps me up nights. Am I an incorrigible fussbudget? A chronic fuddy-duddy? Is my blanket henceforth doomed to remain wet? Regardless, the people have spoken, a plan is in place, and I will fall in line. As I choose which of my remaining clean T-shirts to stuff in my backpack, a new smell wafts in through the Yellow Room's open window: the rich oleaginousness of some choice domestic doja. It's ten o'clock in the morning. The day brims with promise.

McMinnville's an hour and a half away and I sit shotgun up by James. He's texted with Mitch, who didn't come out to campus because of the weather. He's decided to spend the day with his wife and her family.

"I think he feels too old for the water park," James says.

"His loss," I say, following what I intuit to be the script.

There's a cooler tucked in the space behind the front seats. It holds energy drinks and beers and Four Lokos, a soon-to-be-illegal energy drink–cum–malt beverage that is the crew's a.m. potation of choice. Two other counselors have also joined us, off-duty because of the rain, and there is much sportive jesting during the drive about the possibilities for the night. With each passing day, Sparrow has refined his campaign on Tinder, fishing the considerable pond of girls he's connected with, trying to suss out whether there is actual intent behind their flirting. He, of course, is one big walking intention. Facundo has borrowed my phone to text with a girl he met at a music festival and who lives in Portland. He is tight-lipped and bashful about their history together in a way I find winning, particularly juxtaposed with Sparrow's carpet bombing. I know I probably shouldn't, but I secretly read all their texts anyway and as we pass my phone back and forth I start to feel like the Cyrano de Bergerac of the Information Age. Wednesday night Facundo writes,

> "Hey Kate! I'm Chino . . . tomorrow with the crew of Windells we are going to eat some sushi and hit some bars at Portland, may be we can meet somewhere, that's ok? Text me to this number."

Chino? Had I missed something? Had he, like me in my Gap days, once been a khaki maven? When he has not heard back by morning, he writes,

> "Kate it's chino again, when you read this message text me here or Facebook, we should meet tonight at downtown Portland."

As we pull off the highway in McMinnville, she texts back asking for our plans.

"We are going first to the us store, at 8 we have reservations at the sushi. 11 we are going to the area of voodoo doughnuts to hit some bars for 25 minutes and then to casa diablo."

She works late but will try to meet us. They promise to keep in touch via text. Facundo tries to hide his smile. And even my heart sets to pitter-pattering a tad.

Deeper into primo Oregon wine country and rain's off in the distance in every direction, but here the sun is out and seems bound to the earth by diaphanous ribbons of light fragile as haikus. We pass estimable travel-brochure views of the vineyards, rows and rows of vines laid out like a maze for the mentally infirm. Around a bend and we spot the water park. You can't miss it. Evergreen Wings & Waves shares a plot with the Evergreen Aviation & Space Museum, whose collection includes, most famously, the Spruce Goose, Howard Hughes's mammoth wooden airplane. Does this not typify America? I wonder as we pull up. This nostalgia for the colossal failures of our hyperrich? This memorializing of pure ambition? The water park itself has been made to fit the museum's aeronautical theme. Perched on the roof and incorporated into the structure of the building is a 747. Not a replica or model, but an actual plane, a plane that once actually flew. The cabin has been gutted and retrofitted with four tubular and tentacular slides: "Sonic Boom," "Tail Spin,"

"Nose Dive," and "Mach 1." This I know from the website I looked up on my phone when curiosity overcame me and I wanted a better sense of what I'd gotten myself into.

We park and the guys finish what's left of their second or third Lokos and we collect our gear. Before we get to the entrance, we seem to pass through a permeable membrane of chlorine, an ammoniac field that only intensifies inside and that recalls the summer days I spent at our little neighborhood pool as a kid. The air is heavy, humid. It makes you aware of the fact that you're breathing and so induces a low-level claustrophobia in those thus disposed. And the noise. Imagine the noise Twitter would make if indeed Twitter could make actual noise. Imagine a cartoon devil's collections of souls—it's a literal Pandemonium in here. Over the Top 40 tunes piped through the place by speakers I cannot see, shrill peals of delight and terror echo endlessly. You can't tell where they're coming from, fore or aft. Meanwhile the wave pool issues a salvo of beachy sound effects. A giant bucket perched atop a forest-themed jungle gym that's reminiscent of the Swiss Family Robinson tips and three hundred gallons of water hit the ground with concussive force—two teenage guys stand below it and brace against the impact. The blue and yellow and green and orange slides spiral like silly straws out from the belly of the 747. Even this simple and stationary recon of the park, laid out like a giant Rube Goldberg device, sets the kettledrum of dread beating inside me.

Admission is thirty-two dollars and I realize I've stupidly forgotten a towel, so for another twenty-four dollars I pick up a commemorative one that portrays a spacewalking astronaut. We change and grab inner tubes and head for the stairs that lead to the slides. A quick scan of the demographic reveals that we are easily the oldest people here without children of our own and, in this, we seem to charge the water park with an electric and mildly dangerous current. Families have come from afar to frolic unselfconsciously in various states of undress and our very presence seems to have corrupted this simplicity, to have turned the mood interrogative. When we reach the upper level, we find colored lines on the floor that correspond with the different colored slides, a system I know from trips to the emergency room to treat skateboarding-related injuries. James compels me to do the "Nose Dive" with him in a tandem inner tube, so we follow the green line. When it's our turn, we hold the grab bars at our sides in the little eddying pool in front of the tube's opening and wait for the signal that the father-son dyad who plunged before us have cleared the pool below. The bidet-like jet under the water behind me burbles upon my undercarriage in a way that is decidedly not unpleasant.

Maybe this is what it means to grow, making myself available to experiences like this. Maybe I'm sitting at the mouth of no mere slide but a portal, a Super Mario–like warp to another world, one in which my fun force field has been disassembled and I'm able to cut loose like the good old days. The days of backyard birthday parties marshaled by Dad. This is healthy, I think. Necessary. I will consent to being swallowed by this monstrous plastic nematode in order to emerge out the other side a new man. And though we know it to be verboten,

283

James pulls a rogue GoPro out of his bathing suit's pocket. It is apparently his intention to film our descent.

What percentage of the truth does video footage really tell? Does James's tiny waterproof camera capture the anxiety I feel as we release the grab bars and are propelled gently tubeward? Or only the smile I force for the camera's sake? Does the darkness that follows convey any of the speed and the jouncing we experience as we plummet down drops and bank around turns we cannot see? Any of the inner-ear disquietude I feel when we then debouch into an open-topped funnel structure halfway through? Or my tachycardia as we circle as though caught in a whirlpool, the jets spinning us around in such a way that by the time we enter the maw at the funnel's center we do so backward? Can you place the moment when the timbre of my screams shifts from simulated fear to the actual thing?

After what qualifies as an eternity, the tube expels us and we hit the sarcophagal pool of water. Relief and vertigo overwhelm me in equal measure. James hurries out of the pool and grabs our tube and makes for the stairs. He must sense my absence and turns to find me well behind him.

"Go on ahead," I say. "I'm gonna scope out the wave pool." Barring extreme circumstance, like if I have to evade a predator or something, I have just ridden my last waterslide.

He seems disappointed and whatever thrill of acceptance and camaraderie I feel at that is overshadowed by my disappointment in myself. Why can't I seem to get out of my own way? "I and me are always too deep in conversation." Will it take having a child of my own for me to be able to enjoy myself at a place like this again, to pay fifty-six dollars and receive something more in return than a commemorative towel and a panic attack?

I walk over and stand on the granulated concrete of Splashdown Harbor. The waves don't break on the shore so much as just sort of surge mellowly forward as they do at small lakes. At the back of the pool, where in real life the ocean would meet the sky to form the horizon, there's a humongous television screen. It's broadcasting trivia questions about water. Surrounding the screen is a mural of a US spacecraft hitting the ocean and a ship on its mission to retrieve it. The stairs on either side of the pool are encased in silos painted to resemble NASA rockets. On the wall above and to the right of the screen are the Ten Commandments. Among many other Bible verses, I once memorized these in Sunday school, but when I try to run through them now I can recall only six. A Big Brothery voice comes over the loudspeaker, interrupting the Top 40 playlist, and reminds parents to increase the frequency with which they take their kids to the bathroom. And for a moment I can almost see them, the urinous nebulae swirling about the midsections of the under-sevens.

How many times in history has a man stood on a beach and dug his feet into the sand and gazed out at the horizon and been awed by the immensity of the ocean and the sky? Been humbled by thoughts of the starry heavens beyond? Been frightened and appraised himself as small? Why is my knowledge limited? Why my stature? By whose order and direction have this place and time been allotted to me? And how many times has a man stood on granulated concrete meant to simulate sand and let lakelike swash lick his ankles as he looked out over manufactured waves and a tremendous trivia game and, over pop tunes, thought likewise?

Everything about this place seems to encourage thinking about Big Words. History. Morality. Science. Humanity. The latter is especially difficult to avoid. I'm unfamiliar with the social codes that govern water parks, but I'm trying to use my best judgment when it comes to people watching. I'm trying my best not to stare. But there are so many bodies here, so much skin on parade. Anywhere my eyes land, there it is. Spectrally thin adolescents with ribs like monkey bars. Obese children of the sort medieval ogres would eat, with Chubby Bunny cheeks and tummies that already look like botched soufflés. Adolescent girls whose bathing suits are real close to being inappropriately loose. A man-titted grandpa wearing a Speedo is splayed out in an inner tube in the center of the pool, a buoy of self-esteem, calling out the answers to the trivia questions that play over the screen. There are a plethora of faded and bad tattoos—in startlingly short order, I spot three depicting Taz. Stretch marks on men and women both that look like shark-attack scars. Women in two-pieces when one would probably be more flattering—and as a straight man with feminist sympathies, I don't know what my proper response to this should be. Should I be proud of these women for fighting the good fight against the impossible body standards our media propounds? Or is it sad that they're having to fight that fight with the media's same weapons of revelation and display? That modesty isn't an option? And then I think I'm probably already some class of asshole for wondering this in the first place, like they need my sympathy. I know what's called for here is an absence of judgment, but as a male animal there are some things that no matter how hard I try I cannot shut all the way down. A ropy-muscled teenager walks past me and enters the pool and his back is so full of acne that it looks like a shotgun wound. And now I also feel like an asshole for gawking at it and then doubly an asshole for feeling pity for him and then trebly an asshole for wondering whether it's sanitary for him to be swimming in Splashdown Harbor in the first place and now I kind of just want to cry. Because what are bodies but fucked-up vessels of time, the testimony of a being's passage through life, and so the record and messenger of private loves and joys, nostalgias and pains that we on the fake concrete sand at the wave pool's edge cannot even begin to guess at?

I haul my own hideous skin into the undulating pool, add my hateful body to the teeming crowd. I make my way into the breakers, where the chop is at its mild heaviest. The density and distribution of bodies force me to wade by a group of sixteen- or seventeen-year-old girls who are jumping over the waves. They're all wearing bikinis and have their hair in sloppy and coquettish updos. As I pass I smile a smile that's meant to be disarming and avuncular and totally unthreatening, but at that moment a wave catches one of the girls off guard and knocks her back and we seem to see it at the same time, that her bathing suit top has been set askew and her young left breast sits exposed. An involuntary and maybe autistic part of me immediately gauges the breast's firmness and heft, cross-references the diameter and hue of the areola and indexes the ambitious nubbin of its nipple, categorizes it as nice and files it away in the basement of my id. The girl has seen me smiling and a look of embarrassment and horror comes over her face as she frantically tries to return the breast to its papoose, but the nipple boings out the other side. My mirror neurons start firing on overdrive as I watch this, for, of course, I realize, *the* breast is really *her* breast, not part of *a* body but *her* body, the bearer of a unique matrix of time and circumstance, that is, a soul, and I'm filled with a tender sympathy for her caught in this dilemma and feel guilty for taking even a scintilla of pleasure in something that has caused her distress or psychic pain. And yet I know that the damage has been done and whatever I do now doesn't matter. I cannot be of comfort because surely any move toward her would be interpreted as one of pervy weirdness and possibly aggression, so I turn, embarrassed now myself, and hurry away, managing that task with the run-paddle that is perhaps the least artful form of water aerobics.

In the middle of the pool the water is warm, amniotic, and I lie on my back and for a while I rise and fall with the gentle swell of the waves. I shake off the disturbance of moments ago and my suspicions of subaqueous nebulae of urine. My thoughts then seem to catch the rhythm of the pool and there's something hypnotic about it all. This is nice, I think. It's soothing, feels safe. Floating in the gently rolling water like this, I experience a moment of deep respect for Human Ingenuity and seem to be approaching an almost Buddhist zone of Plenary Emptiness.

Then the whistles are blown. The sound effects abruptly cease. The waves calm and flatten as though rebuked. I stand in the chest-high water and there is much confusion in the pool as the lifeguards leap to action. It is then I see what looks to be a Mexican man floating facedown near the center of the pool. Did I not but moments ago see him disporting gleefully? When the two lifeguards reach him, they flip him over and slide their safety orange foam tubes in place and begin the process of ferrying him to shore. They follow a protocol I'm familiar with from all the episodes of *Baywatch* I saw as an adolescent. A solemn and reverential mood overtakes Splashdown Harbor. Molecular clusters of children in inner tubes go quiet. Whispers and hushed concern circulate among the adults. I ask, but no one around me knows what's going on—everyone's as clueless as I am. What could have possibly happened here? What manner of tragedy are we witnessing? If the lifeguards are not able to save him, what story will his kids tell? And what of his poor wife? Is death experienced as somehow more real and more unjust if it happens under this Disneyfied dome? In a theme park whose many architectural features have been engineered to provoke a fear similar to that of death? Whose tubes could be said to mimic the experience of death, transporting one as they do through darkness to a different plane of existence? Other guards are waiting near the beach, holding a buoyant stretcher in place. When they maneuver the man onto it and secure his neck, they carry him out of the pool and begin tending to him on the granulated concrete.

I then notice people around me pointing to either side

of the pool and shaking their heads, their faces filled with disbelief. And there I see them, too, the small signs above the lifeguard stands. They inform us that a drill is under way, that the drama has been staged.

Fuck.

This.

I wade out of the pool. I'm careful to avoid the huddle of teenage girls and pass the man strapped into the stretcher on the ground and any pity I felt for him moments ago has turned to disdain, even rage. Some delicate balance has been upset here, I feel, some social contract violated. What should remain implicit in a park like this (that is, the fear of death) has been made explicit and I could almost scream at all these budding Hasselhoffs. Spit and fart on them both. Could they not have made it more obvious that this was all pretend, make-believe, or did they want to do their best to simulate the variable of a crowded wave pool? Were we all just unwittingly duped into working for the theme park? And if so, should we not then be compensated somehow? Maybe with commemorative towels, for example?

While the other guys continue to tube, I spend much of the rest of my time at Evergreen Wings & Waves sitting in the hot tub, luxuriating in an experience the Adult House had promised but failed to deliver. Time to time they join me, modern Marco Polos, bearing fantastic tales of their travels on the slides, reveling in the wondrous sights they've seen.

"Chick in the white bikini," Sparrow says, and stands to look for her. His back has a weal across it from the joints in the Mach 1 slide, which you ride tubeless. "Major camel toe."

"And this one woman in green," Ben says. "Her bush is hanging out the bottom of her bathing suit. Needs to take a Weedwacker to that shit."

"It was gross," Zach confirms.

Is it enough that I resist the temptation to bro out over the boob I've seen? Does this little bit of self-denial count as a form of atonement for the pleasure I took from something that caused the girl grief? I choose instead to tell them about the staged death of the Mexican man but I must fail to convey the weight and strangeness of it because when I finish they just laugh and laugh. And after a while my skin has pruned up so much it aches. It's like even my body is trying to retreat inside itself.

XII.

Portland's all misty wet with rain when we arrive in the late afternoon. We park the van downtown, in the southwest part of the city I'm rarely ever in. For reasons that are obscure to me, I've decided not to tell anyone that I'll be back for the night. And as we walk around, everything begins to take on an uncanny Rip Van Winkle quality, like I've been away for a generation or more. I keep feeling like I should know people we pass on the sidewalk, like I should recognize their faces, but I don't. Or maybe it's that I keep wanting them to know me, to recognize my face and embrace me and welcome me home, but they walk on by, eyes ahead like I'm not even there. That I can't even get some harmless human eye contact suggests an obscure but pointed failure. Street names have an eerie, familiar-foreign ring to them. Alder. Stark. Burnside. I automatically correct Zach on the pronunciation of "Couch." "It's said like 'cooch,'" I tell him, and everyone laughs and I'm slow in remembering why that's funny. Sparrow asks why it's called the Pearl District, like did they used to sell a lot of them here, and I don't have a good answer for him.

"How long have you lived here again?" he asks.

"Eight years," I say, but while I know that's right, I'm sure it can't be true.

"Hey, guys," Zach says at one point. "Remember Mo?"

"Yeah," Sparrow says, catching the wave of nostalgia. "Remember Pat?"

Facundo disappears while we're browsing in an outdoor store. After we leave, we stand around outside wondering where he could have gone. He comes out and says he's not feeling well. It's his stomach. James gives him the keys to the van, where he wants to lie down for a spell.

Not Facundo, too, I think, pleading with whatever vindictive god has been lording over Session 2. He'd been looking forward to this night all week. Sushi. Fernet. Casa Diablo. Perhaps a sweetly little tête-à-tête with Kate? Given everything that's happened, it occurs to me that in signing up for camp I might have been unknowingly enrolled in a tontine and that this week will end with but one man standing. The way things are going, I'm not sure I have it in me to be that man.

The rain eases and the clouds clear and the sky's high up and pellucid, the light somehow clearer and sharper because of the day's storm and for it being so close to sundown. We hit a music store, where I pick up a handful of used CDs for

James—he'll be driving the van all summer and has only one album, Biggie's *Ready to Die*. They're dirt-cheap and I end up getting six for nine dollars, but for James it's like I've gifted him a kidney, he's so grateful.

"For sure? You sure?" he effuses as he shuffles through the midnineties sampler I've picked out. "I remember my brother listening to these. Back in the day."

"How old's your brother?" I ask.

"Twenty-nine," he says. And then he asks how old I am and looks surprised when I tell him. "Crazy. I thought you were closer to our age. Twenty-six. Maybe like -seven at most."

"Thanks," I say, and flush with pride. And while I know I've worked for this, taken all the little steps I've taken to ensure I look younger than I am, the pride I experience in the moment confuses me. Because what's at work here really? What was fueling this initial desire of mine? The easy answer would probably stop with the obvious: in our culture, it's better to be young than old. Go a little deeper and I think this has something to do with the fact that we're suckers for potential, promise. To be young means that you're undespoiled, that time has not imprinted you with the failures inherent in becoming who you are. This compliment seems to elide the past five years, implicitly returning all the possibilities that sat before me at twenty-six. Marriage, a house, a dog, a steady job. And maybe it's all the Nietzsche, but after the flash of pride wears off, the question looms: would you do them again, these five years that have been so easily erased? I don't really have a choice, at least according to Nietzsche. "There is a great year of becoming, a monster of a great year, which must, like an hourglass, turn over again and again so that it may run down and run out again; and all these years are alike in what is greatest as in what is smallest; and we ourselves are alike in every great year, in what is greatest as in what is smallest." But in the moment this seems like a loop- or wormhole and I'm still trying to sort out what to make of it as we head back to the van.

Facundo is in the way back with his legs canted, hugging his stomach. The last text message to Kate looms there on my phone, the promise it held now frozen in time, a spit of information preserved in the cloud. We end up at a divey sports bar called the Silver Dollar Pizza Company in Northwest Portland, right on Twenty-First Avenue. It's game seven of the NBA Finals and the place is packed but we find a spot up by the entrance, near the Ping-Pong tables. We order pitchers of beer and cheers one another and toast "To Facundo" and drink. We watch the ten or so TVs that line the walls. They're all playing the same channel, so the images dance a synchronized dance on the screens. The incessant plink-plink of the Ping-Pong ball puts me back in the basement of my childhood home, the ranch house, where I skated on rainy days and where we had a table and a running round-robin, a prime source of so much family fun. Dad would keep a tally of the wins and losses and goad us, talk his waggish and goofy shit, hoot when he hit a winner, when we hit a winner, and he'd cavil at shots that nicked off the back or clipped the net, bitching histrionically, laughing and calling out "chip-chip-chipper," and all of this is to say that it was eminently clear then that there was no place in the world he'd rather be—as heart-hurty and as clear as it is now, actually. Given that the family has fallen apart, it's difficult not to imbue memories like this with a sense of foreboding, to fight off the fatalism of the present and preserve the joy they've always held. To not search them for signs of where the train may have jumped the rails, not ask how in the world this present could have possibly developed from that past. One of the knocks against nostalgia is that it glosses over whatever was difficult about the past and focuses only on the good stuff, leaving a spiced gumdrop of sentimentality. But my question is something like: is there any difference between a simple good memory and doe-eyed nostalgia?

After the Heat win the championship we make for the sushi place, which is on the same block. This is my old neighborhood, where I lived when I was twenty-five, and ghostly traces of significance haunt the streets. I've had enough to drink that everything has begun to take on a fuzzy stereoscopic quality, with impressions coming in pairs, like a double exposure. There's the shitty bar where I once had my heart broken. Up this street is where a friend used to live, where one time, drunk at a party, I made out with his girlfriend, in his pantry, feeling smugly vindicated because I believed he was hooking up with another girl I was in love with then. (I found out later he wasn't and that I was just being paranoid and an asshole.) We walk by the bar outside of which Alexis and I first kissed. Down the block is the arty movie theater where we went on some of our earliest dates and a couple streets the other way is the bakery we can thank for the weight we put on during our honey-moo phase. We'd sometimes get takeout from this very sushi place and eat it in my living room while watching Blazers games. Is it a defect of my personality that I can find regret in even my most joyous memories? Joy in my most regretful?

Sparrow's Tinder-brokered date meets us at the restaurant. Her name is Ashley and she's in her midtwenties. For some reason I'm relieved to find that she's more cute/pretty than sexy/hot, although given the run-up to tonight, I'm wary of making any sweeping generalizations about Sparrow's taste in women. She's brought two friends along, Rachel and Nicole, and neither seems that psyched to be there. Rachel has thick and wavy chestnut-brown hair—it's straight out of a shampoo commercial. But she's shaved the whole left side of her head and I catch myself in a Mitch-moment, trying to get my mind around why she could've possibly wanted to do that. Sparrow and Ashley waste no time. They're holding hands and kissing before our table's ready. This has got to be a record, I think. And half of me wishes this app had been around when I was twenty-five and single. The other half, though, is exceedingly grateful it was not. Sparrow is so amped up that when the hostess seats us he orders a round of sake bombs from her, too eager to wait for our server. When they arrive he gives us a tutorial on how to do them and checks the table to make sure everyone's got the ceramic shot glass balanced on the chopsticks properly. Then he makes a toast: "To new friends and beautiful women." He's so earnest and genuine that Rachel rolls her eyes, but this has got me second-guessing myself. Maybe I've figured Sparrow all wrong. Maybe he's simply a yes-sayer, a man who welcomes with open arms all that life currently has on offer. Maybe he is, indeed, our culture's version of the nesta. We all hit the table and our sakes clunk in our beers and we drink.

And from that moment on the night begins to feel like it's speeding up and slowing down at once. Time's gone viscous and slippery both and I get caught in its web.

Chinatown. I'm in line for a small club with Sparrow and the girls. Apparently annoyed, the other guys have ditched us without letting us know where they're headed. I text them but they don't reply. James has gone to take Facundo back to the Adult House. He'll drop him off and turn right around to come pick us up. As he was leaving, I promoted a spliff from my pack of cigs and presented it to him with a face like *vaya con dios* and he took it and thanked me and pulled away, the copy of *Nevermind* I got him playing on the stereo.

Sparrow slinks up and lets me in on the angle he's been working: we're pro snowboarders, in town to shoot part of a video.

"Cool," I say, feeling like this is my chance to make good on the promise of reinvention I passed on during the week's introductions. "I got this."

It's not yet crowded inside and we spot a table in back against the wall. On our way we pass the DJ. He's playing house or techno or trance or dubstep or whatever—I've never bothered to learn the difference. Two muscled Asian men whose short shirtsleeves are tourniquet-tight and who have their hair gelled into dorsal fins are cruising around the bar, taking pictures of people partying and then handing these people business cards. Rachel has to tell me that the cards alert folks to where they can buy the images online. That's a business model? When did Portland get this scene? Further still, can Portland have this scene and still be considered Portland? How much about a place has to change before it is an entirely new place, only nostalgic for the old? Sparrow takes our drink orders and dances toward the bar, grooving to the music's aggressive pulse. His arms do like he's shaking imaginary maracas. Big red fireman suspenders dangle (fashionably?) from his pants like a torturous sling. When he's out of earshot, Ashley turns to me and says, "Okay, the truth. Are you guys really here for a snowboarding video?"

"Yeah, for sure," I say without a moment's hesitation. "It's called *License to Shred*."

She looks at me a long while, reading my face.

"But you gotta keep that on the DL," I add, hoping people still say that. "Hasn't been announced yet. At least not officially."

They all seem to buy the story and start peppering me with questions about life as a snowboarder.

"It's pretty sick," I tell them. "But tough. Lot of travel. I mean, I'm twenty-seven and I don't know how much longer I can keep it up."

"God. When did we get so old?" Rachel asks.

"I know, right?" I say, and feel I've made great strides in winning her over.

Sparrow returns and we drink our drinks and then he goes to get more. I'm drinking like I'm both running away from and chasing something. Whatever it is, it's a doomed and contradictory state of consciousness that I conceive of as a place, a site inside me. If only I can run far enough away from the place, I will at long last arrive at the place. The two Asian guys sidle up to our table, dancing their own version of the groovy bobbleheading maraca dance, and I pull my orange trucker hat down low and am firm about not wanting to appear in any of their pictures and this seems to win me an obscure cred around the table. It's a forceful coyness that suggests I really am known. Sparrow approves and then Sparrow dances. The girls and I watch. He gets up and dances on a chair until he's told not to. Conversations dissolve into other conversations. Rachel complains about how all the guys she meets are assholes and I'm sure she would also mean me if she knew the truth. One Bible verse I still have down: "I do not understand what I do. For what I want to do I do not do, but what I hate I do." I have a beautiful wife I love at a home I own not five miles from where I sit playing wingman to a *Pirates of the Caribbean*–looking guy I've known all of five days, letting a lovely and sad young woman with a third of her head shaved believe I'm a single pro snowboarder and letting her talk openly about her life, knowing full well I will not reciprocate. While I'm listening to Rachel and thinking about Alexis, my contact lens tears, probably dried out from being exposed to all the day's chlorine. It's still in my eye and I'm winking, trying to work it free, but I only get half of it out. The other half continues to float around and every so often its jagged edge jolts my eye and sometime in here I finally hear back from Ben. His text reads, simply, "Spyce." We seem to arrive at the strip club around the corner without having to leave the first place. It's like we've morphed there. The place is PG-13, topless only, and I have to explain to the others that this is an oddity in Portland. That going to a topless place in this town is like driving a Countach in second gear. Zach spills his drink onstage and is asked to leave. He disappears. Ben offers me a beer from his cargo shorts and explains that he bought a case of PBR and has been smuggling them in because, duh, it's cheaper that way. Then James returns and it's after one in the morning and the stages we're watching become the stages of a different strip club across the river, an all-nude outfit called Sassy's, where I came for friends' bachelor parties and no special occasion whatever back in my twenties. Zach has reappeared as mysteriously as he left and we have lost all the girls but Ashley and there may or may not have been an awkward parting with Rachel and my vision is blurred and my depth perception's all off and the contact-half is still in my eye like the prick of conscience and I'm worried that the dancers think I'm winking at them as they summit and leg-lock the poles and lean back and cork-screw listlessly down them, or as they lie on the ground and spread their legs wide so one and all may survey the inguinal folds of their depilated hoohoos and then scissor their legs back together so that their platform heels clack over the music like a woodblock. The sexiness of this theater, so thick with impassivity as to be practically opiated, remains beyond me. I can't ken it. And after a long while, I think that I've seen maybe a baker's dozen hoohoos and like thirty-seven nipples today and none of them my wife's and whatever marriage is about it isn't this.

Mo's ex-boyfriend comes to mind, flying all that way to pick her up. Mitch comes to mind, out in some hotel by the airport playing Yahtzee or Uno or Sorry! with his wife and her family. And though I've never had one, what I think I could really go for about now is a nausea pop.

Outside the club at night's end and Sparrow is waving us off and we leave him with Ashley to figure his own way back to the Adult House in the morning. The van, now, is on its way. Zach passes out almost immediately. I ask James how the spliff was and he laughs and says it was among the worst he's ever had and he's had his share of bad spliffs. Truly.

"So what you're saying is that you want to run it back?" I ask as I promote another one from my pocket, and we both laugh as I light it.

In the way back, Ben keeps repeating that he's had his age in beers tonight, nineteen. "I might have to yak. Guys, I'm just sayin'. I might have to yak."

He and James bicker about whether he should throw up out the window in the back of the van, which cracks open maybe two inches max.

"I've done it before," he says. "Get your lips up in there like you're you-know-what if you know what I mean." A raspberry sound then issues from the way back and Ben can then be heard laughing and laughing.

We leave the city behind us and it's two thirty and there are no other cars on the road. Without being prompted or asked, James puts on another of the CDs I got him, *Third Eye Blind*. I drum the dashboard and sing the first verse of "Losing a Whole Year." But as the spliff begins to work its sort of shitty work the excitement bleeds into something more muted and complex. The music is turned up loud and I can't stop my mind from replaying the day's events. They roll over me: the rain and the water park and the strip clubs. "I come back eternally to this same, selfsame life, in what is greatest as in what is smallest." We Pac-Man the highway's dotted yellow centerline. The darkness beyond the reach of the van's headlights seems almost unnaturally dark. It seems to enter the van, the windshield becoming a viscous, sticky membrane, and then it enters me. It blooms and spreads, envelops. The van shrinks and the air goes out of it and I am sure I've become part of some black box experiment. I tell James I have to pee. Then I tell James to pull over, I have to pee. He does and I hop out of the van and hurry over the gravel gully beside the highway and into the grass at the edge of the woods. The darkness is in me then and I am the dark. It's the wild and loamy dark of the sea at night, strange and frightful and unfathomably deep. There's a thickness to it and I am aware in a way past words that the shroud of darkness is a glut of gunky time. It is where I've come from and where I'm headed and is this impossibly alive and imbricated moment between. It is the love of my father and my father's pain and the embrace of his weakness because his weakness and his pain are my weakness and pain also. It is the pity and sorrow and compassion I feel for him and myself and the fear that pervades and subsumes me, the beautiful and doomed sadness of this life, the gift of its long leave-taking and the splendid and awful ache as it passes through us. It is the hurt and hardship of family and the beautiful futility of joy. And it is the vain hope that it all doesn't one day have to end.

I piss for what feels like forever and when I turn around, I discover that the van is farther away than I remember scurrying. It's glowing there against the night and is both blurry and in focus because of my contact situation and looks a little like a UFO, like something from an ancient and primordial dream. In either direction the highway stretches into textured darkness. And the stars, I don't remember the last time I saw so many or when they meant so much. The sky's bedazzling, the Milky Way a stark blur above me. I've left the van door open and as I approach I almost can't believe my ears. It's the chorus of "Jumper," everyone who's still awake in the van singing along. "Maybe today / you could put the past away . . . You could cut ties with all the lies / That you've been living in." And if someone tried to tell me this, I don't think I'd believe it. It's too perfect, too neat. But I don't have to believe it. I just have to live it. And as I climb back up into the van and we pull off down the highway, I add my voice to the others' and sing so loud that mine's the only one I can hear. The words have been alive inside me for years.

XIII.

Four hours after we get in, after we carry Zach to his bed and take our places in our own, James barges in to wake me. I'm still in the grips of a soul-nullifying sleep and it takes a second for me to remember where I am. I wave him off and text Jamie, saying that I'll meet up with them later, that I'll drive myself to the day's park. He texts back saying that's cool and tells me where they'll be. He wishes me a Happy Go Skate Day, a holiday I didn't know existed but that Congress has apparently recognized. The Situationists had a word for when the official culture of capitalism takes an idea from the avant-garde and incorporates it into itself, and in the process neuters whatever was once radical or powerful about it: they called this recuperation. And a Congress-approved skateboarding holiday held at eunuchoidal skateparks the nation over is about as good an example as any you could dream up on your own.

I get up out of bed and look around the room. My dirty jeans and T-shirts and socks are piled on the floor of the alcove and I now have to confront the fact that the smell of the Yellow Room can no longer be attributed to anyone but me. I shower and dress and after that I fold up the rest of my clean clothes and pack them in my suitcase and toss my dirty gear in a black plastic trash bag. As I do I get an image of the guys at the beer pong tourney that night and at Disorientation tomorrow. Will they wonder, with the same speculative tone we used to talk about the others, "Remember Cheston?" And if so, what exactly will they remember? I doubt very much. And yet memory and imagination have already started to work their obscure magic and I realize that even though I've had more than enough of skateboarding camp and am leaving early, I'm already nostalgic for my time here. Can that be possible? With my car packed, I do a final walk-through of the place and on my way out, I leave my last spliff next to the half-eaten package of Double Stufs on the kitchen counter.

The campers are at a park in Newberg, Oregon, over an hour from campus. I'm not there for more than ten minutes before Jamie begins rounding everyone up to head to another park in Forest Grove. I follow the vans out of the parking lot and we cruise north. His question comes back to me then: what am I doing here? At the beginning of this week, I think I wanted to reexperience the salvific aura I'd always associated with the language of skateboarding, to return to a time when I hadn't yet been disabused of the notion that talent or skill could save me, when identity was something other and more meaningful than a pose. In a certain sense, the genius of skateboarding's language is that everything that can be imagined can be said. And be said clearly, denotatively. If a new trick comes along, room is made for it. It is named, codified, made part of the parlance. As much as I've been wanting it to talk about something else, though, it cannot. The language collapses in on itself. There is no metaphysics in skateboarding. At least not for me. Not anymore. One writer defines nostalgia as the "repetition that mourns the inauthenticity of all repetitions and denies the repetition's capacity to define identity." And this calls to mind one of my favorite passages in Faulkner, one of our most nostalgic writers: "There is no such thing as memory: the brain recalls just what the muscles grope for: no more, no less: and its resultant sum is usually incorrect and false and worthy only of the name of dream."

When we arrive in Forest Grove I pull in behind the vans. As they get out, some of the cooler-seeming teenagers appear to admire my car but they don't say anything to me directly. I note that this is a street-heavy park, a plaza, with a good amount of open concrete and I decide I'm going to push myself. Thus far I've progressed to the point of being able to spin the 360-flip but haven't yet been able to land it cleanly. I can get my back foot on it, easy, but not my front, which is always off to the side, to the left. There are a few other tricks that have eluded me, too.

I take to the concrete and after thirty minutes my muscles have warmed and I have a nice perspiratory lather going. Can the kids can smell booze on me? I wonder. Am I sweating out the night? If only it were possible to dispense with one's past like that, to excrete it from one's pores and be done with it. Loose now and with growing confidence, I have my kickflips on lock, as they say, and then land several halfcab kickflips and fakie frontside flips. We're at over an hour in and my T-shirt is drenched. It's pretty much an entirely different color. One of the teenagers, a small and quiet Asian kid whose name or nickname I haven't caught, rides over and says, "Man. You really got a sweat on, huh?" And I just laugh and he laughs, too, and we start skating together. His earbuds hang loose from the neck of his T-shirt and helicopter like demonic clock hands when he pops a trick. He matches everything I do. I land a regular frontside flip and then a hardflip and these are not easy tricks and though they were a little janky, a measure of the old pride comes over me. He does them like they're nothing. And though I know it's lame, I ask him how old he is. Fifteen, he says. I don't know what I hope to prove by saying it, but I tell him I landed my first hardflip before he was born.

"Word?" he says, unimpressed.

"Word," I say. Word.

I spend fifteen minutes or so trying the 360-flip. It's late afternoon and I can tell the session's coming to an end. More campers are sitting around watching than are skating. A couple times I land on the board and it slips out from under me or my heels hit the ground and I stumble off the board. I'm close. I can feel it. And then on one pass I crouch and pop my board and I couldn't tell you what I've done differently on this try but it spins perfectly under me. My feet are there when it finishes and they land over the bolts and I ride on. The Asian kid and a handful of the other teens watching knock their boards against the ground and cheer and call out "Sick!" and "Tight!" and "Dope!" The trick feels nothing like I thought it would, nothing like I remembered. It's way, way better. It is the real thing.

I call Jamie over and ask him to film me. He's using the camp's fancy HD camera and high-fives and hugs me when I stick another one clean. This is enough to get my hopes up that I will make the edit of Session 2. Months later, when I call the video up on my computer and watch it, I will relive Boston's hardflip and many of the other improbable things I witnessed, and I will be convinced that my 360-flip is coming up next, that surely they'd put it in for the other prospective adult campers to look on with respect, fomenting a desire of their own. But no. I will sit in disbelief as the clip ends and I have not seen myself.

As a fail-safe, I ask Jamie to get some extra footage on my phone and he says for sure. It takes me a few tries, but when

I land another one I take my phone back and immediately shield it from the late-afternoon light and watch. There I appear on-screen, rolling almost laughably slow toward the camera. The trick itself looks labored and the landing's a little sketch but I don't care. It's still pretty fucking dope.

The campers begin to pile back into the vans and I share a few parting words with the one I've hit it off with.

"Later," he says.

"Yeah. Later," I say, and wave what I realize is not only Dad's air piano wave, but mine now, too.

Then the vans peel away. Because I followed them here, I wasn't paying attention on the way into town and so didn't orient myself, didn't register any landmarks or record how to get out of here. So when I attempt to leave, I get turned around in the neighborhood behind the park and end up right back where I started. I stop and laugh to myself and then pull out my phone to get directions, but first I sit through beaucoup viewings of my 360-flip. I can't wait to show Alexis, can't wait for her to share in my pride. Then I call up Google Maps and as I start to plug in my address, the app finishes it for me—it's almost like my phone knows before I do that where I'm headed is home.

Acknowledgments

Upper rung gratitude goes to Daniel Loedel and the Whole Sick Crew at Scribner. Likewise to my argus-eyed agent, Bill Clegg, whose enthusiasm buoyed me through nauseating chop. For their unwavering support, profuse appreciation is due Win McCormack, Holly Macarthur, and my entire Tin House family. And I have benefited immeasurably from the wise and generous counsel of the following folks: Christian Shiflett, Garth Swanson, Ryan Boyd, Scott Binkley, David Shields, Tony Perez, Lance Cleland, Alex Morris, Kyle von Hoetzendorff, Karen Russell, Jim Guida, Thomas Ross, Emily Bliquez, Rob Spillman, Elissa Schappell, Wells Tower, Ben Percy, Jon Raymond, Michelle Wildgen, Sarah Burnes, Pauls Toutonghi, Tony Doerr, Pete Rock, Arthur Bradford, Curt White, Chris Yates, Scott Phelps, and David Smith—to all of them I extend a fist-bump of thanks.

My family has supported me through all of my identities, especially Lee Knapp, who gave more of herself to these essays than she had to. The invaluable example of her life kept me from becoming a feckless stockbroker with iffy taste in neckties. Or something.

Finally, without Alexis Knapp, well, nothing. Period. This book is as much of as for her.